Contagious holiness

Titles in this series:

NEW STUDIES IN BIBLICAL THEOLOGY 19

Series editor: D. A. Carson

Contagious holiness

JESUS' MEALS WITH SINNERS

Craig L. Blomberg

APOLLOS

INTERVARSITY PRESS
DOWNERS GROVE, ILLINOIS 60515

Inter-Varsity Press, England
Norton Street, Nottingham NG7 3HR
Website: www.ivpbooks.com
Email: ivp@ivpbooks.com

InterVarsity Press, USA
P.O. Box 1400, Downers Grove, IL 60515-1426
World Wide Web: www.ivpress.com
Email: email@ivpress.com

InterVarsity Press®, USA, is the book-publishing division of InterVarsity Christian Fellowship/
USA® <www.intervarsity.org> and a member movement of the International Fellowship of
Evangelical Students.

Inter-Varsity Press, England, is closely linked with the Universities and Colleges Christian
Fellowship, a student movement connecting Christian Unions in universities and colleges
throughout Great Britain, and a member movement of the International Fellowship of Evangelical
Students. Website: www.uccf.org.uk.

UK ISBN 978-1-84474-083-3
USA ISBN 978-0-8308-2620-9

Set in Monotype Times New Roman
Typeset in Great Britain by CRB Associates, Reepham, Nofolk
Printed in the United States of America ∞

Library of Congress Cataloging-in-Publication Data has been requested.

British Library Cataloguing in Publication Data
A catalogue record for this book is available from the British Library.

P   23   22   21   20   19   18   17   16   15   14   13   12   11   10   9   8   7   6   5   4   3   2

Y   27   26   25   24   23   22   21   20   19   18   17   16   15   14   13   12   11   10   09

for Jan and Bob Williams,
who have hosted special meals
with Christian grace and unaffected hospitality
for more different people and more different kinds of people
in more different situations
while intentionally ministering to the outcast
than anyone else I personally know.

Contents

Series preface

New Studies in Biblical Theology is a series of monographs that address key issues in the discipline of biblical theology. Contributions to the series focus on one or more of three areas: 1. the nature and status of biblical theology, including its relations with other disciplines (e.g. historical theology, exegesis, systematic theology, historical criticism, narrative theology); 2. the articulation and exposition of the structure of thought of a particular biblical writer or corpus; and 3. the delineation of a biblical theme across all or part of the biblical corpora.

Above all, these monographs are creative attempts to help thinking Christians understand their Bibles better. The series aims simultaneously to instruct and to edify, to interact with the current literature, and to point the way ahead. In God's universe, mind and heart should not be divorced: in this series we will try not to separate what God has joined together. While the notes interact with the best of the scholarly literature, the text is uncluttered with untransliterated Greek and Hebrew, and tries to avoid too much technical jargon. The volumes are written within the framework of confessional evangelicalism, but there is always an attempt at thoughtful engagement with the sweep of the relevant literature.

In the unlikely event that they do not know him from his long list of publications elsewhere, readers of this series will recognize the name of Dr Craig Blomberg from his earlier contribution to this series, viz. *Neither Poverty Nor Riches* (vol. 7). The topic he addresses here may not be as 'hot' as questions about poverty and wealth, but perhaps it deserves to be. The people with whom we eat say a great deal about us. Even if 'table fellowship' is not as intrinsically freighted with symbolism in Western culture as in cultures in other places and times, much more is being said than the numbers of calories we are taking in. Dr Blomberg not only addresses current disputes about the 'table fellowship' practices of the historical Jesus, but traces out the historical and theologically-laden implications of table fellowship across the canon of Scripture and issues a call to contemporary Christians to reform their habits in this matter. And, once again, Dr Blomberg accomplishes all this while simultaneously engaging with the most recent literature and writing with the limpid clarity for which he has become known.

D. A. Carson
Trinity Evangelical Divinity School

Author's preface

In early 2001, Darrell Bock, representing the Jesus Group of the Institute of Biblical Research, graciously invited me to write an article for the *Bulletin for Biblical Research* on the topic of 'Jesus, Sinners and Table Fellowship'. For several years this study group has convened every June in Dallas to discuss various essays on the historical Jesus and to make suggestions for revision as they are prepared for the *BBR*. Ultimately, a dozen or so of these will have surveyed representative swaths of each major section of the ministry of Jesus, and the hope is to update and collect them together into a single edited volume that will demonstrate how sizeable the database for research into the historical Jesus actually is, and how a coherent understanding of his intentions can emerge when the Gospels are studied against the Jewish backgrounds of his day.

When I realized I had until June of 2004 to complete my first draft of this article, I readily agreed to the assignment. Within a few weeks of that invitation came another one – to deliver the Moore College Lectures in Sydney in the summer of 2002. Acknowledging what a rare honour this was, but explaining that I had already committed myself to teaching two different overseas courses during that same period of time, I reluctantly declined the invitation. I was similarly scheduled for the next year as well. Admitting my presumption, I did, however, add that I had no commitments yet for the summer of 2004, and would be delighted to prepare those lectures if they still wanted me. For months I heard nothing, and I became more and more convinced that I had lost all chance of participating in what might have been a once-in-a-lifetime opportunity.

Nearly a year later, to my astonishment, Moore College did in fact take me up on my offer. Of course I should have interpreted their silence quite differently. They had obviously been plenty busy arranging the lectureships for the intervening years, but were now ready to think that far into the future. What topics might I be willing to address? I suggested several, all based on various research in which

I was engaged (or in which I soon hoped to be engaged), and we settled on 'Jesus, Sinners and Table Fellowship', a biblical-theological survey that would grow naturally out of my shorter article.

My work began in earnest in 2003. Knowing that IVP's *New Studies in Biblical Theology* series had first right of refusal on all the current Moore College Lecture series, I contacted the editor, Don Carson, to see if he thought there would be interest in my topic. He encouraged me to proceed. I subsequently learned that he had something to do with recommending me to the kind folks at Moore in the first place! Anticipating my next sabbatical in the spring semester of 2004, it seemed reasonable to me that not only could I complete the article by June 2004 and the lectures by August of that same year; I could have the book in reasonably good shape by the end of that summer as well.

Normally the order of my deadlines (the last of the three being self-imposed) would have dictated the order of the projects. But with 'plenty' of time in advance, and an immediate return to all of my regular seminary duties after my sojourn to Australia, I thought it better to work backwards. I would write a draft of the book, excerpt the lectures from it, and then choose and reword the most important sections, particularly on the Gospels themselves, for the article. Little did I know that in February 2004 I would re-aggravate a repetitive stress injury in my shoulders and neighbouring body parts that I had contracted seven and a half years earlier (and from which I had largely recovered six years previously), thus losing the equivalent of at least two months' sabbatical-time work. Mercifully, thanks to a series of 'coincidences' so extraordinary that I can attribute them only to God's providential intervention, I was able to get extra help in transcribing dictation; I was introduced to a state-of-the-art voice-activated word-processing program, which Denver Seminary agreed to pay for (along with the new computer I would need to run it); and a student directed me to a local chiropractor who is one of only three in the Denver area conversant with the 'Active Release Techniques' that speeded up the healing process almost tenfold compared with the first time I had been injured. Without this set of events, I would have lost far more than two months.

Notwithstanding these mercies, it became clear that I would not get the book done in time to create separate, carefully crafted lectures for Moore College, much less a succinct article for the IBR Jesus Group. The conveners of the latter amazingly agreed to postpone my deadline with them for a year, while my audiences in Sydney had to put up with the less than ideal format of my alternating between reading portions of my overly long manuscript and summarizing intervening sections. But God seemed to work in spite of it all, for which I am enormously grateful. Here then is my book, even though, as of this writing (October 2004), I have yet to produce the article! Lord willing, that will occur between now and next May.

In view of this narrative, I obviously must thank co-conveners Darrell Bock and Bob Webb and the entire IBR Jesus Group for their confidence in me three and a half years ago and for their understanding when I ruined their plans last spring. Principal John Woodhouse and the entire Moore College community could not have extended a warmer welcome, not only to me but to my entire family, as we spent almost two weeks on their campus (and in the Woodhouses' home). The week prior to coming to Sydney, we had an equally warm welcome at the Bible College of Victoria, thanks to the recommendation of my former D. Min. student Mike Grechko, now Administrative Pastor of Crossway Baptist Church in Melbourne, and the invitation of Principal David Price (in whose home we likewise experienced warm hospitality). At BCV I was able to teach a number of classes from the material in this book in a more informal setting. Not surprisingly, a large portion of the hospitality in both Australian colleges involved food, and it was encouraging to see how both institutions had largely preserved the often-vanishing tradition of eating together regularly as an entire college community.

It goes without saying (but I will say it anyway) that I am grateful to Denver Seminary's generous sabbatical programme and to its faculty, administration and board for granting me my fifth term (three quarters and two semesters) in my eighteen years with the school away from classroom duties this past spring, so that I could work more steadily on this project. My colleague and the director of our Doctor of Ministry programme, David Osborn, gave me a demo copy of Dragon Works' program Dragon Naturally Speaking, which convinced me of the enormous advances voice-activated software has made in the seven years since I last attempted to use it. My student Tom Hall appeared at my office door on Good Friday like an angel of mercy, referring me to Dr Glen Hyman for what he called my 'miracle cure'. Only God knows how direct an answer this was to the prayers of the previous day by my charismatic Romanian friends Elena Bogdan and Ana Ploscaru, when they laid hands on me and pleaded for God's healing, though undoubtedly they were hoping for on-the-spot results such as they have frequently seen in other similar situations.

Many other individuals and groups deserve my profound thanks for their help in this enterprise. Drs Philip Duce of Inter-Varsity Press and D. A. Carson, with the NSBT series overall, have been most cordial, prompt and helpful editors. As she has done for so many years on so many of my writing projects, Jeanette Freitag, Assistant to the Faculty of Denver Seminary, happily typed numerous notes and drafts of specific sections of chapters, while also helping with various phases of the editing process en route. In successive years my research assistants Jeremiah Harrelson and Mariam Kamell helped with the actual research, particularly in tracking down and surveying primary source material. My colleague and fellow Greek instructor Elodie Emig rechecked countless quotations and references for accuracy and spared me numerous mistakes that the dictation process inevitably introduces. And my adult Sunday School class, 'Bridges' at Mission Hills Baptist Church (whose property sits on either side of the border between the townships of Greenwood Village and Littleton, Colorado), tolerated three of the crazier Sunday mornings I have ever inflicted on them as I tried out selected portions of this material with them just before leaving for Australia.

I probably would never have agreed to begin studying this topic in depth in the first place were it not for my former MA student Michelle Stinson, who had just completed under my supervision her thesis on the topic of Jesus' table fellowship in Luke the year before the IBR invitation first came. I am thrilled to watch her career advance as she embarks on the final stages of a PhD in Old Testament at Wheaton College, and I am immensely grateful for her close scrutiny and critique of this entire manuscript, along with her particularly thorough analysis of my treatment of meals in the earlier Testament which has now become her specialty. That analysis read like the product of a seasoned veteran and colleague, as her own dissertation research continues her interest in the topics addressed in this volume. Her subsequent work will no doubt correct whatever errors remain in mine and will have the space to go into considerably greater detail.

After I had completed the final draft of this manuscript, Scot McKnight's outstanding new work *The Jesus Creed: Loving God, Loving Others* (Brewster, MA: Paraclete, 2004) appeared. His pioneering synthesis of cutting-edge historical Jesus work with issues of spiritual formation regularly echoes convictions I had come to about the nature of Jesus' table fellowship in its Jewish setting and even uses the expression 'contagious holiness'. While unable to utilize

McKnight's insight in this work, I am grateful to find a fellow scholar who has synthesized much of the same material in so similar a fashion. This book may be viewed as the detailed support for the brief generalizations that McKnight repeatedly makes.

All unlabelled New Testament Scripture quotations in this volume follow Today's New International Version published by Hodder & Stoughton in 1996. Quotations from the Old Testament follow the New International Version, published by the same company in 1984. Citations from the Apocrypha adopt the translations of Metzger (1977). Pseudepigraphical references mirror the standard English edition of Charlesworth (1983, 1985). Renderings of passages from the Dead Sea Scrolls utilize the Hebrew–English compilation of García Martínez and Tigchelaar (1997, 1998). Josephus, Philo and the various Greco-Roman authors quoted come from the Greek–English volumes of the Loeb Classical Library, unless otherwise specified.

I dedicate this study to my good friends Dr Bob and Jan Williams. My wife, Fran, and I met them in the fall of 1986, just a couple of months after moving to the Denver area. Bob is one of three co-founders of the Inner-City Health Center in Denver, a not-for-profit private Christian healthcare clinic for the particularly needy, which last year celebrated its twentieth anniversary. Jan, a second co-founder, was the administrator of the clinic for many years, has been active in work with numerous non-profit organizations and societies concerned with Christian community development, and today is the administrator for Joshua Station, an arm of Denver's Mile-High Ministries that provides low-cost, temporary housing for people who would otherwise be homeless, in the context of Christian love, counselling and job-placement aid. For nearly fifteen years, Fran and I have been part of a small group with the Williams, which has met as often as every other week (for several years), as little as once a quarter (for a couple of years), and now aims at a gathering every six to eight weeks. Two other couples who joined shortly after we did have remained throughout these years, as other couples and singles have come and gone for various multi-year stretches at a time.

Together we have studied Scripture, discussed important Christian books, brainstormed on ministry-related issues, prayed, laughed, cried, loaned each other substantial sums of money when needed, celebrated family milestones, renewed wedding vows, and acted as a surrogate church for various individuals during periods of time in which they needed to recover from less than Christian treatment at churches of which they had been a part. All of us have shared an interest in, commitment to, and experience of inner-city ministry, and all of us have recognized the special dynamic that attaches to the intentional Christian meals (or portions of meals) which we share together every time we meet. But none has hosted as many, with us and with many other individuals and groups, as the Williams. Thanks, Jan and Bob, for your friendship; for your model of Christian sacrifice and service; for your faithfulness over the years to God, to his people and to so many who have not yet become his people; and for all the wonderful events you have hosted or celebrated with us at other venues (not least in Greece and Turkey). If anyone knows the potential of Christian meals, you do. I can't wait until we can celebrate together forever at the wedding feast of the Lamb!

Craig L. Blomberg

Abbreviations

ABR	*Australian Biblical Review*
ARTS	*Arts in Religious and Theological Studies*
ATR	*Anglican Theological Review*
BAR	*Biblical Archaeology Review*
Bib	*Biblica*
BR	*Biblical Research*
BTB	*Biblical Theological Bulletin*
CBQ	*Catholic Biblical Quarterly*
EJT	*European Journal of Theology*
ET	*Expository Times*
ETL	*Ephemerides Theologicae Lovanienses*
HBT	*Horizons in Biblical Theology*
HeyJ	*Heythrop Journal*
HTR	*Harvard Theological Review*
HUCA	*Hebrew Union College Annual*
Int	*Interpretation*
JBL	*Journal of Biblical Literature*
JETS	*Journal of the Evangelical Theological Society*
JJS	*Journal of Jewish Studies*
JITC	*Journal of the Interdenominational Theological Center*
JR	*Journal of Religion*
JRT	*Journal of Religious Thought*
JSJ	*Journal for the Study of Judaism*
JSNT	*Journal for the Study of the New Testament*
JSOT	*Journal for the Study of the Old Testament*
JSS	*Journal of Semitic Studies*
JTS	*Journal of Theological Studies*
Neot	*Neotestamentica*
NovT	*Novum Testamentum*
NTS	*New Testament Studies*
PRS	*Perspectives on Religious Studies*
RB	*Revue Biblique*

RQ	*Revue de Qumran*
SBL	*Society of Biblical Literature*
SEÅ	*Svensk Exegetisk Årsbok*
SJT	*Scottish Journal of Theology*
SLJT	*Saint Luke's Journal of Theology*
TJT	*Toronto Journal of Theology*
TynB	*Tyndale Bulletin*
UBSGNT[4]	United Bible Societies' Greek New Testament, 4th edition
VT	*Vetus Testamentum*
WW	*Word & World*
ZAW	*Zeitschrift für die alttestamentliche Wissenschaft*
ZNW	*Zeitschrift für die neutestamentliche Wissenschaft*
ZPE	*Zeitschrift für Papyrologie und Epigraphik*

Chapter One

The current debate

'Sinners who need no repentance'
and Did Jesus really eat with the wicked?

A casual perusal of contemporary New Testament scholarship would suggest that Jesus' practice of sharing table fellowship with the outcasts of his society is one of the most historically reliable pieces of information that can be extracted from the Gospels. J. D. Crossan (1991: 344), co-chair of the famous Jesus Seminar, determines that Jesus' 'open commensality' lay at the heart of his programme of 'building or rebuilding peasant community on radically different principles from those of honor and shame, patronage and clientage' and 'based on an egalitarian sharing of spiritual and material power at the most grass-roots level.' Joachim Gnilka (1997: 105), in a standard liberal German text on the historical Jesus, agrees that 'those whom Jesus accepted were flagrant sinners, or were viewed as such', so that his eating with them symbolically expressed the forgiveness of sins brought about 'less by means of the message than by the manifest personal acceptance, the effective restitution and granting of a new beginning in the context of fellowship.'

More evangelical scholars generally concur. N. T. Wright (1996: 149), bishop of Durham, explains that Jesus ate and drank with all sorts of people, often in an atmosphere of celebration.

> He ate with 'sinners', and kept company with people normally on or beyond the borders of respectable society – which of course in his day and culture, meant not merely social respectability but religious uprightness, proper covenant behaviour, loyalty to the traditions and hence to the aspirations of Israel.

Not surprisingly, 'this caused regular offence to the pious.' Even as staunch a conservative as the South African David Seccombe (2002: 240) declares:

Once we see that Jesus construed his eating with sinners – his offer of friendship and their acceptance of it – as tantamount to entrance into the kingdom of God, we see how appropriate was the conviviality and celebration which got him his reputation as 'a wine drinker and a glutton' as well as 'a friend of tax collectors and sinners'. Their meals together were an expression of their new relationship with Jesus, which was celebrated as though it was a new relationship with God.

This apparent consensus across the theological spectrum does not lack a good foundation. The theme of Jesus' table fellowship with sinners permeates every layer of the Synoptic tradition. In Mark 2:13–17 and parallels, Jesus calls the tax collector Levi to be one of his disciples and then attends a party with Levi's associates. In Mark 6:30–44 and 8:1–10 and parallels, he feeds the five thousand and the four thousand, crowds that would have included very heterogeneous groupings of people. In the so-called Q-material, Jesus indeed acknowledges that his critics consider him a glutton and drunkard, a friend of tax collectors and sinners (Matt. 11:19 par.), and he predicts a coming eschatological banquet in which Gentiles will come from all over the world to eat at table with the Jewish patriarchs (Matt. 8:11–12 par.). At the end of a passage unique to Matthew, the parable of the two sons, Jesus observes that tax collectors and prostitutes are entering the kingdom ahead of the Jewish leaders (Matt. 21:31–32). In material unique to Luke's Gospel, Jesus commends the faith of a disreputable woman who anoints him during a meal at the home of Simon the Pharisee (Luke 7:36–50); dines with Mary and Martha but puts spiritual priorities above culinary ones (10:38–42); unleashes a bitter invective against the Jewish leaders at another dinner with a Pharisee (11:37–54); upends conventional standards about whom to invite to a banquet (14:1–24); justifies his scandalous behaviour by telling the parable of the prodigal son (15:1–2, 11–32); takes the initiative to eat with the chief tax collector Zacchaeus (19:1–10); and discloses himself as resurrected to the unnamed disciples in Emmaus during their breaking of bread together (24:30–32). Distinctively Johannine passages include Jesus' turning water into wine in the context of a wedding feast (John 2:1–12) and appearing to his followers in order to eat breakfast with them by the Sea of Galilee (21:1–14).

The theme of Jesus' table fellowship with a broad cross-section of people thus clearly satisfies the criterion of authenticity known as multiple attestation. It similarly appears to pass the dissimilarity criterion with flying colours: it is not quite like anything else in Jesus' Jewish world or in early Christian practice.[1] And it fits the principle of coherence with other authentic teachings of Jesus, particularly those which focus on the arrival of the kingdom of God (see esp. Franzmann 1992). Notice how many parables involve meals and/or sinners: in addition to those already cited, compare especially the wedding banquet in Matthew 22:1–14; the faithful servants in Luke 12:35–38; the rich man and Lazarus in 16:19–31; and the Pharisee and tax collector in 18:9–14. At the same time, Jesus' practice satisfies the criterion of Palestinian environment, as it proves to be a natural extension of hospitality practices deeply embedded in Ancient Near Eastern and Mediterranean cultures.[2] Indeed, as recently as 1998, Hungarian scholar János Bolyki could write an entire monograph on *Jesu Tischgemeinschaften*, defending the substantial authenticity of this theme passage by passage throughout all four canonical Gospels.[3]

Several important recent challenges to this consensus, however, clamour for attention. Pride of place among these must go to Dennis Smith's Harvard dissertation (1980) and numerous articles (see esp. 1987; 1989; 1991), now conveniently summarized in his 2003 volume *From Symposium to Eucharist*. Smith argues that the Greco-Roman form of banqueting known as the symposium had become a model so pervasive throughout the empire that Jewish and early Christian meals would have adopted at least parts of this structure as well: a formal meal during which participants reclined on couches, followed by a time for drinking wine, discussion of controversial topics and entertainment of various kinds, usually musical and often sexual. Smith thinks he can detect elements of this format in the Corinthians' practice of celebrating the Lord's Supper. On the basis of pre-Christian hints from the Wisdom of Sirach and post-Christian details of the prescriptions for Passover in the rabbinic literature, he believes that Jewish feasts had adopted this format as well. Thus both Jesus'

---

[1] For a detailed analysis of this theme in light of both of these criteria, see Brawley 1995: 18–23. Cf. also Bartchy 2002.

[2] For a book-length study of the New Testament practice of hospitality, see Koenig 1985. For an analysis limited to Luke's extensive presentation of the practice, cf. Byrne 2000.

[3] A more classic tradition-historical perspective is reflected in Kollmann 1990, but he still retrieves substantially authentic cores from most of the relevant passages. For other important treatments coming to similar conclusions, see Hofius 1967 and Chilton 1992.

Last Supper and his festive meals more generally must be understood as forms of symposia. For our purposes, only the second of these two claims requires analysis, but it is precisely here that Smith argues that the Gospel portraits are primarily unhistorical. Employing both an older form-critical dissection of the pericopae and a more recent literary-critical analysis of the theme of table fellowship in the Gospels in general and in Luke in particular, Smith concludes that the theme is largely the construct of the Evangelists themselves.[4]

In both instances, Smith is fairly quickly rebutted. The form-critical analyses assume a fallacious and now outmoded kind of historical research. The very literary-critical approach to which Smith subsequently appeals has demonstrated that one cannot strip un-historical layers from a historical core of Gospel pericopae, as once was thought. And demonstrating that a theme is crucial to a Gospel writer's literary purposes bears no relation to the probability of its historical authenticity (for both points see, e.g., Green 2003). But Smith's research opens the door for others to make more challenging assaults. Is it really the case that the symposium model had become pervasive in first-century Jewish society *in Israel*? If not, and if the model *is* reflected in the Gospel tradition, then it may be unhistorical, because it does not fit the Galilee of Jesus' day. Alternatively, it is striking how infrequently Jesus' eating with sinners appears in Mark or Matthew by comparison with Luke. On the standard theory of Markan priority, this distribution of material could suggest that the theme is primarily of Luke's creation.[5]

A second challenge comes from Kathleen Corley. In her two books on women, meals and the historical Jesus (1993b; 2002; cf. also her article – 1993a), she adopts Smith's symposium hypothesis but then explores in more depth the label 'tax collectors and prostitutes'. Corley notes how Roman women during the late republican and early imperial periods were increasingly emancipated, taking the initiative to be seen in public, including at banquets. This in turn triggered a conservative backlash, so that such women were often viewed as

---

[4] For a strikingly similar volume from recent German scholarship, see Klinghardt 1996.

[5] Numerous studies analyse Jesus' table fellowship in Luke. See Via 1985; Karris 1985: 47–78; Moxnes 1986; Esler 1987: 77–86; Neyrey 1991; Kelley 1995; Kayama 1997. Moritz (1996) explicitly defends its authenticity. Elliott (1991) extends his study to include Acts as well. Klosinski (1998) believes he finds the theme prominent already in Mark but still considers it a literary construct. Neufeld (2000) does the same but from a sociological perspective. Stinson (2000) finds important foreshadowings of the Messianic banquet.

unscrupulous. The term 'prostitute' could thus be just a slanderous label for what Bruce Winter (2003), in a different context, has recently called 'the new Roman women'. They were not in most cases literally sexually immoral, just unconventional by attending public banquets. Because literal prostitutes were often licensed, and taxes on their 'profession' were collected by tax farmers, it was natural for 'tax collectors and prostitutes' to be joined together into a rhetorical vilification, even when those actual occupations were not represented by the persons slandered (Corley 1993b: 152–158). If Corley is right, then a key piece of the consensus that Jesus fraternized with the worst of his society's outcasts is undermined.

On the other hand, the mere fact that the terms could be used in broader senses does not mean that literal tax collectors or prostitutes are not in view in the Gospels. J. Gibson (1981: 430) cites evidence from Josephus and the Babylonian Talmud to suggest that these terms were linked together because 'both groups were regarded by their contemporaries as prime examples of the type of Jew who collaborated with the occupying forces of the Roman government' (soldiers being a principal clientele of the 'courtesans'). Dorothy Lee (1996) stresses the strong contrast in the three Gospel accounts that portray women as sinners (Luke 7:36–50; John 4:4–42; and John 7:53 – 8:11) between the faith of those women and the misguided behaviour of the male authorities surrounding them, suggesting that extreme examples have been chosen (like literal prostitutes or unfaithful wives) to highlight the surprising reversal of praiseworthy roles. And Sean Freyne (2000: 271–286) observes that even when the slogan 'tax collectors and prostitutes' (or 'sinners') was not meant literally, it still represented serious vilification, such that its targets were being viewed as wicked. At the same time, our picture of Jesus' fraternizing with the outcast does change considerably if we imagine him dining with the wives of his peers rather than with inherently immoral women.

Just as there have been questions about the identity of the women who surrounded Jesus in the intimate context of table fellowship, so also recent scholarship has disclosed considerable interest in identifying the 'tax collectors' more precisely. It has been recognized for some time now that these were not the true Roman *publicani*, the very wealthy and influential government officials who oversaw the entire tax collection process (on which, see esp. Badian 1972). Rather they were tax farmers, or middlemen: Jews working for Rome, in charge of the collection of tolls, customs duties or certain yearly taxes in specific locations; men who made their money by charging more than what they had to pass on to their imperial overlords. Thus, except in some very limited circles, their ostracism had far more to do with their making a living – at times via considerable greed and extortion – to the detriment of their own country than with any supposed laws of ritual impurity that they might have transgressed (see Youtie 1937; Donahue 1971; Herrenbrück 1981, 1987). Fritz Herrenbrück has completed the most thorough investigation of this topic, concluding that 'tax contractors' might be the best English rendering of the Greek *telōnai* (1990: 25) and that the heart of the historical Jesus' ministry to these people involved his sense of mission to 'all Israel', including the nation's most despised (1990: 285). Even studies that engage in more radical tradition-historical dissection usually come to similar conclusions (e.g. Völkel 1978).[6]

From analysing the two groups denoted by 'tax collectors and prostitutes', it is a small step to considering what the Gospels mean by the more common epithet 'tax collectors and sinners' (or the term 'sinner' or 'sinners' by itself). Precisely who is and who is not included under this broad heading? For much of the twentieth century, the stereotypical response to this question was the *'am-hā-'āres*, the 'people of the land': the vast majority of simple Jewish farmers and fishermen, housewives and artisans, who were not aligned with any Jewish sect and did not follow the purity laws that the Pharisees had superimposed onto the Torah to contextualize the commandments of Moses for their day.[7] Specific studies that investigated the problem in more detail often considerably narrowed the scope of who would have been called a 'sinner', focusing, for example, on those guilty of an immoral mode of life or who practised a dishonourable vocation (Jeremias 1931).[8] Others added Gentiles of various categories, or the priestly aristocracy who had compromised too much with Rome, or other non-Pharisaic leadership sects (see Perrin 1967: 93–94; Borg 1984: 83–86, esp. 84–85; Westerholm 1978: 69–71).

[6] Farmer (1978) thus thinks that 'tax collectors' in the phrase 'tax collectors and sinners' refers to the social, economic and political constituency of the outcasts, while 'sinners' indicates their religious status. Rau (1998) believes he discerns two stages in Jesus' ministry, so that his initial popularity among the people symbolized by 'tax collectors' eventually becomes a key catalyst in his later rejection by the religious authorities.

[7] See classically Raney 1930; Horsley (1987: 217–221) claims it as a consensus a half-century later.

[8] But Jeremias (1969: 259, 26–67) later confused things by moving more in the direction of seeing all the *'am-hā-'āres* as sinners.

In the mid-1980s, however, E. P. Sanders' blockbusting *Jesus and Judaism* challenged these approaches head on. Building on an earlier article (1983), Sanders (1985: 174–211) argued that the Pharisees had too little influence and were too few in number to have successfully stigmatized as 'sinners' all non-Pharisees, or even the majority of the people of the land. What is more, why would Jesus be criticized for eating with what amounted to his own cultural subgroup, since he was not a formally trained teacher or aligned with any of the leadership movements? Rather, the 'sinners' in the Gospels must be seen as the flagrantly wicked. The Greek term employed, *hamartōloi*, in the Septuagint regularly translated the Hebrew *rěšā'îm*, a word consistently used for serious forms of immoral or evil behaviour. Now one can understand why Jesus would be severely criticized.

Sanders goes even further, to allege that by eating with the wicked, Jesus demonstrated his acceptance of them *without* calling them to repentance. Sanders points to the paucity of references to 'repentance' in Mark and Matthew; the few references that do occur he believes prove historically suspect. Mark 1:15 and parallels are the Evangelists' creation of a kind of headline over Jesus' ministry, summarizing how he went around telling people to repent in light of the imminently arriving kingdom. The majority of explicit references to repentance occur in Luke, several in demonstrably redactional additions to Mark or Q, so that it would appear this is a favourite theme of Luke and not necessarily of the historical Jesus (cf. also Sanders 1993: 231–232).[9]

Now Sanders does not deny that, if asked, Jesus would have responded that turning from sin was a good thing to do; he just does not believe it formed the distinctive or dominant core of Jesus' message. Rather, what stood out was Jesus' pronunciation of God's forgiveness of sins to people without requiring of them the standard Jewish signs of true repentance: the offering of animal sacrifices in the temple; restitution where crimes, particularly financial ones, against people could be compensated for; and a period of penance. or probation during which one's change of heart and behaviour could be tested.

Scholars have responded to Sanders' claims in several ways. This last point, that Jesus bypassed the provisions in both written and oral Torah for demonstrating true repentance via the temple cult and

---

[9] Without always coming to the same historical conclusions, see the detailed unpacking of the concern in Luke for tax collectors by Ford (1984: 65–78) and for sinners more generally by Neale (1991). For an entire monograph on the theme of repentance in Luke, with detailed consideration of Jewish backgrounds, see Nave 2002.

specific restitution or penance, has been widely accepted. Herein may well have lain one of the major 'scandals' of Jesus' ministry (see esp. Chilton 1992). On the other hand, Sanders has probably overly minimized both the impact of the Pharisees in Jesus' world and the pervasiveness of a desire for ritual purity, even on the part of the ordinary people (whose scrupulous concern for the Law can, at the same time, certainly be overestimated). Jacob Neusner's many writings provide a counterpoint to Sanders at this juncture,[10] while Roland Deines has provided perhaps the most balanced analysis seeking a middle ground between exaggerating and overly minimizing the role of purity in Pharisaic thought and practice.[11] The rejection of any widespread concern for repentance, finally, is the weakest link in Sanders' chain of argument. The claim that Lukan theological emphasis implies unhistorical fabrication is again a *non sequitur*, and, even apart from specific uses of the term in the earlier Gospels or Gospel sources, the whole thrust of Jesus' ethical teaching highlights stringent moral living, in contrast to many prevailing trends of his day, as the sign of the transformed lives the in-breaking kingdom generates among his followers (see esp. Chilton 1988; cf. N. Young 1985).

William Walker (1978) offers a more sweeping challenge to the conviction that Jesus' acceptance of tax collectors formed a central and authentic part of his historical mission. He itemizes six reasons for rejecting this theme in its entirety.

(1) The tradition appears only in the Synoptic Gospels within the New Testament.

(2) The most authentic Synoptic material presents Jesus holding a very negative view of the tax collectors (grouping them with sinners and prostitutes in pejorative slogans: Matt. 5:46–47; 18:15–17; 21:31–32).

(3) The references to Jesus' positive association with them appear mostly in accusations by his critics, which therefore cannot be trusted (Matt. 11:18–19 par.; Luke 15:1–2).

(4) The two narratives that actually portray Jesus dining with tax collectors (Mark 2:15–17 pars.; Luke 19:1–10) can be viewed as artificial constructions.

---

[10] See esp. Neusner 1991. For a balanced, mediating perspective see Dunn 1990; for a similar approach in dialogue with the ongoing debate between Sanders and Neusner, see Hengel and Deines 1995.

[11] See esp. Deines 2001. Cf. also Hengel and Deines 1995 and Dunn 1990.

(5) There is confusion surrounding the identity of one of those tax collectors, Levi, since Matthew's Gospel refers to him as Matthew instead (Matt. 9:9–13).

(6) Finally, an Aramaic word *tĕlānê*, which means something like 'playboy', could have been confused with the Greek *telōnēs* for tax collector.

None of these arguments seems strong. Regarding (1), the Synoptic Gospels are overwhelmingly the place where even fairly sceptical scholars turn to find the *most* reliable historical information about Jesus. In response to (2), the negative uses of 'tax collector' all involve Jesus echoing the conventional views of his day in teachings that also challenge his listeners to a quite different ethic. Concerning (3), stereotypical charges, even when they include an element of caricature, are usually built on a core historical truth. Argument (4), about artificial constructions, is called into question by the integrity and logic of the relevant passages that emerges when we examine them in depth one at a time (see chapters 4 and 5). Point (5), dealing with the different names assigned to the tax collector Jesus calls as a disciple, makes the Synoptists' agreement on his identity as a tax collector that much more significant and secure. One can also be uncertain of people's names yet still remember accurately a lot of other information about them, as anyone who has begun to age even a little can attest! As for (6), it is improbable that an Aramaic word would ever have led to a Gospel writer rendering it with a similar-sounding Greek word on that basis alone. On any theory of Gospel authorship, the writers knew they were *translating* Jesus' teaching from one language to another, not looking for similar-sounding words. Aramaic *can* be shown to influence our exegesis of the Greek of the Gospels when a specific nuance in the Aramaic word Jesus most likely used does not automatically carry over to the Greek term, but that is not what Walker is proposing.[12]

Yet even if wholesale rejections of Jesus' welcome of the outcasts of his world can be fairly readily dispensed with, it is clear that the current state of scholarship is more in flux on this topic than many introductory overviews concede. Moreover, even after eliminating the idiosyncracies of the Jesus Seminar, it is increasingly recognized that the standard criteria of authenticity used in Gospels scholarship – multiple attestation, dissimilarity, coherence and Palestinian

---

[12] For a similar but independent critique of Walker, see Neale 1991: 110–115.

environment – cannot bear all the weight that has often been placed on them.[13] In fact, N. T. Wright and a trio of German scholars (Gerd Theissen, Dagmar Winter and Annette Merz) have independently developed a four-part criterion that holds out considerably greater promise for valid historical-Jesus research. Wright (1996: esp. 131–133) calls it the criterion of 'double similarity and dissimilarity'. The Germans refer to it as the *Plausibilitätskriterium*, which in English translation has been rendered 'the criterion of historical plausibility' (Theissen and Merz 1997: 115–118; Theissen and Winter 2002). In short, the criterion suggests that when an element of the Gospel tradition (1) makes sense in the first third of the first century in Israel, yet (2) depicts Jesus challenging conventional Jewish thinking in some respect *and* (3) shows signs of having been followed by early Christianity either inside or outside the New Testament, yet (4) seems to have changed in some significant way in that later context, *then* we have powerful support for believing it to be authentic. That is to say, other early Jewish or Gentile Christians are unlikely to have created it and read it back onto the lips of Jesus.

What happens to our theme of Jesus, sinners and table fellowship when this four-part criterion is applied to it?[14] We may deal with two of the four parts quite briefly because there is little controversy attached to their application. Celebrating communal meals together continued to play a central role in early Christian living. The first summary of Christian fellowship in Acts 2:42 describes the believers 'breaking bread' together, a practice subsequently stated as occurring in their homes on a daily basis (v. 46). Acts 6:1–7 depicts a daily distribution to needy believers, which may well have involved food (the other possibility is money). Peter's 'breakthrough' with Cornelius involved his recognition that by declaring all foods clean, God was declaring all people clean, so that there could no longer be valid objections to Jewish Christians residing and eating with Gentiles (Acts 10; cf. 11:3). Paul and Silas enjoyed a meal with the Philippian jailer and his family, on which occasion the latter were baptized (16:34). Paul and his companions likewise 'break bread' with the church in Troas, after which Paul preaches into the night

---

[13] I have summarized the state of research already in Blomberg 1987: 246–254, with updates in Blomberg 2001: 63–66.

[14] In very sketchy form, Rau (1998) has done this for Jesus' association with sinners more generally. Cf. his generally positive results with the fairly meagre conclusions of Fiedler's book-length work (1976) on Jesus and sinners using the older criteria of authenticity and tradition-critical dissections of each passage.

(20:7–12).[15] While not pervasive, the motif of Christians eating special meals with each other and extending table fellowship to outsiders appears just often enough to demonstrate that Jesus' practice was not something unique to his mission or ministry but remains a model for Christians everywhere.

The most significant meal for early Christians, of course, was the Lord's Supper, which may already be referenced in Acts 2:42. Important epistolary teaching on its practice occurs in 1 Corinthians 10:14–22 and 11:17–34, in which Paul rebukes the Corinthian Christians for the way they are eating food sacrificed to idols in the context of pagan temple worship and are profaning the Lord's Supper by not caring adequately for the poor and needy in their midst.[16] Hebrews 13:10 may also allude to the Eucharist when it avers, 'We have an altar from which those who minister at the tabernacle have no right to eat,' but this is disputed. Hebrews 13:2 certainly reflects the need for early Christian hospitality more generally, as it alludes to Abraham's experience of entertaining angels 'unawares' (KJV).

Revelation 2:14–16 and 20–22 contain further reproof of early Christian communities improperly eating food sacrificed to idols, again because they confuse pagan worship with Christian. In 3:20, Jesus introduces the precious metaphor of coming in to eat with those who open the door to him when he knocks. And perhaps the most important reference to a Christian meal in the New Testament outside the Gospels is the glorious picture of the wedding feast of the Lamb (Rev. 19:7–9), a stunning portrait of the intimacy of table fellowship that all God's people will enjoy with all the company of the redeemed of every age when Christ returns. A number of Jesus' meals with his disciples even before the Last Supper may well have intentionally foreshadowed this banquet, especially given the imagery Jesus utilizes in Matthew 8:10–11 and parallel, of people coming from every direction of the compass to eat with faithful Jews when the kingdom comes in all its fullness.[17] There is thus no doubt that lines of continuity proceeded from Jesus' dining customs into early Christian meal practices in the rest of the New Testament (cf. further Oden 2001). •

[15] For a similar overview, see Bolyki (1998: 208–210), who adds the meal on board the ill-fated ship in Acts 27:33–38. But there is no indication that Paul here is 'breaking bread' with any other Christians, or that the meal is anything other than an ordinary one after so many days of fasting.

[16] On both passages, see further Blomberg (1994a: *ad loc*).

[17] For a more detailed survey of the texts presented in this paragraph (along with a few others), see Bolyki 1998: 210–215.

At the same time, significant discontinuity appears. Precisely because Jesus' Last Supper (Mark 14:12–26 pars.) took on such central significance and became prescriptive for the repeated celebration of the Lord's Supper, the unambiguous evidence of Christians continuing to go out of their way to have ordinary meals with the sinners and outcasts of their communities remains comparatively meagre. Jude 12 affords the lone New Testament reference to the *agapē* or love feast, terminology which is repeated in Ignatius, Tertullian, Clement of Alexandria, the *Sybilline Oracles*, the *Epistula Apostolorum*, the *Apocalypse of Paul* and perhaps a few other early Christian sources. But while there is a diversity of meals to which this terminology is applied, none unambiguously describes a fellowship meal *apart from* the celebration of the Eucharist (McGowan 1997; cf. Bolyki 1998: 223–227). *Didache* 11 offers instructions on how long to provide hospitality for itinerant Christian prophets, but these seem to apply only to ordinary meals in private homes. Otherwise this document's various references to table prayers and fellowship meals point to eucharistic practices (cf. further Bolyki 1998: 222–223). None of this is to say that believers cannot combine some of the objectives of Jesus' table fellowship with outsiders with the celebration of the Lord's Supper, but the caution that not everyone should partake of the latter (1 Cor. 11:27–32),[18] contrasting with the radical inclusiveness of the former, makes it more difficult to combine the two kinds of meals than to keep them separate.

Ironically, it is actually non-Christian Judaism that appears to preserve a somewhat closer parallel to the format of Jesus' original festive meals, particularly in the Pharisaic *ḥăbûrôt* (White 1988). But of course these were not open to 'sinners', whether the ritually impure or the morally wicked, while the Christian celebration of the Lord's Supper, precisely because of the warnings of 1 Corinthians 11, became increasingly limited first to believers only and then, in even narrower fashion, to Christians of certain theological traditions or to 'believers in good standing' with the Lord, as we might say today. Within a few centuries after the beginning of the Christian era, no context remained in which Christians re-created the conflicted

---

[18] This is true regardless of one's interpretation of precisely who should exclude themselves from the Lord's Table and for what reasons. A fair number of recent commentators argue, persuasively in my opinion, that 'discerning the body of the Lord' in v. 29 refers to truly recognizing who God's people are and thus caring for the poor in their midst (contrast vv. 17–22) (see further Blomberg 1994a: 231). But non-Christians by definition cannot truly understand who Christ's body is, or they would become Christians.

dynamic of what Jerome Neyrey (1996: 160) calls 'Jesus' own eating customs, his choice of table companions, his disregard for washing rites preceding meals, and his unconcern for tithed bread': precisely the behaviour that 'provoke[d] controversy with other religious reformers'.

Because there is such a vast literature already on the Last Supper and the Lord's Supper, I have chosen not to focus on those meals on this occasion. What have been comparatively neglected are the *other* meals that Jesus celebrated and the company he kept at them. It is true that the Gospels do describe one notorious sinner, namely Judas Iscariot, participating for a portion of the Last Supper with Jesus (cf. Matt. 26:20–25 with John 13:18–30), but it is doubtful if we can make any generalizations for Christian practice based on this one exceptional figure who had a unique role to play in the events that led to Jesus' death. But what about the various kinds of 'sinners' who regularly graced the table with Jesus and his disciples on other occasions? What of the other two parts of the double similarity and dissimilarity criterion, comparing the teachings and actions attributed to Jesus with Jewish backgrounds? After all, here will appear answers not only to questions of authenticity but also to those of meaning. Later Christian practice may help us evaluate the former, but it cannot be used to determine the latter. Jesus could have assumed knowledge only of that which already existed during his lifetime, either by comparison or contrast with the practices of his contemporaries, if he wanted his audiences to understand his behaviour.

Our way forward, therefore, will be as follows. First we will survey the different kinds of Old Testament meals that potentially provide background for Jesus' teaching and behaviour, highlighting the texts that offer important illustrations of those meals. Then we will turn to developments in the intertestamental period, from both Jewish and Greco-Roman contexts, that may shed similar light. For if Smith and Corley are right, the symposium model had so permeated the ancient Mediterranean world that even orthodox Jews adopted forms of it. But it will have to be determined if indeed those scholars *are* right. Finally, we will proceed to analyse in greater depth the key texts in the Gospels mentioned at the outset of this introduction and grapple with questions both of their authenticity and of their meaning. In closing, we will briefly suggest some possible contemporary applications of our findings.

Chapter Two

Forming friendships but evading enemies

Meals in the Old Testament

Prominent as is the role dining plays in the Hebrew Bible, there are surprisingly few sustained studies of the topic. Dictionary and encyclopedia articles often helpfully survey selections of references, under headings such as 'meal customs' or 'eating and drinking' (see esp. Schramm 1992; Jenks 1993). Books on life in biblical Israel typically have short sections on topics like hospitality, furniture, food preparation, bread making and daily meals (as in King and Stager 2001: 61–68; cf. Grimm 1996: 14–20). Studies on meals in the Gospels occasionally have significant Old Testament background material (see esp. Mosca 1985), and larger works on hospitality in one or both testaments usually contain helpful introductions to dining (see esp. Duke 1980; cf. Douglas 1975: 249–275; Denaux 1999). Diane Sharon (2002) *has* recently written an entire book on meals in the Hebrew Scriptures, but her interest is in a structural analysis that defends the thesis that unless eating and drinking appear as what she calls a variable in a separate literary form, the meal at hand will form part of an oracle of either 'establishment' or 'doom'. That is to say, one will recognize a prophetic or foreshadowing element in the meal, for either good or ill for the protagonists. Sharon's study proves reasonably persuasive for the meals she examines, but she assigns so many others to more tangential roles which are thus excluded from her analysis that it is hard to be sure she has really identified a consistent pattern.

Perhaps the best summary of our topic to date appears in Philip King's short article on 'Commensality in the Biblical World' in the Ernest Frerichs *Festschrift* (1998). There King observes that 'the two basic obligations of hospitality are to feed and to protect the guest or stranger' (53). Old Testament meals frequently occur in this context, but King also surveys key texts that illustrate festive meals, royal banquets, the eschatological banquet and the 'daily fare of stew'. But King's article spans a mere nine pages, so clearly there is room for more to be said. And it is not obvious that feeding the stranger happens very often in the Old Testament at all.

Moreover, none of the studies of dining in the Hebrew Scriptures of which I am aware treat them in either canonical or historical order, allowing one to observe whether different emphases emerge at different times in biblical history or within different literary genres. So it would appear crucial to embark on a survey of key Old Testament texts *in sequence*[1] and see what emerges. Because our ultimate interest is in making sense of Jesus' teaching and actions in the Gospels, we too must be comparatively brief and leave more space for the fuller analysis of Gospel texts. But we must engage the Old Testament in enough detail to ensure that any generalizations about Jesus' similarity or dissimilarity with the Israelite religion that preceded him prove valid. While not having room for separate discussions of every minor reference to food in the Hebrew Scriptures, we have tried to highlight every passage in which a meal plays a particularly significant role. We also refer to a fair number of other texts in which dining occupies at least a moderately important position.

The Pentateuch

As with many topics in the Hebrew Bible, the Torah (or five books of Moses) lays the foundation for the majority of subsequent motifs involving meals. Food, of course, plays a crucial role from the creation of Adam and Eve in the garden onward. The one prohibition God gave the first human couple was not to eat of the tree of the knowledge of good and evil, precisely what they went ahead and did anyway (Gen. 2:17; 3:6). Inasmuch as food normally sustains life, the choice of this particular restriction as a test of human obedience proves understandable. In this case, disobedience, in eating the forbidden fruit, brought the onset of death rather than eternal life. The later purity laws are also foreshadowed in the early chapters of Genesis, when Noah is commanded to bring two of every kind of animal onto the ark, but to bring seven of every clean animal (7:2–3).[2] Yet neither of these accounts narrates a full-fledged meal.

---

[1] Because it more closely approximates chronological order and more consistently groups books of like genre together, we will proceed through the sequence of Old Testament books following the arrangement of the Protestant rather than the Jewish canon.

[2] Mathews (1996: 372) rejects the common critical complaint of anachronism here, arguing that such an early distinction was appropriate, given 'the same understanding of God and his relationship to the righteous (e.g., Sabbath, Exod. 16:23–29)' as would later distinguish Israel from the nations.

The first such meal appears when Abram tithes his spoils of war to Melchizedek, king and priest of Salem. On that occasion, this pagan who nevertheless seems to know God Almighty[3] brings out bread and wine (14:18): fare for a royal banquet honouring a returning conqueror (Wenham 1987: 316; cf. Waltke 2001: 233). An even more extensive description of an elaborate meal emerges when Abraham encounters three visitors at the entrance to his tent near the great trees of Mamre (18:1–8). The 'three seahs of fine flour' (v. 6) represent a large amount of food. The lavish meal continues with curds, milk and a tender choice calf (vv. 7–8), showing either Abraham's 'relative prosperity and social standing, or his desire to give his best to his guests, or both' (Hamilton 1995: 11). The extent of the meal is surprising after Abraham's initial offer merely of 'something to eat' (v. 5). Nahum Sarna (1989: 129) cites the Talmud (*Baba Metzia* 87a), 'Such is the way of the righteous; they promise little but perform much.' Sarna also alleges that 'Abraham's openhearted, liberal hospitality to the total strangers knows no bounds.' But this goes considerably beyond what is actually narrated. In light of texts still to come, what is worth observing is that while the guests are initially unknown to Abraham, nothing in the passage gives him any reason to be suspicious of them, as with potential enemies.

Genesis 19 narrates what is almost certainly intended as a direct contrast to chapter 18. Here Abraham's nephew, Lot, likewise tries to provide hospitality for two of the three strangers, now identified as angels, who had visited his uncle. But the wicked inhabitants of Sodom surround his house and demand that the visitors be sent out as sex toys. Lot refuses, offering his virgin daughters instead, a proposal that does not interest anyone, and has to be rescued by the angels striking the outsiders with temporary blindness (vv. 1–11). Whatever we make of Lot's bizarre offer,[4] commentators are generally agreed that Lot is going out of his way to be as hospitable a host as possible to his meal-guests. At the same time, a meal of 'bread without yeast' (v. 3) foreshadows the haste with which Lot and his family will have

---

[3] Sarna (1989: 109) describes Melchizedek as a monotheist, one of the few select non-Israelite individuals in the Old Testament who are depicted as preserving the original religion of the human race in the face of what had almost universally degenerated into pagan polytheism.

[4] Bechtel (1999) may be best in suggesting that Lot's offer violates both his standards (as a godly person) and the community's (as desiring homosexual rather than heterosexual intercourse), and that both know it. The totally offensive offer is an attempt to 'defuse the tension, stop the action and prevent possible aggression' (32). Unfortunately it fails.

to flee (vv. 12–22) because of the imminent destruction of Sodom. In both chapters 18 and 19, then, meals do more than illustrate abundant hospitality; they prefigure the well-being or doom of those who eat them.[5]

Another series of passages in Genesis may be grouped together under the heading of feasts to celebrate special family occasions. In 21:8 Abraham throws a banquet to celebrate Isaac's weaning, though the festivity is marred by Sarah's jealousy of Hagar and Ishmael (vv. 9–10). In 24:54 Bethuel's family enjoys a festive meal in honour of Rebekah's engagement to Isaac. A generation later, a wedding feast for Jacob and Rachel is held in the same home, this time complicated by Laban's deceit in at first giving Leah to Jacob instead (29:22–23). Such occasions would continue to be times of feasting throughout the Israelites' history.[6]

The pair of events by which Jacob stole Esau's birthright involved meals as well. First Esau traded his birthright for some bread and lentil stew (25:29–34), an episode in which he is portrayed 'as a boor' and 'self-gratifying glutton' who asks for soup to 'gulp down' or 'swallow greedily' (Sharp 1980: 166). Then Jacob feeds his father a meal of game, tricking him into thinking he is Esau and receiving the blessing Isaac thought he was giving to his older son (27:1–40). The importance of meals is highlighted by the covenant-making and -breaking activities that occur during them. Bruce Waltke (2001: 363) recapitulates: 'Adam fails in eating, Noah in drinking, and Isaac, a gourmand, in tasting. God's sovereign grace must now prevail over Isaac's efforts to thwart the divine intention.'

A different kind of covenant is sealed when Isaac and Abimelech eat together, swear an oath, and depart in peace, no longer at odds with one another (26:30–31).[7] Likewise Jacob and Laban signal an uneasy truce between them with a sacrificial meal in the company of relatives (31:54). In each case, the individual giving the banquet admits (or re-admits) the other into their 'family' circle (Hamilton 1995: 207). Or as Sarna (1989: 188) explains, 'In the ancient world,

---

[5] Matthews (1992) takes a minority view, arguing that Lot should be partially implicated in this judgment as well, for taking aliens into his home from a position of sitting in the city gate (v. 1) as if he were an official representative of the town, and that is one reason for the Sodomites' anger. But nothing in the text enables us to determine Lot's role in the city one way or the other.

[6] For a brief survey of ancient Israelite wedding and marriage customs, see King and Stager 2001: 55–56.

[7] Nicol (1996: 359) explains that the feast and oath create a transformation 'as the result of an appropriate recognition of the source of Isaac's blessing; threat and aggression are converted to peace and security.'

treaty-making often was accompanied by a ceremonial meal, the purpose of which was to create an auspicious atmosphere of harmony and fellowship for the pact to go into effect.' One thinks of Proverbs 16:7: 'When people's ways are pleasing to the Lord, he makes even their enemies live at peace with them' (Wenham 1994: 193).

The last significant meal in Genesis is the one at which Joseph and his brothers are reunited in Egypt. While Joseph is still testing them, by returning their money and hiding a silver cup in Benjamin's sack, the meal is also the first step toward their ultimate reconciliation with each other (43:24–34).[8]

Eating and drinking in Genesis are thus never ordinary matters. That is not to say that Abraham and his descendants did not normally eat ordinary meals. But the ones chosen for inclusion in this book all convey additional meaning,[9] usually in the establishment of harmony or peace where there has been estrangement, or in celebrating important gifts of God to his people. At times, however, they turn into occasions for treachery and deceit (most notably between Jacob and Esau), sins made all the more heinous because of their link with the meals at which they occurred, which should have been completely happy occasions.

Eating and drinking do not occur with the same frequency in the rest of the Pentateuch, but the references that do appear prove significant. One gets a sense of the pervasiveness of ancient Near Eastern hospitality customs when Moses helps seven young Midianite women drawing water from a well by driving hostile shepherds away from them. When they report the incident back home, their father asks them, 'Where is he?' and 'Why did you leave him? Invite him to have something to eat' (Exod. 2:20). A meal is the expected 'payback' for this stranger's kindness. The fact that he is a stranger does not change the cultural expectation.

Exodus 12 narrates the Passover event, providing the precedent for what would become an annual festival for the Israelites. Here is the beginning of the formation of the actual nation, even if it would be the next generation that would cross into and take possession of the Promised Land (cf. Durham 1987: 154). Here are key roots for the children of Israel developing a distinctive ethnic as well as religious identity, even if the realities of each would regularly involve a mixture of other peoples and beliefs as well. Deuteronomy 16:11 insists that

---

[8] Waltke (2001: 552) observes, 'At the peak of reconciliation in this scene the brothers freely feast with Benjamin, whom Joseph has lavished with favoritism.'

[9] This may well turn out to be the case for the entire Bible.

resident aliens celebrate the Passover along with the Israelites, but these are still those who have become partially assimilated to Jewish lifestyles (the *gērîm*) and not the temporarily visiting foreigners (the *nokrîm*).[10] Like the other Israelite festivals that would be prescribed in the Mosaic legislation, Passover would help forge a sense of Israel being separate and different from the other nations that surrounded it.

More so even than the other festivals, Passover focuses on a particular meal of remembrance to be celebrated by family units. 'By means of this sacrificial meal, kinship ties are strengthened, and family and neighborly solidarity is promoted, while communion with God is established' (Sarna 1991: 55; cf. Cassuto 1967: 138). But, more important than strengthening a sense of kinship, almost each item of the meal highlights another feature that sets off its celebrants from outsiders: ritual purity. The lamb must be without defect (v. 5); the bread (and homes) without yeast (v. 15: a symbol of corruption); the meat must be roasted (not eaten raw or even boiled: v. 9) to ensure the impurities are removed; and leftovers must be burned the following morning (v. 10).[11]

As the Israelites began their trek through the wilderness, supernatural provision of manna, quail and water (Exod. 16:1 – 17:7) further delineated their recipients as the objects of God's special provision (cf. also Num. 11:4–9 and 20:1–13). Rather than judging them for their grumbling, God shows remarkable restraint and grace (Enns 2000: 324; Ashby 1998: 75), even if in the case of the quail the people have to learn the lesson that too much of a good thing can become repulsive. As they receive the Law, numerous commandments enshrine ongoing concern for the dispossessed, including the foreigners in their midst (see Blomberg 1999: 48 for texts and topics), which no doubt included feeding them, though not necessarily in the context of dining together.

The next two meals in Exodus contrast strikingly with the last one. In 18:12, Moses, Aaron, Jethro and the elders of Israel all celebrate a sacrificial meal as part of the fresh start for their people that the escape from Egypt has made possible.[12] In 24:9–11, as part of a

---

[10] C. Wright (1996: 200) highlights the 'social inclusiveness of Israel's worship' here, but still it is to be 'shared throughout the whole *community*' (italics mine) and thus is not indiscriminately available to outsiders.

[11] The various elements of the meal served other purposes as well, some explicitly stated in the text, others added in Jewish tradition. But the motif of purity does seem to be a unifying one, on which see further Bergant 1994.

[12] Durham (1987: 244–245) stresses that Jethro receives the sacrifices 'as the presiding leader of worship and not in token of his acceptance of a covenant or treaty' (citing others who have argued for the latter).

covenant meal with God himself – a common practice elsewhere in the Ancient Near East but unique in Israel because of the single, pre-eminent Mosaic covenant – Moses and Aaron, Nadab and Abihu, and the seventy elders of Israel go part-way up Mount Sinai, eat and drink, and in some sense see God himself. But later, while Moses is receiving the Ten Commandments, Israel, including its leaders and even Aaron, is busy worshipping the golden calf, complete with sacrificial offerings, a festive meal, and 'revelry' which may have included sexual immorality (32:1–6).[13]

These contrasting meals set the stage for the various kinds of sacrifice for which Leviticus 1 – 7 proceeds to legislate. All of them involve food of one kind or another that Yahweh was believed to consume. In some cases, the priests who officiate can eat a portion of the meat, while uniquely in the fellowship or peace offering even those offering the sacrifice can join in the meal (7:11–21). But all who eat must be ritually clean, just as the sacrificial animals must be unblemished. Purity and wholeness or holiness remain the dominant objectives throughout (for details on all the sacrifices, see esp. Averbeck 2003).

Even more exclusivist in orientation were the dietary laws, introduced in Leviticus 11. One could maintain ritual purity only if one ate strictly clean food. The rationale behind the specific animals barred from consumption continues to be debated. Jirí Moshala (2001) itemizes no less than fourteen suggestions that compete for acceptance. But a fair consensus has emerged around Mary Douglas's views that the clean animals exhibit normality or wholeness in some element of their behaviour, as against abnormal or unexpected practices (see esp. Budd 1996: 158–184; following esp. Douglas 1966; modified by Firmage 1990, who disputes means of locomotion as an operative principle). Also influential in designating something as unclean seems to have been that which threatened nature or culture (M. Carroll 1985), in contrast to domesticated animals, which were more likely to be viewed as clean (Houston 1993).

But, whatever the precise rationale, the biblical text itself explicitly declares in Deuteronomy 14:2, immediately before its presentation of

---

[13] So most commentators. Knoppers (1995), however, observes that while *śāhaq* can elsewhere carry sexual connotations, it need not. Rather than overtly orgiastic rites, Knoppers (99, n. 15) thinks we are meant to envision a ritual banquet followed by sports, miming and antiphonal singing to honour a god, consistent with a broad pattern of worship in the ancient Near East.

the 'kosher' laws, 'Out of all the peoples on the face of the earth, the Lord has chosen you to be his treasured possession.' As Gene Schramm (1992: 650) elaborates:

> the effects of practicing kashruth, from a socio-religious stand-point, are clear: the strictures of kashruth make social intercourse between the practicing Jew and the outside world possible only on the basis of a one-sided relationship, and that is on the terms of the one who observes kashruth.

John Hartley (1992: 163) even more emphatically points out the boundary lines that these laws would have drawn between Israel and other nations nearby:

> In following these dietary laws, the Israelites obeyed God's instructions several times each day, developing deep in their consciousness an attitude of obedience to God. That all the people observed these laws at every meal was a mighty force of solidarity, uniting the people as God's special treasure (Exod. 19:5). It separated the Israelites from their polytheistic neighbors and became a distinguishing mark of their national identity ... They erect a high barrier against assimilation and amalgamation of the Jewish people, which would lead to the loss of their racial identity.

By the time one reaches the New Testament era, keeping a kosher table was one of the top three or four boundary markers that visibly set Jews apart from their neighbours and kept them from most table fellowship with Gentiles. The significance of the fact that Jesus would set the stage for the abolition of these laws in early Christian practice can scarcely be overestimated, a theme to which we will return when we reach the Gospels (see chapters 4 and 5).

Numbers and Deuteronomy pursue a topic introduced already in Exodus: that of looking forward to entrance into Canaan as a 'land flowing with milk and honey' (see Ashley 1993: 239, n. 18 for a complete list of references). Particularly crucial is Numbers 13, in which the spies confirm the report of the bounty of the land but the majority of them, terrified of the Canaanites, consign the people to wilderness wanderings for forty years. The bounty will be experienced by later generations, however, and will become a type of the eschatological blessings of a new age (see 'The prophets', below).[14] In the shorter term, it paves the way for the central Deuteronomic theology that, as Israel in general and her leaders in particular are more obedient to God's Law than not, they will collectively experience long life, abundance, prosperity, and peace from their enemies in the Promised Land (see classically Deut. 28:1–14).

A more tangential reference to meals occurs in Deuteronomy 23:3–4, in which the Ammonites and Moabites are prevented from entering the assembly of the Lord because they did not meet the Israelites 'with bread and water' on their way into Canaan. At first blush, this might seem to have been an unreasonable expectation, since these were entirely separate nations that may have recognized the purpose of the Israelites' march toward the Promised Land. On the other hand, Israel had specifically requested peaceful passage through the territory outside Canaan and had even promised not to eat or drink anything from those lands (Num. 20:14 – 21:35). The conventions of hospitality, even for strangers, or at least for those who came in peace, were deeply enough embedded in that region that these countries should have responded differently.

The Pentateuch thus presents a diverse array of purposes for special meals. They include celebrating military conquest, demonstrating personal hospitality, marking family milestones, sealing covenants, offering sacrifice to God and commemorating his mighty acts in history. In a significant number of contexts, the meals depicted include outsiders to the chosen line of Abraham and they create varying levels of peace and well-being with Abraham's descendants. Yet the outsiders in many instances, with a few noteworthy exceptions, have some pre-existing relationship to the people with whom they eat. Meanwhile, another collection of texts, culminating in the dietary laws, sets the stage for dining among the Israelites to become a much more exclusive practice. Meals can also form the setting for treachery against Yahweh and his commandments; in such contexts they usually exacerbate the seriousness of that deceit.

The historical books

The extent to which meals play a central role in the books the Hebrew Scriptures call 'the former prophets' (or in the other 'historical books'

---

[14] A minority view is represented by Levine 2000, who thinks that a 'milk and honey' economy in the Bible often reflects survival at a subsistence level, but this flies in the face of most of the contexts in which the expression appears.

in the arrangement of the Christian canon) varies considerably from one volume to the next. Although Joshua finally brings the children of Israel to Canaan and they begin to enjoy the land flowing with milk and honey, there is no eating *per se* in the book that merits our attention. Judges, on the other hand, contains numerous significant meal narratives. Like the book more generally, most of them contain considerable negative elements.

In Judges 4:18–24, we read the gruesome account of Jael's treachery. Purportedly offering refuge in her tent to Sisera, general of Hazor under King Jabin, she drives a peg through his temple, killing him as he sleeps. Doubtless Sisera's willingness to trust Jael was enhanced by her volunteering to slake his thirst and by her offer of milk when he asked merely for water (v. 19). Perhaps illustrating the principle that all is fair in love and war (or at least in war!), Deborah's victory song proceeds to extol Jael precisely for her duplicitous ploy (5:24–27).[15]

In an uncharacteristically positive narrative in Judges, Gideon offers a sacrifical meal for Yahweh which God entirely consumes by fire (6:21). This event forms Gideon's commission and consecration for his unlikely role as a judge in Israel. At the place where his family had erected an altar to Baal, Yahweh orders him 'to reclaim this apostate shrine locale by himself' (Younger 2002: 178; cf. vv. 25–26). The next meal contrasts strikingly with this one, as practices revert to the pagan. In 9:27 the Shechemites rebel against Abimelech in the context of a festival to their god, one marked specifically by 'eating and drinking'.

Judges 14:10 introduces the customary week-long wedding feast, as Samson marries a Philistine bride, but this merely forms the setting for his riddle and its aftermath, remaining tangential to the overall narrative. Judges 19, on the other hand, presents a meal that plays a far more central role in its context. A syncretistic Levite, trying to reclaim a concubine from her parents' home, is invited to eat and drink with her family for five days. Repeatedly he tries to leave, but her father persuades him to stay longer. The Levite's father-in-law is still lavishing this kind of hospitality when the couple insist on breaking away to return to their home. From this point on, things go from bad to worse. They cannot make it home by nightfall; they reject the idea of staying in the still foreign city of Jebus and make

---

[15] Block (1999: 209–210), however, points out several features in the narrative of Judges 4 that make Jael a more ambiguous figure and not necessarily one that the narrator intends others to emulate.

their way to Gibeah instead. But only a newcomer to town welcomes them. The meal he offers and the subsequent demand by the towns-people to have sex with the Levite are meant to make us recall the strikingly similar episode in Genesis 19. Once again the host, in vain, offers his virgin daughter as a replacement for his guest. But this time no supernatural protection appears, while the Levite proceeds to give his concubine to them, who is raped and then murdered. As graphically as any episode in the entire book of Judges, this text reflects the degenerate state of Israel during the period in which there was no king and 'everyone did as they saw fit' (21:25).[16] In retrospect, the father-in-law's hospitality no longer seems excessive;[17] was he (wittingly or unwittingly) protecting the Levite and his daughter from the grave danger that lay ahead? Once again, meals form the heart of the two episodes of countercultural hospitality that temporarily relieve the horror of this era.

Food and meals likewise form an important part of the hospitality that Boaz offers Ruth in the little book that bears her name. Set in this later period of Judges, he unquestioningly reflects atypical, positive behaviour in treating this newly arrived Moabite woman with great kindness, including gracious gleaning arrangements (Ruth 2:8–9, 15–18) and a privileged position with him at mealtime (v. 14).[18] All this occurs before he finds out that he is a potential kinsman-redeemer for her mother-in-law Naomi. Robert Hubbard (1988: 173) rightly speaks of Boaz as 'a model of racial and religious tolerance'. At the same time, Boaz is not showing kindness to the truly 'other'. He *does* already know at this stage that Ruth has bound herself to Naomi and her (Jewish) God (2:6, 11–12; cf. 1:16–18).

Turning to the period of the monarchy, the narratives of Samuel and Kings are filled with significant meals. Elkanah's faithful doling out of food portions to his wives at the annual Shiloh sacrifice, according to the number of children they had, proved a regular embarrassment to barren Hannah (1 Sam. 1:3–8). The NIV's 'double portion' for Hannah (v. 5) is probably a mistaken translation of an obscure Hebrew phrase that more likely means only one portion (Bergen 1996: 66), but either way she would still have received

---

[16] On this material, as on chs. 17 – 21 more generally, cf. esp. Satterthwaite 1993.

[17] Block (1999: 527) notes that it exceeds even that of Abraham in Genesis 18.

[18] Bush (1996: 128) thinks Boaz's behaviour welcomes Ruth into his intimate circle of close companions and that the provisions for gleaning formed 'an unheard-of favor'. Cf. also Sasson (1979: 55), who muses that offering her the first handfuls of roasted grain may have been 'ceremonial, perhaps quasi-legal in nature'.

far less than Peninnah with her many children. And the intimate contexts of meal and worship would have heightened Hannah's sorrow.

In 1 Samuel 9:12–24, an even more formal commissioning of Saul than that which Judges depicted for Gideon takes place immediately after a sacrificial meal. It includes Samuel and about thirty specially invited visitors, with designated seats and portions of food intended to honour Saul above all of them (vv. 22–23; cf. Hertzberg 1964: 83). Robert Gordon (1986: 115) rightly suggests that 'the meal takes on the character of a coronation supper', even if the participants other than Samuel do not yet recognize this aspect. Clearly this is a select company, not open to everyone.

More minor references to food include the honey that Jonathan consumed, not knowing about his father's ban on eating during battle, an edict that almost got him killed (14:24–45); David's offering the culturally appropriate gifts, including things to eat, when he began his service to Saul (16:19–20); and his errand to his brothers in bringing them food when he was sent to check up on their welfare in the conflict with the Philistines (17:17–19). Missing a meal can also prove significant, as when David repeatedly does not come to Saul's table and the king finally intuits his rebellion (ch. 20).[19]

The next major meal comes in 1 Samuel 25. In fact, this chapter presents the antithesis between two meals: Nabal's 'feast of fools', which cannot be interrupted to meet the needs of David and his men, and Abigail's gifts of food for them, which stave off certain destruction of her household. The absence and presence of expected hospitality are abruptly juxtaposed. In the words of Ralph Klein (1983: 251), Nabal's 'gluttonous eating and drinking are in stark contrast with his denial of David's request for provisions for his starving, thirsty band. Nabal feasted like a king, but rejected the legitimate request of the future king.'[20]

The last two meals in 1 Samuel contrast Saul, soon to die for his sins in combat (28:21–25; cf. ch. 31), with an Egyptian captured in battle and revived by a meal (30:11–12). The very warfare that slays the legitimate king is prolonged by a foreigner, who is reinvigorated

---

[19] On the motif of refusing to eat and drink here and elsewhere in the Old Testament, see Sharon 1999.

[20] For intriguing intertextual comparisons between Eve, Abigail and the Lady Wisdom of Proverbs 9, see McKinlay 1999. Abigail may be a redemptive counterpart to Eve, foreshadowing the later personification of Wisdom as a quasi-divine feminine.

to become an informant. Where there should have been hope, despair takes its place, and vice versa.[21]

The privilege attached to dining at the king's table reappears in 2 Samuel 9 as David extends kindness to the house of Saul by inviting his crippled grandson, Mephibosheth, to eat with him. This kindness parallels David's later command to his son Solomon to treat the sons of Barzillai in similar fashion (1 Kgs 2:7). A. A. Anderson (1989: 142) notes that 'it is less certain whether this royal patronage meant that' the persons in question 'shared the king's personal table' or whether each 'had his own establishment in Jerusalem' (cf. 2 Sam. 16:3). It seems probable, however, that both privileges were granted. Compare also the arrangements made for Jehoiachin in exile in 2 Kings 25:27–30 and Jeremiah 52:31–34.

David's practice of fasting while his dying son was still alive, but then eating normally after his death, surprised those around him, but it makes good sense in light of the chronology of when prayer and fasting can and cannot move God to act (2 Sam. 12:15–23).[22] The sacrificial meal in 1 Kings 1:9–10 highlighted Adonijah's attempt to claim David's throne. While internally trying to unite those on his side (Ishida 1987: 174–175), Adonijah's ploy backfired and David installed Solomon as his successor instead (vv. 11–53). 1 Kings 4:22–28 and 8:62–66 itemize the vast quantities of foodstuffs and animals for sacrifice that Solomon's faithfulness helped him to amass. Here is Deuteronomic theology working as it should: God showering his blessings, including material resources, on his people (cf. 4:25) and especially on their leaders in response to covenant obedience. Despite the huge quantities of the provisions, Solomon has an enormous retinue for which to care, so the amounts are not as fantastic as some commentators allege (rightly House 1995: 117). And while the total consumption could be criticized (cf. Brueggemann 2000: 62 with 116), its role in the narrative underlines God's blessing. As Paul House comments on 1 Kings 8 (1995: 150), 'the whole celebration is so historically and symbolically important that the festival lasts fourteen

---

[21] Klein (1983: 273) sees Saul's willingness to eat after first refusing to do so as simply the last of his many inconsistencies. The narrative does not intend to offer hope for Saul's survival here (*contra*, e.g., M. Evans 2000). Bergen (1996: 269) further observes that 'the woman's generous gift of food in behalf of the king and his men is reminiscent of Abigail's even more bounteous gift to David and his men (cf. 25:18–27). The comparison of the women's gifts invites a comparison of the women: whereas Saul was nurtured by a woman under the Lord's curse (cf. Lev. 20:27), David was nurtured by a woman under the Lord's blessings (25:33).'

[22] On which, again see Sharon 1999.

days. When the people finally leave, they praise the Lord and bless the king for all that has happened. Indeed, this entire event has served to unify Israel as one people, under one king, serving the one true God.'

This unity, unfortunately, proves short-lived; Solomon's faithlessness later in his reign marks the beginning of the demise of Israel, which in subsequent generations will lead to the divided kingdom and ultimately to the conquest and exile of both north and south. 1 Kings 13, during Jeroboam's day, reminds us of Adonijah's rebellion, in which eating with someone demonstrated one's loyalty to that person, in this case again someone who does not side with Yahweh. There are many strange features of this chapter's description of the anonymous 'man of God' who first obeys God's commands not to eat with the apostate king or his supporters, but then is tricked by a false prophet into violating the command. But his obedience should have been unflinching; in its place he loses his life instead (cf. further Wiseman 1993: 146).

1 Kings 17 – 19 contain four texts that further illustrate either the dangers of eating in the wrong place with the wrong people or God's provision for those who resist that temptation, even if it produces dire consequences. 1 Kings 17 contains the two accounts of Elijah being fed by ravens, while staying out of the public limelight (vv. 1–6), and of the miraculous provision for the widow of Zarephath and her son, who later housed Elijah (vv. 7–24). The latter passage is noteworthy because Zarephath was part of Sidon in Gentile territory. Presumably the widow and her son were Gentiles as well, a point Luke 4:25–26 appears to highlight. Still, the narrator of 1 Kings never spells out their ethnicity, and the point of the passage surrounds Elijah's miracle-working activity, not any boundary-breaking with foreigners.[23] Indeed, to the extent that the geography is significant, the narrative highlights Yahweh's power over against Baal's impotence in the homeland of the Baal-worshipping queen, Jezebel herself (cf. Long 2002: 206; R. Hubbard 1991: 94–95). Chapter 18 refers to the false prophets who sold out to the pagan queen and who were about to be executed as those 'who eat at Jezebel's table' (v. 19; on which, see esp. Appler 1999). And chapter 19 shows God's care for Elijah on the run from Jezebel, when he suddenly discovers a bread cake and a

---

[23] Fretheim (1999: 97) notes that 'God acts through both the word of the prophet and the food and deed of a widow (those pursued and neglected by the political power structures) to provide life-giving food for both prophet and widow. Note Jesus' appeal to this story in a context of opposition (Luke 4:25–26).'

jar of a water under a tree in the desert a day's journey south of Beersheba (vv. 6–8).

In 2 Kings, several of Elisha's miracles form important historical background for Jesus' wondrous deeds in the Gospels. Two of these, in consecutive passages in chapter 4, involve meals. First Elisha orders flour to be put into a pot of poisonous stew and it becomes safe to eat (vv. 38–41). Then he feeds one hundred people with only twenty small hand-sized barley loaves and a few ears of corn, and still they have leftovers (vv. 42–44). Combined with the earlier events narrated, 'as a whole, chapter four stresses God's power to provide for those who trust Him amid poverty, death, and famine. That implied that He was superior to Baal, who claimed to control fertility, vegetation, and life itself' (R. Hubbard 1991: 152). More specifically, 'this contact between Elisha, a threatened widow and orphans (vv. 1–7), a bereaved woman (vv. 18–37), and hungry companions (vv. 38–42) ... reflects the ideal society in which such care is commonplace', along with 'the very character of God himself, who "executes justice for the fatherless and the widow, and loves the stranger, giving him food and clothing" (Deut. 10:18)' (Hobbs 1985: 55). But the needy people here are still Israelites. We do not see Elisha feeding Gentiles, as Christ will,[24] even though in the next chapter he will heal a Syrian from his leprosy, but on Jewish terms (5:1–27).

Chapter 6 comes as close as any text in the Old Testament to exemplifying love for actual enemies; many have thus seen it as important background to the parable of the Good Samaritan (Luke 10:25–37). In verses 22–23, Elisha responds to those who want to kill a group of Aramean prisoners of war in Samaria by ordering them instead to 'set food and water before them so that they may eat and drink and then go back to their master.' Indeed, 'he prepared a great feast for them' and then 'sent them away'. Donald Wiseman (1993: 210) casts this in the most positive light possible, arguing that 'the giving of a *feast* followed a covenant-agreement and in principle precluded revenge (so Rom. 12:20–21)' and that 'clemency often leads to peace' (cf. also Long 2002: 36). But T. R. Hobbs (1985: 78) suspects that Elijah was 'more intent upon embarrassing his foes with kindness than sparing them for purely humanitarian reasons,' noting that the peace did not last very long. And on either reading, Elisha has already successfully besought the Lord that these enemies be

---

[24] Specifically in the feeding of the four thousand. Of course, the make-up of this crowd is debated, but see below (pp. 109–111) for details of why it seems probable Gentiles were included.

struck blind for a time (vv. 18–20), a noteworthy contrast with Jesus' rebuke to his disciples when they want to call down fire from heaven against hostile Samaritans, shortly before the narrative about the Good Samaritan (Luke 9:52–56).

Three texts in 2 Kings, 2 Chronicles and Ezra all feature the re-establishment of regular Passover festivals in Israel.[25] In 2 Chronicles 30 Hezekiah commands the feast to be celebrated, but several anomalies remain: the date is later than it should be; ritually unclean laity are allowed to participate; and an extra week of feasting is added (vv. 15–23).[26] The second of these anomalies is of most interest to us, demonstrating that the community of celebrants was more inclusive than on some occasions. Verse 25 goes on to add that various resident aliens participated as well (see esp. Graham 1999; cf. Thompson 1994: 355). But limitations still remain: the uncommitted outsider is not present, and the priests and Levites have to undergo all of the purification rituals on behalf of their unclean kin. In 2 Chronicles 35:1–19 (cf. 2 Kgs 23:21–23) is narrated a similar renewal of Passover practice under Josiah. The accounts do not rule out earlier, more private celebrations in less faithful eras (rightly Brueggemann 2000: 558), but now the feast is enacted in public and fully in accordance with the Law (House 1995: 390; cf. 2 Kgs 23:21), so that the boundaries specifying who could participate in what condition would have been drawn more narrowly.

After the return from exile, Ezra 6:19–22 describes yet one more re-establishment of Passover in a context of God's people fully rededicating themselves to the Law. Here the distinctiveness of Israel is explicitly stressed: the participants were all those 'who had separated themselves from the unclean practices of their Gentile neighbours' (v. 21; cf. esp. Clines 1984: 97). The festival was designed to mark a key turning point in the history of Israel and a fresh start for the uniquely chosen people of Yahweh (Fleishman 1998: 17–18). Nehemiah 5:15–18 demonstrates that leadership in this new era could still prove remarkably generous, including to the needy in the community, especially with provisions of food. Some of the recipients were also visiting dignitaries from the surrounding nations (v. 17). But still the major concern was meeting the needs within Israel (cf. Breneman 1993: 207 with Fensham 1982: 198–199).

---

[25] On the festival emphasis more generally in 1 and 2 Chronicles, see DeVries 1997.

[26] These anomalies were unlikely to have been created if they were not historical, and they may explain why Josiah's later Passover can still be said to have been unique. On both points, see Selman 1994: 494.

Finally, the historical books introduce us to numerous banquets within the narrative of Esther. Here we must recognize the Persian context and conviction that even the gravest matters were to be deliberated over wine and drinking parties, because they 'believed intoxication put them in closer touch with the spiritual world' from which they could receive guidance (Jobes 1999: 67). Esther 1:5–12 introduces us to segregated parties: Xerxes and the men wanting to see Vashti 'display her beauty' (v. 11), while Vashti and the women were dining by themselves, unwilling to further the men's agenda (cf. v. 9 with v. 12; Baldwin 1984: 59). The feast in Esther 2:18, in which Xerxes takes Esther as his new queen, contrasts with both of those in chapter 1: neither decadence nor disobedience appears (cf. Clines 1984: 290–291). Two banquets that Esther orders for the king and Haman increase the suspense as to whether God's people will be rescued or not (Levenson 1997: 90), but likewise form the culturally appropriate vehicle for impressing on the king the seriousness of Esther's request (cf. Bush 1996: 405–406).

The impromptu celebration after the king's edict protecting the Jews (8:17), like the more formalized and ongoing celebration of Purim after their victories in battle (9:18–22), prove more relevant to understanding *Jewish* rather than Persian practice. On the one hand, 8:17 stresses that some among the Gentiles were converted when they saw the providential intervention on behalf of Esther's people. Moreover, 9:22 stresses that the celebration of Purim had to include 'giving presents of food to one another and gifts to the poor'. On the other hand, Purim, though not commanded in the Pentateuch, would take its place with the Torah-based feasts as an annual Jewish festival highlighting Jewish national identity and recalling God's unique deliverance of his people. Not until medieval Christian times would a quite different understanding emerge on a widespread basis. In that era, many Christians began to see Esther's banquets as a key foreshadowing of the eschatological banquet or Messianic feast that later Scriptures foretold (Vrudny 1999; see below, pp. 58–60).

It is difficult to summarize this almost bewildering diversity of contexts in which meals feature prominently in the historical books of the Old Testament. Provisions of food along with full-fledged meals often establish one's human loyalties through the people with whom one associates or from whom one separates oneself. On the rare occasions when treachery occurs in these contexts, it is made that much more ignominious by virtue of violating the cultural expectations of table fellowship. Dining and offers of food to the hungry also demonstrate one's faithfulness to Yahweh, his laws, and his appointed sacrifices and festivals. The Lord, in turn, honours his Deuteronomic covenant by showering material blessings – even gourmet meals – on his people as they demonstrate widespread obedience to him. As in the Pentateuch, festive meals continue to mark milestones in family life, especially at weddings, and in national life, especially at coronations and after conquests. Numerous other meals simply form the backdrop for significant events that could perhaps as easily have occurred in other contexts.

The wisdom literature

While the wisdom literature interrupts the chronology of the history of Israel in the Christian canon, grouping these books together does reveal some distinctive themes. Meals do not play a dominant role in Job. Indeed, during much of the narrative Job's suffering makes him loath to eat at all. At the same time, before he was afflicted by God, his regular practice was to share his wealth, including provisions of food, with the needy (Job 31:17–18). What is more, this story's narrator illustrates Job's original wealth by including the observation that 'his sons used to take turns holding feasts in their homes' (1:4). This formed part of God's blessing on his life; no criticisms of his affluence were implied (cf. Hartley 1988: 69; Andersen 1976: 80). But the only people mentioned as invitees are Job's daughters, and Job was equally concerned that these family members subsequently offer sacrifices for purification (v. 5). Interestingly, when Job's fortunes are finally restored, nothing is mentioned about any banquets resuming (42:10–17), though too much should not be inferred from this silence. At any rate, especially since Job may well not have been Jewish (being from the unknown land of Uz), we cannot infer much about Israelite table fellowship from the account of his experiences.

The Psalms contrast with Job by presenting us with an overabundance of material on our topic. Stephen Reed (1987) has surveyed 'Food in the Psalms' in comprehensive detail in his Claremont dissertation, noting that the dominant theme is Yahweh's provision for his people, for the whole world of human beings, and even for the animal kingdom. Here we can unpack only a few representative highlights.

Psalm 22:26–29 represents a passage that may provide precedent for Isaiah's vision of an eschatological banquet (Isa. 25:6–9).[27] Here poor and rich alike feast and are satisfied. Here

> All the ends of the earth
>> will remember and turn to the LORD,
> and all the families of the nations
>> will bow down before him.
>> (Ps. 22:27)

Clearly there is a universal offer of salvation and plenty here; what is less clear is whether all who come do so by voluntary conversion, or whether some are forcibly subjected (contrast Kidner 1973: 109 with Wilson 2002: 422). After all, verse 28 describes the Lord's dominion and rule over all the nations, language that elsewhere in Scripture often looks beyond those who become believers from every nation to the day when every knee shall bow, including some against their will (Isa. 45:23–24; cf. Phil. 2:10).

The beloved Psalm 23 paints the intriguing picture of God preparing for the shepherd a table in the presence of his enemies (v. 5). While many commentators think this verse marks a scene change from pasture to temple (as in v. 6), Samuel Terrien (2003: 241) shows how it could fit the setting of the preceding verses. The Arabic equivalent of the Hebrew word for 'table' here, 'even in modern times, continues to mean, not a piece of wooden furniture, but an animal skin or a woven rug thrown on the ground to keep food away from sand'. One's enemies are far more likely to threaten in the wilderness than in the temple, so perhaps this psalm is depicting the shepherd spreading out his lunch on a mat while God protects him and his flock from any nearby predators. On either view, though, it is clear that the psalmist is not sharing his bounty with his enemies![28]

Psalm 36:8–9 reflects the more common theme of the righteous feasting in the abundance of God's house. As regularly in the Psalter, this theme contrasts with the ultimate demise of the wicked (here see v. 12). If God's house is the temple, then sacrificial meals may be in view. Drinking from God's 'river of delights' and 'fountain of life'

---

[27] One also thinks of Isa. 2:2–4, though no reference to eating occurs there, and of 55:1–5, which probably elaborates on 25:6–9.

[28] For the view that this takes place in a banqueting hall, see VanGemeren 1991: 218. For the possibility that this is 'a victory celebration, where the enemies are present as captives; or an accession feast with defeated rivals as reluctant guests', see Kidner 1973: 112.

may allude to the Garden of Eden and/or the river flowing from Ezekiel's new temple (Ezek. 47:1). Anderson (1972: 290), following Mitchell Dahood (1965: 222), thinks 'that these verses may have provided the background of the messianic banquet'.

Psalm 41:9 clearly presents a backdrop for the Gospel writers' interpretation of Judas' betrayal of Jesus (see esp. John 13:18), as the treachery of one who shared the intimacy of table fellowship with David is seen, typologically, as fulfilled on an even grander scale. Indeed, John attributes this interpretation to Jesus himself, recognizing that 'in this, as elsewhere, He saw in the experiences of David the pattern, writ small, of His own calling' (Kidner 1973: 162).

Psalm 78 well represents the major emphasis in the Psalter on Yahweh's provision for his people, including the material provision that sustained them during their wilderness wanderings (vv. 15–31). He continues to sustain the faithful; 111:5 declares that

> He provides food for those who fear him;
> he remembers his covenant for ever.

Again, in 128:2–3, those who fear the Lord and walk in his ways 'will eat the fruit' of their labour, while 'blessings and prosperity' will be theirs. In 104:10–30, this graciousness is praised because God's provision extends to all humanity and even to the world of nature (cf. also 145:16).[29]

The psalmists are also aware of the dangers of going to dine with the wicked, despite the attraction of their 'delicacies' (141:4). The term is a biblical *hapax*, but it appears in extra-biblical inscriptions with apparent reference to banquets. Robert Davidson (1998: 454) likens this setting to the enjoyment of 'the fruits of high society living', while Anderson (1972: 920) adds that these 'dainties' (another possible translation) probably stand more generally for the hospitality of the godless. Finally, while not as dominant in the Psalms as in many parts of Scripture, the affirmation does recur that Yahweh 'upholds the cause of the oppressed and gives food to the hungry' (146:7). In so doing, he 'lives up to the highest ideals of kingship as the source of justice and vindication (cf. 99:4). Food and freedom are

---

[29] Kidner (1975: 482) describes this last text as an 'exuberant provision – so unlike the standardized dietary units of farming technocrats' and one that 'reflects the Creator's generous joy in His world' (precisely as 'developed at length in Psalm 104') and that is 'used for our emulation and encouragement in the Sermon on the Mount (Mt. 5:45; 6:25ff.)'.

his gifts; wholeness is his blessing. The defenseless can find in him their royal champion' (Allen 1983: 303).

Unquestionably the most significant contribution of the Proverbs to the theme of table fellowship is a metaphorical one. Chapter 9 presents the invitations of Lady Wisdom and Dame Folly as if two women were issuing literal appeals to come and dine in their homes (on which see esp. Stallman 2000). Given the rarity of meat in an ordinary Israelite's diet, the banquet laid out by Wisdom is clearly special: 'She has prepared her meat and mixed her wine; she has also set her table' (v. 2). In keeping with the custom at large feasts, she sends out her servants to call to all the townspeople to join the festivities (v. 3). The meaning of the metaphor is then explained more prosaically: ' "Let all who are simple come in here!" she says to those who lack judgment' (v. 4). Folly likewise calls from the highest point of the city to invite all who hear to dine with her (vv. 14–16), but the only fare that she specifies is 'stolen water' and 'food eaten in secret' that is alleged to be 'delicious' (v. 17). The contrast in foodstuffs remains striking (Clifford 1999: 105; Aitken 1986: 90–92); the results of choosing the one invitation over the other quite literally involve matters of life and death (cf. v. 11 with v. 18). Roland Murphy (1998: 61) goes so far as to claim that despite the deliberate parallelism between the feasts of the two hawkers, 'Woman Folly does not offer a menu. In what sounds like a proverb, she throws out a suggestive advertisement that promises, at the same time that it deceives.' The picture of Lady Wisdom, on the other hand, probably forms background for Jesus' parable of the great banquet in Luke 14:16–24, 'emblematic of life, health, and celebration' (Garrett 1993: 115).

Other proverbs treat the motif of meals more briefly. A representative sampling would include honouring the Lord with our firstfruits so that our 'barns will be filled to overflowing' (Prov. 3:9–10); preferring the simplest of meals with peace and love to banquets with hatred and strife (15:17; 17:1);[30] demonstrating wisdom by preserving choice stores of oil (21:20); showing generosity to the poor by supplying them with food (22:9); being wary of craving the meals of kings or stingy people (23:1–3, 6–8); and avoiding over- or under-eating (24:13; 25:16, 27; 27:7). Among the many exemplary features of the noble wife in 31:10–31 is her tireless provision of food for her family, including the most menial of her servants.

[30] Cf. Koptak (2003: 399): 'While the best situation would be to have both meat and love, if we must choose, a good relationship is always more important than material gain.'

One additional proverb stands out from the rest. In 25:21–22, we read:

> If your enemies are hungry, give them food to eat;
> if they are thirsty, give them water to drink.
> In doing this, you will heap burning coals on their heads,
> and the LORD will reward you.

Like Elisha's culinary kindness to his prisoners of war, here is a rare Old Testament command to show compassion to one's enemies. Kidner (1964: 160) views this saying as 'the topmost of a cluster of peaks (see 24:11, 12, 17, 18, 29) which are all outcrops of an underlying care for others and faith in God presupposed throughout the book.' Of these texts, however, only 24:17 mentions enemies, and there only in the context of not gloating when they fall. Even in 25:21–22, we are probably not meant to imagine actual table fellowship with one's enemies, but merely the provision of bodily sustenance in the hope of shaming them into repentance (cf. the New Testament's appropriation of this text in Rom. 12:20).[31] As R. N. Whybray (1994: 367) perceptively observes, 'like many other passages in Proverbs, these verses are concerned with the harmony and well-being of the local community, which ought to override the selfish interests and feuds of individuals. *Love* of enemies, however, is not prescribed.'

The book of Ecclesiastes regularly instructs its readers to find enjoyment in the ordinary tasks of daily life, including eating and drinking at meals. The interpretation of these commands depends on one's view of the book overall. Does Qoheleth intend to punctuate his otherwise bleak assessment of the futility of life 'under the sun' with more hope-filled reminders of the potential for experiencing fulfilment in the tasks of this age? Or are these seemingly more positive intrusions simply part of the author's overall strategy of ultimately criticizing even the best of what this life appears to offer? Although the latter seems to have garnered a current consensus, I tend to side with those who argue for the former (e.g., Kidner 1976; Kaiser 1979; Eaton 1983).

The first of these passages is Ecclesiastes 2:24–26. 'People can do

---

[31] The meaning of the metaphor of heaping burning coals on their heads is disputed. Koptak (2003: 580) surveys the main options: a gift to the poor, a sign of repentance, punishment, healing wounds, and relieving suffering. In context, however, the meaning must be a reversal of what was expected and hence something positive.

nothing better[32] than to eat and drink and find satisfaction in their work' (v. 24a), and 'to the one who pleases him, God gives wisdom, knowledge and happiness' (v. 26a). While it has been argued that this 'positive counsel rests under a cloud', because 'the ability to enjoy life is not in anyone's power, coming as a gift from God' (v. 24b; Crenshaw 1987: 90), God does promise to give the gift to those who do what pleases him, so it is hardly an 'arbitrary' process (as alleged by Murphy 1992: 26). And the final line of the paragraph, 'this too is meaningless, a chasing after the wind,' makes more sense as modifying its immediate antecedent – the fate of the sinner who has to give up his wealth to the one pleasing God (v. 26b) – rather than referring back to the entire pericope.

Ecclesiastes 3:13 echoes earlier sentiments: that each person 'may eat and drink, and find satisfaction in all their toil – this is the gift of God.' The larger passage in which this verse is embedded again underlines the transience of this life, affirms that God will judge the righteous and the wicked according to their works, and ends with characteristic Old Testament uncertainty about the nature of the afterlife (vv. 9–22). But Tremper Longman's pessimism (1998: 123) considerably outruns what the text actually says when he claims, 'it is fair to deduce ... that from his frequent expressions of pain and frustration Qohelet did not himself feel that God granted him this *gift*, which serves as anesthesia toward the problems of the present fallen world ... This insight points to Qohelet's underlying problem: he feels unfairly treated.' The immediate context of verses 12–15 in fact divides into two units each beginning with the confident 'I know' (vv. 12 and 14), leading to affirmations of the possibility of happiness and the promise of equitable final judgment. Much more on target is Michael Eaton's remark (1983: 82) that in verse 13 'the decisive new factor is the sovereignty of God. Secularism gives way to theism, pessimism to optimism, human autonomy to human faith.'

Similar debates recur in the other key texts on eating, drinking and enjoying life in Ecclesiastes. The context of 5:18 repeats the theme of pleasure as a gift from God but does not include any negative, qualifying remarks (vv. 18–20; cf. esp. Lohfink 1990). The setting of 6:7–8 remains more negative, noting how one's appetite is never satisfied, another meaningless 'chasing after the wind'. But verse 9a returns to the theme of preferring what is at hand to what is only desired. Once again, the subsequent declaration that 'this too is

---

[32] On the 'nothing better than' formula in Ecclesiastes, see esp. Ogden 1979.

meaningless, a chasing after the wind' (v. 9b) makes most sense as modifying only the immediately preceding 'roving of the appetite', rather than 'better what the eye sees' as well.[33] In 8:14, what is declared futile is clearly the inequity of the righteous and wicked at times getting in this life what the *other* deserves. Verse 15 then provides the positive contrast: 'So I commend the enjoyment of life, because nothing is better for people under the sun than to eat and drink and be glad. Then joy will accompany them in their work all the days of the life God has given them under the sun.' Nothing else in the following verses casts any shadow over these specific statements.[34]

Ecclesiastes 9:7 is the last of the disputed verses on dining in this book, enjoining us to go and eat our 'food with gladness' and drink our 'wine with a joyful heart, for it is now that God favours what' we do. This enjoyment is coloured by two subsequent references to our meaningless life (v. 9), but Eaton (1983: 127) again seems correct in stressing that

> the basis of contentment is that *God has already approved what you do*. This almost Pauline touch is the nearest the Preacher came to a doctrine of justification by faith. Man has but to receive contentment as God's gift (*cf.* 3:13); God will approve of him and his works.

The Song of Songs refers to table fellowship only in its many splendid metaphors for loving romance and sexual relationships. Athalyah Brenner (1999) categorizes the relevant references under five headings: verbs for eating and drinking, terms denoting wetness, foodstuffs, general terms for edible entities, and locations of food production. By analogy, however, this little book's author would undoubtedly agree that dining can become another delight in this earthly garden.

The wisdom literature thus introduces us to several new emphases not as central to other Old Testament documents. Food is the utterly gracious gift of God, with which he blesses his faithful followers in particular and all people at times. But in a fallen world there is no

---

[33] 'If the comparison in the verse is between immediate pleasure and illusory desires, the image of chasing the wind applies to a roving desire' (Crenshaw 1987: 130).

[34] It is not clear that 'each time the commendation of enjoyment occurs in the book it is expressed with increasing emphasis ... here by the use of the verb *šbḥ* (Piel, commend), which elsewhere in the Old Testament means "praise" (cf. its meaning in 4:2)' (Whybray 1989: 138), but there is even less justification for Longman's claim (1998: 221) that we should read this as some kind of elaboration of v. 14 so that v. 15 'takes on a tone of strident desperation, or perhaps of resignation'.

exceptionless correlation between piety and prosperity (and what does exist does not carry over to New Testament arrangements: see Blomberg 1999: 82–84). Feeding the hungry remains the responsibility of God's people, but far more attention is given to praising God for the food he has provided already and to enjoying life, even in its material and physical dimensions, within the guidelines God has laid down for their proper use. Correct attitudes to eating and drinking are simply a subset of the larger domain of living a wise life more generally. At times, our texts foreshadow a coming age in which there will be an endless supply of plenty for God's chosen, and all his enemies and every other evil that prevents full enjoyment of his provisions in this age will be vanquished.

The prophets

With the writing prophets, a broad chronological order returns which overlaps with the later centuries covered in the historical books. But again, the distinctives that emerge from treating this material as a corpus justify the procedure. For example, a new category of meal appears: the *marzēaḥ*.[35] Marvin Pope (1972: 193) has well defined this as 'a social and religious institution which included families, owned property, houses for meetings and vineyards for wine supply, was associated with specific deities, and met periodically, perhaps monthly, to celebrate for several days at a stretch with food and drink and sometimes, if not regularly, with sacral sexual orgies.'[36] Though pagan in origin, its growing encroachment into Israel forced the prophets on numerous occasions to denounce the people's participation in its profligacy.

Isaiah 5:11–12 introduces us to the problem:

> Woe to those who rise early in the morning
> to run after their drinks,
> who stay up late at night
> till they are inflamed with wine.
> They have harps and lyres at their banquets,
> tambourines and flutes and wine,
> but they have no regard for the deeds of the LORD,
> no respect for the work of his hands.

---

[35] For a summary of recent literature on this topic, esp. as it relates to Amos 6, see Carroll R. 2002: 20–21, 40, 173 and 176.

[36] The most oft-cited study is that of King 1988.

John Oswalt (1986: 159–160) elucidates:

> By virtue of their abundance, [the wealthy] can spend the entire
> day ... pursuing their own pleasure, particularly in drinking. It is
> important to notice the reason why the prophet opposes these
> practices. He does not oppose them because they are wrong in
> themselves, but because they have become all-absorbing to the
> point where spiritual sensitivity has become dimmed. The revelers
> no longer have any interest in or ability to recognize how God is at
> work in the world. When the passion for pleasure has become
> uppermost in a person's life, passion for God and his truth and his
> ways is squeezed out. Furthermore, the use of alcohol in the quest
> for pleasure can only heighten the degree to which one becomes
> insensitive to responsibilities and values.

Isaiah 5:22–23 brings up the theme again:

> Woe to those who are heroes at drinking wine
>   and champions at mixing drinks,
> who acquit the guilty for a bribe,
>   but deny justice to the innocent.

It is probable that we have further allusions to the *marzēaḥ* in Isaiah
22:13 and 28:1–6 and Ezekiel 8:7–13.[37]

Perhaps the most famous prophetic lambaste against the *marzēaḥ*
appears in Amos 6:4–7. Here wealthy leaders in Judah are berated as
lounging on their couches, dining on choice lambs and fattened calves,
strumming away on their harps like David, drinking wine by the
bowlful, and using the finest lotions, all without grieving over the ruin
of the northern kingdom. Thus Amos promises that they 'will be among
the first to go into exile'; 'your feasting and lounging will end.'[38] Daniel
Carroll R. (1992: 260) explains that 'these were pagan ritual feasts, and
this fact points to an idolatry among those in power, a paganism which
only they could enjoy because of the high costs.' But he stresses that
'Amos is more concerned with the injustice that makes the *marzēaḥ*
feast possible than in the idolatry associated with it' (261).[39]

---

[37] On the latter two texts, see Asen 1996 and Ackerman 1989, respectively.

[38] B. Smith (1995: 119, n. 261) doubts whether the *marzēaḥ* is indeed in view here, but
see Finley (1990: 265) for an adequate, even if earlier, defence of this position.

[39] A somewhat related theme that will not be developed here involves the prophetic
judgment passages that utilize the metaphor of 'sour grapes', on which see esp. R. P.
Carroll 1999.

Probably the most important kind of meal depicted in the prophets is that which eventually developed into the concept of the Messianic banquet. Beginning with the vision of all humanity coexisting peacefully on this planet (see already in Isa. 2:2–4), the picture emerged of former enemies, even in the animal world, enjoying meals with one another. Isaiah 11:6–9 demonstrates this development with its portrait of wolf and lamb, leopard and goat, calf and lion, infant and cobra all living happily together. Thus 'the cow will feed with the bear ... and the lion will eat straw like the ox' (v. 7). Coming immediately on the heels of the prediction of the divine ruler from the lineage of Jesse (vv. 1–5), this depiction sketches 'the restoration of creation by a new act of God through the vehicle of a righteous ruler ... that focuses on the eschatological deliverance of God's people' (Childs 2001: 104).[40]

But it is not until Isaiah 25:6–9 that this vision is presented in all its splendour. By common agreement, this is the single most influential passage for the development in both Second Temple Judaism[41] and early Christianity of the idea of a Messianic banquet.[42] Here we read:

> On this mountain the LORD Almighty will prepare
>   a feast of rich food for all peoples,
> a banquet of aged wine –
>   the best of meats and the finest of wines.
> On this mountain he will destroy
>   the shroud that enfolds all peoples,
> the sheet that covers all nations;
>   he will swallow up death for ever.
> The Sovereign LORD will wipe away the tears
>   from all faces;
> he will remove the disgrace of his people
>   from all the earth.
>   The LORD has spoken.

---

[40] Cf. Widyapranawa (1990: 70) for incisive contemporary application.

[41] Jews obviously prefer the use of 'Second Temple Judaism' to the 'intertestamental period', since they do not acknowledge the New Testament as a sacred corpus parallel in authority to the Hebrew Scriptures (or Christian Old Testament). But, writing as a Christian, and largely for the sake of stylistic variety, I use these terms as synonyms, just as I do 'Hebrew Scriptures' and 'Old Testament', while not unaware of the technical distinctions between terms in each pair.

[42] For an excellent, succinct overview, see G. Miller 1995.

In that day they will say,

'Surely this is our God;
  we trusted in him, and he saved us.
This is the LORD, we trusted in him;
  let us rejoice and be glad in his salvation.'

Within this chapter itself, no royal or Messianic figure appears separate from Yahweh himself, so it is perhaps better to label this simply 'the eschatological banquet'. But the picture calls to mind inaugural feasts for various ancient Near Eastern kings (Oswalt 1986: 462), while deliverer figures have appeared earlier in Isaiah, so either title seems apt. What is most striking is the repeated emphasis on the presence of all peoples on this glorious occasion (Motyer 1999: 171). Yet the larger context of this vision makes plain that, while we see here a universal offer of salvation, Isaiah is no universalist (Goldingay 2001: 144). Moab, representative of the enemies of God's people, will be trampled down (vv. 10–12); chapters 26 – 27 go on to describe the redemption of *Israel* and the destruction of its opponents. Even here, in 25:8, the singular form returns when Isaiah prophesies that God will remove the disgrace of his *people*. Walter Brueggemann (1998: 200) captures the twin emphases: 'The work of this God is both positive and negative. The positive is a welcoming feast that signifies the new governance of abundance and well-being. The negative is the elimination of that which threatens and precludes festivals of generosity.'

Isaiah 35 offers another stunning portrait of the peace and joy of the Messianic age. No meal metaphor emerges *per se*, but we do read of water gushing forth in the wilderness and streams in the desert to relieve both parched ground and parched throats (vv. 6–7).[43] Similarly, 55:1–2 depicts salvation as an invitation to those longing to eat and drink:

Come, all you who are thirsty,
  come to the waters;
and you who have no money,
  come, buy and eat!
Come, buy wine and milk
  without money and without cost.
Why spend money on what is not bread,
  and your labour on what does not satisfy?

---

[43] On the various debates surrounding this chapter, see esp. Harrelson 1994.

> Listen, listen to me, and eat what is good,
> and your soul will delight in the richest of fare.

'By likening his message to water, wine, milk, and tasty, nourishing, life-giving food', Isaiah

> makes it clear that it is not mere intellectual cognition he desires, but a chewing and digesting, an inner appropriation in which the total self is involved (cf. Ez. 2:8 – 3:3). He also wants to emphasize that the acceptance of his message is not like eating spinach or some other distasteful food. Not only is it tasty and life-giving; it brings joy.
>
> (Rice 1980: 23)

Once again the invitation is extended to those who would often be excluded from gaining literal physical nourishment because of the price it usually cost (on which see esp. Motyer 1993: 452). Verses 3–5 explicitly mention the positive response of nations that have not previously known God when the recipients of his everlasting covenant witness to them. One suspects that Jesus' parables of the great supper (Luke 14:16–24) and the wedding feast (Matt. 22:1–14) were drawing on precisely such imagery (Watts 1987: 246), just as his feeding miracles acted out foretastes of this plenty for highly diverse crowds of his followers (see below, 'Feasting in the wilderness', in ch. 4).

The last key description of a meal, literal or metaphorical, in Isaiah involves the glorious predictions of a coming new heaven and earth (ch. 65). Verses 13 and 25 prove particularly relevant for our interests: God's servants will eat and drink, while those who have rejected him will go hungry and thirsty. In conscious repetition of some of the language of 11:7 (van Ruiten 1992),

> The wolf and the lamb will feed together
> and the lion will eat straw like the ox,
> but dust will be the serpent's food.

As Oswalt (1998: 650) summarizes, 'to be blessed is to have enough to eat and drink, to have reason to rejoice and exult out of a glad heart … To be cursed is to suffer hunger and thirst, to be ashamed and in despair with a broken spirit.'

A darker side of dining reappears in one additional passage in Isaiah, as well as several in Ezekiel and Daniel. In a text that probably influenced Jesus' so-called parable of the sheep and the goats (Matt. 25:31–46), Isaiah 58 reminds his seemingly recalcitrant listeners of their responsibility to meet the social needs of the dispossessed among them, including the provision of food for the hungry (v. 7). One of Ezekiel's many prophetic object lessons involves cooking a meal for himself over manure to symbolize for the people the judgment coming upon them (ch. 4). Initially, God commands him to use human excrement for fuel (v. 12) to display in shocking fashion how the nation will eat defiled food in exile. When Ezekiel protests that he has never so desecrated himself, God relents and permits him to use cow dung instead (v. 15). But the results remain a graphic reminder of how Israel should have remained pure and separate from the Gentiles. Since they did not, they will be punished by being taken captive by those very peoples (cf. esp. Brownlee 1986: 78; Duguid 1999: 91).

A similar object lesson appears in Ezekiel 24:1–14, in which a cooking pot illustrates how the nation is about to 'stew in its own juice', so to speak. At first, it looks as if a wonderful feast is being prepared, with choice pieces of meat from the best of the flocks (vv. 4–5; cf. Block 1997: 775). But then we are told that the pot is so encrusted that it cannot be cleansed. The food with the pot will have to be thoroughly purged by fire to get rid of all the deposit and dross (vv. 6–13); cf. Cooper 1994: 236). Thus, only judgment is depicted with this composite metaphor.

Ezekiel 39:17–20 provides the antithesis to the eschatological banquet, portraying what John's Revelation will reuse and dub 'the great supper of God' (Rev. 19:17). Here the Lord tells Ezekiel to call out to the birds and the wild animals to assemble for a sacrifice he is preparing for them, that they might eat the flesh and drink the blood of mighty men and princes, of soldiers and their horses, who form the armies getting ready to attack God's people. Ezekiel's metaphors draw on the partial precedents of texts like Isaiah 34:6–7, Jeremiah 46:10 and Zephaniah 1:7–9 (Taylor 1969: 248; Allen 1990: 208), but none develops the imagery as fully as here. Daniel Block (1998: 474–475) observes that 'while most ancient Near Easterners could speak of sacrifices as food prepared by humans for the deity or for deceased royal ancestors, seldom, if ever, were humans invited to participate in communion meals with deity.' In striking contrast, 'the biblical writers expressed remarkable freedom in their portrayal of Yahweh hosting banquets for earthly guests.' In this case, those guests extend even to the animal kingdom!

The book of Daniel contains two scenes that lead to the drawing of various kinds of boundaries. In 1:8–16, Daniel and his companions refuse to defile themselves 'with the royal food and wine', receiving permission to eat only vegetables and drink only water. Yet after ten days 'they looked healthier and better nourished than any of the young men who ate the royal food.' Commentators debate what was defiling about the king's fare in Daniel's eyes, since it need not have violated the Levitical dietary laws. John Goldingay (1989: 18–19) surveys seven main options, preferring the view that 'pagan food and drink may simply epitomize the pagan uncleanness associated with exile' (19). But Joyce Baldwin's conclusions (1978: 83) make even better sense: 'By eastern standards to share a meal was to commit oneself to friendship; it was of covenant significance.' Thus, those who had 'committed themselves to allegiance accepted an obligation of loyalty to the king. It would seem that Daniel rejected this symbol of dependence on the king because he wished to be free to fulfil his primary obligations to the God he served.' The people with whom one eats, especially when they represent either the powerful or the downtrodden of society, make a huge difference in shaping one's values and character.

Daniel's restraint contrasts dramatically with Belshazzar's extravagant feasting and debauchery in chapter 5. Both Herodotus (1.191) and Xenophon (*Cyropaedia* 7.5.15) attest that a banquet was in progress on the night Babylon fell. Belshazzar's motives may have included a last-ditch attempt to build his people's morale, to celebrate his own coronation despite the ominous circumstances, and/or to commit an act of sacrilege against the holy things of Judaism so as to assert Babylonian religious superiority (S. Miller 1994: 151–152). He may even 'have been making claims to power' by likening himself to Nebuchadnezzar (Longman 1999: 137). But the meal simply forms the setting for the famous handwriting on the wall and its aftermath and plays no further role in the interpretation of the passage.

Apart from their denunciations of the *marzēaḥ* (see above, pp. 56–57), the minor prophets have little distinctively new to add with respect to formal meals. What one does begin to see with somewhat greater frequency, however, are glimpses into the future of an age beyond exile, in which God's people, their fortunes and their prosperity are restored. These portraits often include within them the promise of abundant harvests and foodstuffs aplenty. Thus Joel 3:18 looks forward to the day in which 'the mountains will drip new wine, and the hills will flow with milk,' and 'all the ravines of Judah will run with water'. As Leslie Allen (1976: 123) explains, 'the relationship between Yahweh and his own would be so close that the land would be laden with lavish fruits of grace.' The same sentiments recur in Amos 9:13b, which is surrounded by the additional predictions of reaper being overtaken by plougher, the planter by the one treading the grapes, and all Israel eating the fruit of its own gardens and drinking the wine of its own vineyards, never again to be uprooted from the land (vv. 13a, 14–15).[44] For a third, similar example, compare Hosea 2:21–22.[45] In other texts, the presence or absence of sufficient crops reflects blessing or judgment in the present (cf. Mal. 3:10–12 with Hag. 1:5–11, respectively).

In sum, the prophetic references to food mirror the prophets' messages more generally. More appears about potential judgment than blessing, at least in the short run. But beyond the current crises and their aftermaths comes an age of restoration and abundance. Sometimes the picture is the general one of material plenty, including food and drink. In a number of cases, however, the vision of an eschatological banquet is disclosed: a banquet which, at least in Isaiah, may implicitly include a Messianic figure. In intertestamental and New Testament times, Messiah's presence will become explicit.

Conclusion

Without merely repeating the summaries of each of the sections of this chapter, the following points may be highlighted. In a minority of instances, Old Testament meal texts explicitly point to a certain measure of inclusiveness: not only faithful Jews but sympathetic outsiders may partake. But with one exception, the unrepentant wicked among the Israelites and the full-fledged enemies among the foreigners are never invited. That one exception, the feast for the Aramean prisoners in Samaria (2 Kgs 6:22–23), is fraught with enough interpretative ambiguity that it is hard to be sure of Elisha's motives, and it appears in a context in which the celebrants have been

---

[44] Finley (1990: 326) insists that 'the physical nature of the promised blessings should not be minimized ... Even so, the great prosperity spoken of here mirrors a condition of forgiveness and wholeness that has been hitherto unknown in Israel or throughout the world.'

[45] 'The point here is that Israel will not only have food and shelter but will have an abundance of the best. Furthermore, by describing their salvation in such cosmic terms, with heaven and earth participating in their deliverance, God in effect declares that he will move the whole universe to bring this about ... The return of the exiles is a type for a new order of eternal celebration in a new heaven and earth' (Garrett 1997: 95–96).

previously punished by God's direct, judgmental intervention. There is also one didactic text that differs from the overall trend: Proverbs 25:21–22 on feeding one's enemies. But an element of shaming may be present there, too. In neither passage are God's people ever described as sharing in the meal that they offer their enemies. No formal table fellowship *per se* ever appears.

In fact, the overall impression emerging from the majority of the texts surveyed in this chapter is that meals helped to draw boundaries. Only those who in some sense belonged were included; the total outsider was not welcome. We do not find a single example of the 'uninvited guest' characteristic of later Greek symposia (see below, p. 88) or of faithful Israelites taking the initiative to seek out the ritually or morally stigmatized of their society for inclusion in table fellowship, as would later characterize Jesus' practice (see below, chs. 4 and 5). Hobbs (2001: 20–21) overstates himself only slightly when he concludes, 'In the classic texts of hospitality in the First Testament there are no examples of hospitality being extended to the "stranger" or "resident alien".' Eating and drinking normally appear as signs of a properly functioning life according to the ground rules of the Mosaic Law, with people of whom one approves (or with those with whom one is in the process of establishing ties), and as the foretaste of 'Paradise' both in this age and in the age to come (Smend 1977: 448, 457–458).

Chapter Three

Contagious impurity

Intertestamental developments

Surveying table fellowship in the Hebrew Bible does not provide adequate background for understanding the portrait of Jesus in the Gospels, since numerous developments intervened in the centuries between the testaments. Judaism, of course continued to evolve and splinter into various groups. In addition, the thoroughgoing Hellenization of the ancient Mediterranean world, followed by Roman imperial rule, requires us to look at Greco-Roman as well as Jewish meal customs of this time period. In this chapter, therefore, we will rapidly survey trends in both broad cultural milieux.

The primary literature in both fields is understandably vast. While New Testament scholars continue to mine the rabbinic literature on all sorts of topics, there is growing recognition that only a minority of that encyclopedic body of data reflects practices already in place at the beginning of the New Testament period. Even when traditions are ascribed to very early rabbis or to the earliest Tannaitic period, we can never be entirely sure of the accuracy of the ascriptions. For example, there is a significant debate about the *ḥăbûrôt* referred to in the rabbinica – shared meals by Pharisaic-like groups that have been described alternately as philosophical circles or eating clubs – which *may* provide background for the Gospels, but it is hard to be sure (see Neusner 1982 for a good introduction to the debate). Josephus and Philo are both first century and at times prove very relevant, but on other occasions are either a bit too late or too Hellenized to reflect the life and times of Jesus properly. There is enough information, however, in the three main bodies of demonstrably pre-Christian Jewish literature – the Apocrypha, pseudepigrapha and Dead Sea Scrolls (recognizing that small portions of what are included in these collections are first century or later and must therefore be used with caution) – that a sketch of their portraits of Jewish meals provides enough evidence to determine the principal trends. We will thus look at each of these three bodies of literature, in turn, and then focus on the characteristics of the Greco-Roman symposia. No one, to my knowledge, has undertaken precisely this kind of survey with respect to the specific topic of meals (at least, not with any reasonably full presentation of the relevant texts), though numerous works have highlighted the most prominent passages. Because this study leaves space for only one chapter based on this survey, we too must be selective, but we have worked carefully through the entire three corpora of intertestamental literature, cataloguing and classifying every meal reference, and have attempted to include representative examples of every category.

Old Testament Apocrypha

Dennis Smith (2003: 133–172) argues that pre-Christian Judaism already pervasively adopted the symposium style of dining by observing (the largely critical) references to it in Sirach in the second century BC and the purported assimilation of the Passover haggadah to this format in rabbinic references from perhaps as early as the second century AD (leaning heavily on S. Stein 1957). He then assumes that such practice was uniformly present during the intervening years and reads the other main accounts of Jewish meals as if they were symposia, showing possible points of fit. A more thorough survey of the literature, however, discloses a vastly greater diversity of forms.

Many of the same themes surrounding eating and drinking in the Old Testament naturally recur in the Apocrypha, often in works of comparable contents or genre to their canonical counterparts.[1] First Esdras, overlapping with the later historical works of the Hebrew Scriptures, stresses the Jews' renewed desire to keep the festivals (1:1– 22; 5:51–55; 7:10–15);[2] frequent feasting as a form of celebration – of the restoration of Jerusalem and the temple (4:63), of the day of the re-reading of the Law (9:50–55), or by pagan kings as was the case in Esther and Daniel (chs. 3 – 4); and the Deuteronomic theology of eating well from the produce of the land as a blessing for faithfulness (8:85). One likewise finds wedding feasts in Tobit (7:8–15; 8:19 – 9:6) and a banquet to celebrate Judith's victory over Israel's enemies in the

---

[1] By which I refer to the Hebrew canon. Nothing in this survey depends on resolving the debate between Protestants and Catholics as to whether the Apocrypha should form part of the *Christian* canon.

[2] Indeed, one survey of the 'theological and practical interests' of this document places its emphasis on 'feasts, offerings, and sacrifices' as most prominent of all (Myers 1974: 16).

book that bears her name (Judith 16:20). Second Esdras 1:17–23 recalls God's blessing of Israel by provisions of food during their wilderness wanderings, while Tobit stresses the exemplary giving of bread to the hungry (Tobit 1:17; 4:16; cf. also Sirach 34:21 and contrast the Letter of Jeremiah 6:28).[3] The Additions to Esther and Daniel also expand on some of the meal traditions in their canonical counterparts. First Maccabees 14:10–12, finally, extols the glorious conditions in the days of the Hasmonean ruler Simon with the biblical allusion, 'Each man sat under his vine and his fig tree and there was none to make them afraid.'[4]

Akin to the biblical Proverbs, Sirach extends the dangers of eating with the wicked to include dining with another man's wife (9:9), the powerful (13:8–13), and the stingy (14:10)[5] and warns against feasting lavishly lest one become impoverished by the expense (18:32), while cautioning against simply overeating (37:29–31). Sirach 29:22 echoes earlier themes with its 'better than' proverb: 'Better is the life of a poor man under the shelter of his roof than sumptuous food in another man's house.' By far the most extensive passage on dining in this document is 31:12 – 32:2, focusing on the consumption of wine in moderation rather than in excess.[6] That Sirach knows of banquets characterized by drunkenness may well reflect awareness of the symposium tradition, though even then it appears that these guests are seated (32:1), not reclining, as at symposia (see below, p. 87). But one finds symposia in these other references only by reading in the concept, not from any unambiguous textual data, and the repeated warnings against banqueting in this fashion make it unlikely that it was the normal Jewish practice among those seeking to follow Torah, even if present in these dinners to be avoided (see esp. Kieweler 1998).

Far more common than any of these individual themes, however, are numerous texts that stress the need for ritual purity, separation

---

[3] Again a major theme in this work. Moore (1996: 27) sums up Tobit's understanding of 'true religion' as 'centered in the heart and home, in the day-to-day faith and pious living of the families of Tobit and Raguel ... Feeding the hungry, clothing the naked, giving the condemned a decent burial, preserving dutiful and loving relationships between parents and children – these are the author's primary concerns.'

[4] Perhaps seeing a fulfilment of Ezek. 36:33–35 (so Goldstein 1976: 491).

[5] 'Relationships between unequals are also treacherous (see Eccles. 9.16; Prov. 14.20). The arrogance of another rubs off on you, and association with the rich and great can overstretch you, for as a relationship it is not evenly balanced' (Jones 2003: 107).

[6] For this text as possible background to Judas' betrayal of Jesus at the Last Supper, cf. Bohnen 2000.

from sinners[7] and related boundary markers in the contexts of meals. What Philip Davies (1999: 157) discusses in the context of Qumran becomes equally apparent throughout much other Second Temple Jewish literature as well: 'the physical control over what members eat and drink [and we should add, with whom they eat and drink] is most certainly to be seen also as a symbolic (or perhaps even a real?) maintenance of the integrity of the sectarian society/body.' In Tobit 1:6–12, Tobit avoided the Baal-worship that his relations pursued; he alone went to Jerusalem for the feast, scrupulously offering his tithes and firstfruits; and when he was carried captive to Nineveh and all his family ate Gentile food, he kept himself from eating it because he 'remembered God with all [his] heart' (v. 12). In this he behaves as scrupulously as biblical Daniel and noticeably more stringently than biblical Esther (Moore 1996: 117). Tobit 4:17 proves even more explicit and didactic. Immediately after being commanded to feed the hungry, clothe the naked and give his surplus to charity, Tobit is told 'but give none [of your bread[8]] to sinners.' Clearly boundaries are being drawn.

The whole key to Judith's success in tricking and killing Holofernes, the Assyrian commander, in the delightful little novel about her, involves the Jewish dietary laws. Judith plays on the enemy's conviction that the Israelites' victory can come only when they obey God's Torah (5:5–21). Thus she convinces him that she is truly defecting precisely by alleging that her people are about to violate their law by eating forbidden food since their normal supply is almost exhausted (11:11–15). Thus they will become vulnerable to Holofernes' forces. Judith, therefore, does not want to be judged along with Israel, but for that very reason she brings along her own supply of food rather than eating the impure Assyrians' food and incurring God's wrath (cf. 10:5, 10–13; cf. 12:5–9) (Moore 1985: 218). The very night the general thinks he will finally get to lie with Judith, she gets him drunk over dinner, still consuming only what she has brought (12:10–20), decapitates him, hides his head in her food bag and escapes (13:6–11). The right kind of table fellowship makes the difference between life and death (cf. Jones 2003: 58–59)!

---

[7] Because we are trying to cast as broad a net as possible for background material to the Jesus of the Gospels, it would be premature to limit the search merely to sinners of one particular category: e.g. the ritually impure, the wholly other (e.g. Gentile), or the (grossly) morally wicked. This inevitably leads to the perception of the blurring of some of these categories, which the primary literature itself does not all that infrequently.

[8] So the Greek text. The Old Latin and Vulgate read 'wine and bread', but the principle remains unchanged.

We have already observed that the canonical Esther apparently *did* participate in Gentile banquets. Daniel and Tobit did not; now we have a third example: Judith scrupulously avoided everything but pure food as well. Tellingly, the intertestamental Additions to Esther reflect this 'tightening up' of tradition by completely rewriting its *Vorlage* in this respect. The section numbered 14:17 in the Vulgate and most English translations (= C 28 in some critical editions) has Esther protest, 'And thy servant has not eaten at Haman's table, and I have not honoured the king's feast or drunk the wine of the libations.' Carey Moore elucidates (1977: 212), 'In contrast to the MT, where Esther apparently ate the delicacies from the king's cuisine (2:9), here she avoids eating the king's food, some of which was certainly not kosher.' The drawing of lines between Jew and Gentile increases.

We have already seen some of Sirach's warnings with respect to banquets. Conversely, this book of wisdom insists, 'Let righteous men be your dinner companions, and let your glorying be in the fear of the Lord' (9:16), as part of its larger emphasis on the wise not associating with the unrighteous (Skehan 1987: 220). It echoes Tobit by forbidding gifts of bread to the ungodly (12:5); likens fellowship between a godly man and a sinner to that of lamb and wolf (13:17); and depicts the desire for another man's table as polluting (40:29). That Patrick Skehan (1987: 245) can refer to such injunctions as making 'good sense' because indiscriminate friendship and hospitality may lead to 'unpleasant consequences' shows just how radical Jesus' violations of such wisdom turn out to be (see below, chapters 4 and 5).

Finally, we may point to the major theme in the books of Maccabees of refusing to eat that which was impure, even at the cost of one's own life. First Maccabees 1:62–63 offers an overall summary: despite those who assimilated, 'many in Israel stood firm and were resolved in their hearts not to eat unclean food. They chose to die rather than to be defiled by food or to profane the holy covenant, and they did die.' Jonathan Goldstein (1976: 227) opines that 'our author may have chosen words connoting the utmost in steadfast courage to deny the insinuations at Dan. 11:32–35, that only the Pietist elite were steadfast Jews.' Whether or not we can be that specific, the Maccabean literature clearly does want to portray preserving a kosher table as the general trend in Israel.

Second Maccabees 6:18 – 7:42 then illustrates this trend with the dramatic and memorable stories of Eleazar, an aged scribe, and an anonymous mother with her seven sons, who all endure torture and ultimately martyrdom rather than eat swine's flesh as the Syrian king demanded. The narrator wanted to show Antiochus IV (Epiphanes) fighting God, bringing on himself the destructive wrath of the Almighty, and humiliated by the martyrs. 'He had conquered many peoples, but he could not conquer' even simple youths (Zeitlin 1954: 48). Not surprisingly, when the tide turns in the Jews' favour and Antiochus V proves more conciliatory, the narrator portrays him pledging 'full permission for the Jews to enjoy their own food and laws, just as formerly, and none of them shall be molested in any way' (2 Maccabees 11:30–31).

In going over much of the same material covered in 1 and 2 Maccabees, 3 and 4 Maccabees stress these dietary boundary markers all the more. This is particularly striking in 3 Maccabees, since 'a special effort is made ... to stress the amicable relations of the Jewish community to their neighbors and the mutual respect subsisting between the two groups.' In other words, Antiochus Epiphanes is sketched as 'out of sync' with even his own people. Still, 'the amicable relations do not involve compromises in religious observances on the part of the Jews' (Hadas 1953: 24). Thus in 3:2–5, despite stressing this goodwill between peoples, the narrator adds, 'but because they worshipped God and conducted themselves by his law, they kept their separateness with respect to foods. For this reason they appeared hateful to some.' So, too, we are not surprised when 4 Maccabees greatly expands its retelling of the martyrdoms of Eleazar and the mother with her seven sons, complete with philosophical reflection on the events, to span fourteen entire chapters (5 – 18). The ridicule of Jewish abstention from pork had become a commonplace (Hadas 1953: 170), so that the author goes out of his way to make it appear reasonable from every vantage point he can imagine.

Still other apocryphal texts demand the dissociation of God's people from sinners more generally. 1 Esdras 9 elaborates on canonical Ezra's command to the Israelites to put away their foreign wives. Sirach 11:29–34 warns against bringing the crafty, proud, scoundrel or stranger into one's home,[9] while 37:1–11 inveighs against a whole host of improper companions, including pretend friends, the self-interested, the suspicious, the jealous, a coward, a merchant, the begrudging, the merciless, an idler, and a lazy servant. Instead, verse 12 explains, 'stay with a godly man whom you know to be a keeper of the commandments, whose soul is in accord with your

---

[9] 'No opportunity should be given to those whose traps might disrupt your home, misrepresent you, threaten your life or your reputation' (Jones 2003: 107).

soul, and who will sorrow with you if you fail.' What is more, the Maccabean literature stresses separation from impure practices in many areas besides diet in passages too numerous to list. More generally still, there is a pervasive condemnation of idolatry and idolaters throughout the Apocrypha, particularly in the Letter of Jeremiah, Bel and the Dragon, Sirach and Susannah.

The pseudepigrapha

Because of the sheer size of this literature, our survey has space to present only very select references. But we have thoroughly scrutinized the entire corpus so that we may make valid generalizations. Many of the identical themes that characterized the Old Testament and/or the Apocrypha understandably recur in this body of Jewish literature, especially in works like the various *Testaments*, *Jubilees*, and *Pseudo-Philo*, which in essence form 'expansions of the Old Testament' (thus Charlesworth 1985: 3). In addition, we may highlight four categories of texts.

First, references to feeding strangers or helping the needy more generally with the provision of foodstuffs do still appear, but they remain few and far between and typically are triggered by existing Scriptural texts. Thus the *Testament of Job* expands on the biblical references to Job's generosity (see above, p. 49) by having him claim, 'I established in my house thirty tables spread at all hours, for strangers only. I also used to maintain twelve other tables set for the widows. When any stranger approached to ask alms, he was required to be fed at my table before he would receive his need. Neither did I allow anyone to go out of my door with an empty pocket' (*Test. Job* 10:1–4). Similarly, in the *Testament* bearing his name, Zebulon avows of his fishing practice, 'Being compassionate, I gave some of my catch to every stranger. If anyone were a traveller or sick, or aged, I cooked the fish, prepared it well, *and offered to each person according to his need*, being either convivial or consoling' (*Test. Zeb.* 6:5). The parallel between the italicized portion and Acts 4:35 proves striking, especially since the pseudepigraphal verse does not appear to form part of the Christian interpolations into the *Testaments of the Twelve Patriarchs*. But such references remain rare.

Second, far more common again are texts that set up clear boundaries surrounding Jewish table fellowship. The *Letter of Aristeas* lines 128–171 contain an expansive justification of the Jewish purity laws. Lines 144–153 address the rationale for avoiding the food of the various unclean animals; intriguingly it resembles more the modern explanations of Mary Douglas and others (see above, p. 38) than the common Christian notion that this was all just good, primitive hygiene. The bulk of the rest of the letter, of course, goes on to describe a classic Hellenistic banquet attended by aristocratic Jews in celebration of the inception of the Septuagint (ll. 182–294). But nothing suggests this was a common practice among the Jewish elite, even in the diaspora, and the vast majority of ordinary folk would have had no reason ever to be invited to such festivities. Even here, the upshot of the banquet is the showcasing of Jewish wisdom; the resulting document remains thoroughly nationalistic.[10]

Precise prescriptions for the various Jewish festivals comprise a recurring theme in *Jubilees*, lest God's people 'forget the feasts of the covenant and walk in the feasts of the gentiles, after their errors and their ignorance' (*Jub.* 6:35b). Even more blatantly, Jacob is commanded, 'separate yourself from the gentiles, and do not eat with them, and do not perform deeds like theirs. And do not become associates of theirs. Because their deeds are defiled, and all of their ways are contaminated, and despicable, and abominable' (22:16). Interestingly, in this text at least, it is not the immoral behaviour of Gentiles that is highlighted but their ritual impurity (cf. further Bolyki 1998: 197). Even their wicked deeds are described with adjectives borrowed from the world of the ritually unclean rather than the morally evil. Given that *Jubilees* probably reflects the harsh conditions of the era of Antiochus Epiphanes (Wintermute 1985: 98, n. d), this diction makes good sense.

The delightful novel known as *Joseph and Aseneth* offers a classic example of how the dietary laws should play out in relationships with Gentiles among pre-Christian Jews. The largest portion of the plot, for our purposes, may be summarized in three stages: (1) The faithful Israelite Joseph meets Aseneth, the beautiful daughter of the Egyptian priest Pentephres, who wants to give him to her in marriage. Both of the young people initially refuse: Joseph because he could not marry a foreigner, an idolater and one who ate unclean food. (2) After a time, Aseneth is convinced of her sin, repents, throws away her idols, and asks to be accepted as a worshipper of the one true (Israelite) God, committing to obey his laws, including the dietary

---

[10] Cf. Shimoff (1996: 445), who also notes that 'Philo's disapproval of the ostentation and immorality of Alexandrian Jewish banquets' suggests that some of the aristocrats may have commonly participated in similar feasts. But even if this were the case, it would still be exceptional in Judaism overall.

restrictions. (3) Joseph now accepts her and the two are married. Punctuating the narrative are scenes of the blessing of food, drink and ointment in ways that suggest that these elements can mediate eternal life (cf. Burchard 1987: 117). A heavenly visitor leads Aseneth to discover a honeycomb that miraculously appears, which is specifically dubbed 'the bread of life' (e.g. 16:16). Such texts may also form part of the backdrop for Jesus' later use of the expression in John 6 (Chesnutt 1989).[11] At any rate, they clearly reflect the extent to which the ideal Jew was supposed to go to preserve his or her distinctive ethno-religious purity.

Of many other possible references, we may consider three more. The *Sentences* of the Syriac Menander, while probably post-Christian, may still be mid-second to early third century (Baarda 1985: 585) and thus pre-date most of the comparable rabbinic traditions. This compilation contains the blunt command: 'Do not dine with a bad servant, lest his master(s) accuse(s) you of teaching his (their) servant to steal' (ll. 154–156). The danger increases in lines 333–335: 'Do not dine with a wicked man; for even what is your own he will consume, and in his wickedness he will say about you evil and hateful things.' No thought is given to the possibly positive influence the godly person could have on the evil one! The earlier, first-century *Psalm 154* confirms the converse that is probably implicit in these warnings: meals are an occasion for the righteous to remain with their own kind. Thus verse 13 refers to the 'just ones' (v. 12), insisting that 'concerning their food fullness (is) in truth; and concerning their feast their portions (are) together.' Other manuscripts attempt to clarify by rewriting the second clause as 'and concerning their feast in fellowship (are they [the righteous]) together' (Charlesworth and Sanders 1985: 621, n. u). Yet another possible rendering of verse 13 is, 'When they eat with satiety She [Wisdom] is cited, and when they drink in a community together' (Eshel and Eshel 2000: 658). Yet whatever the precise translation, the 'they' remain the 'righteous' and 'the assembly of pious' Israelites (v. 12), without any indication that anyone else is welcome.

Third, an inordinate number of texts far too numerous to list unleash warnings and woes against sinners of all kinds, with vice lists frequently dotting the pages of the pseudepigrapha. Particularly replete with such references are *1* and *2 Enoch*, the *Sibylline Oracles*,

---

[11] Kügler (1998) thinks the larger picture in this pseudepigraphon, of Joseph as Pharaoh's vizier dispensing corn (and thus ultimately bread) to the people, also forms part of this background.

the *Testaments of the Twelve Patriarchs*, the *Letter of Aristeas*, *Jubilees* and *Pseudo-Philo*. Even in those texts that stress the positive love commands of the Torah and hint at a universal application to all people, dire warnings of what must be avoided lurk close behind. *Jubilees* 20:2–10 proves typical. Abraham commands his sons to behave righteously and love their neighbours, even 'that it should be thus among all men so that each one might proceed to act justly and rightly toward them upon the earth' (v. 2). But the rest of the passage follows immediately with stern reminders to circumcise their sons; to 'not cross over either to the right or left from all of the ways which the Lord commanded us' (v. 3); to abstain from all fornication and pollution; to burn with fire the woman who fornicates; and to avoid all forms of idolatry and immorality, itemized in considerable detail (vv. 4–8). Then and only then will God bless them, including with material blessings that extend even to abundant food and drink (vv. 9–10). Of course, in various places, this central preoccupation of *Jubilees* 'has a uniqueness over against the views put forth by other groups' in Judaism, 'but it was not directed toward a small embattled minority. It was a theology appealing to all of the pious sons of Israel to return to strict obedience to the law' (Wintermute 1985: 48).

Fourth and finally, a number of the apocalyptic pseudepigrapha develop the concept of an eschatological and even a Messianic banquet in further directions. *First Enoch*, of course, includes the highly scrutinized section known as the 'parables' or 'similitudes' of Enoch (chs. 37 – 71), which because of its absence from Qumran texts has often been alleged to be as late as the third century AD and even influenced by Christianity. Particularly intriguing is the repeated reference to an exalted, heavenly, Messianic figure as the 'Son of Man' in these chapters. But the trend today is moving decidedly away from claims of a late date to the recognition of a first-century Jewish provenance. John Collins has led the reversal of this trend in several writings. In a recent summary of his views (2000: 316), he concludes, 'It is unlikely that a Jewish author would have given such prominence to this figure after the "Son of Man" had become widely identified with Jesus by the early Christians.' Collins also thinks he can detect allusions in Josephus to the similitudes. He determines, therefore, that 'the most probable date is the early first century AD, prior to 70,' while 'an earlier date would be difficult to justify in view of the absence of the Similitudes from Qumran.'

In this event, we may turn to *1 Enoch* 62 as a key chapter for our survey. Here the Lord commands the rulers of the earth to look and acknowledge 'the Elect One', 'the Son of Man', who will sit on his glorious throne and judge all the people of the earth. Tribulation described as like the birth pangs of a pregnant woman (the so-called Messianic woes) will precede this judgment, after which the Son of Man, who 'was concealed from the beginning', shall be revealed (v. 7). Unbelievers will then become frantic and plead for mercy, but it will be too late. Only vengeance will await them. But for God's people, the Lord's 'righteous and elect ones', 'they shall rejoice over (the kings, the governors, the high officials, and the landlords) because the wrath of the Lord of the Spirits shall rest upon them and his sword (shall obtain) from them a sacrifice' (v. 12). This will be the day of final and perfect salvation for God's people, no one shall ever oppress them again (v. 13), and 'the Lord of the Spirits will abide over them; they shall eat and rest and rise with that Son of Man for ever and ever' (v. 14) and always wear garments of glory (vv. 15–16). The righteous eating with the Son of Man for ever forms the key allusion to the Messianic banquet and brings us extremely close to language we will read in the Gospels (esp. in Matt. 8:11–12 par.). And the language of 'rising', though disputed, appears to refer to the hope of bodily resurrection, already articulated in Daniel 12:2 and central to the climax of Jesus' ministry and early Christian conviction (cf. Black 1985: 237).

In *2 Enoch* [J], the patriarch ascends into the third heaven and sees the 'paradise of Edem [presumably a variant spelling for Eden], where rest is prepared for the righteous' (42:3). There the angels rejoice as each righteous person dies and arrives (v. 4). Then,

> when the last one arrives, he will bring out Adam, together with the ancestors; and he will bring them in there, so that they may be filled with joy; just as a person invites his best friends to have dinner with him and they arrive with joy; and they talk together in front of that man's palace, waiting with joyful anticipation to have dinner with delightful enjoyments and riches that cannot be measured, and joy and happiness in eternal light and life.
>
> (v. 5)

No Messiah figure appears here, unless one adopts the improbable interpretation that 'the last one' is the Son of Man, a kind of last Adam figure akin to Paul's understanding of Christ in 1 Corinthians 15:45. Much more likely, given verse 4, 'it is the privilege of the last righteous person ... who completes the tally of the elect, and so brings the history of mankind to an end, to bring out the first man and the first sinner' (Andersen 1983: 168). In this case, we may speak of only an eschatological and not an explicitly Messianic banquet here.

Third Enoch is attributed to Rabbi Ishmael of the Bar Kochba era near the beginning of the second century AD, though scholars propose considerably later dates as well. But again, a text emerges that is so clearly Jewish and nationalistic that we can scarcely suspect it of being a Christian interpolation. Here the Messiah explicitly re-appears. In 48A:9, 'the Holy One, blessed be he, will reveal his great arm in the world, and show it to the gentiles.' Then, in verse 10, 'At once Israel shall be saved from among the gentiles and the Messiah shall appear to them and bring them up to Jerusalem with great joy. Moreover, the kingdom of Israel, gathered from the four quarters of the world, shall eat with the Messiah.' Yet a universalist strain can be detected at this point, akin to Old Testament hopes for people coming from all nations to embrace Judaism: 'and the gentiles shall eat with them.' The book closes (minus the later appendices) with three scriptural quotations to support this affirmation of God's sovereign, universal triumph: Isaiah 52:10, Deuteronomy 32:12 and Zechariah 14:9. Interestingly, recension E reverts to a more nationalistic ideology, declaring that only 'Israel will come from the four quarters of the world and eat with the Messiah,' and explicitly adding, 'But the nations of the world shall not eat with them': a striking contrast with New Testament texts like Matthew 8:11–12 or Revelation 21:24 and 22:2 (cf. Odeberg 1973: 159).

Finally, *2 Baruch*, almost universally agreed to be a late first-century or early second-century Jewish theodicy, grappling with the horror of the destruction of the temple and the fall of Jerusalem in AD 70, contains an intriguing description of a Messianic banquet at the end of days (29:1–8). Here we read that 'the Anointed One will begin to be revealed' (v. 3). 'And Behemoth will reveal itself from its place, and Leviathan will come from the sea, the two great monsters which I created on the fifth day of creation and which I shall have kept until that time. And they will be nourishment for all who are left' (v. 4). It is hard to know how literally our author imagined this picture; would something like hippopotamus and crocodile have been viewed as a desirable repast? Especially since these quasi-mythical creatures came to take on more and more diabolical overtones (see Fyall 2002: 157–174), it is possible that we have here a metaphor intended to depict the ultimate conquest of the devil and his realm. The rest of the passage, however, presents an unequivocally attractive picture:

The earth will also yield fruits ten thousandfold. And on one vine will be a thousand branches, and one branch will produce a thousand clusters, and one cluster will produce a thousand grapes, and one grape will produce a cor of wine. And those who are hungry will enjoy themselves and they will, moreover, see marvels every day. Four winds will go out in front of me every morning to bring the fragrance of aromatic fruits and clouds at the end of the day to distill the dew of health. And it will happen at that time that the treasury of manna will come down again from on high, and they will eat of it in those years because these are they who will have arrived at the consummation of time.

(vv. 5–8)

Once again, the text goes on immediately to describe the resurrection of all people to their respective fates in the context of 'the appearance of the Anointed One' (30:1; cf. vv. 2–5).

Other post-Christian Jewish pseudepigrapha have clear Christian interpolations that testify to the ongoing interest in an eschatological or Messianic banquet. Perhaps the oldest of these is *5 Ezra* (= 2 Esdras) 2:33–41. Included in this context is the call to 'rise and stand, and see at the feast of the Lord the number of those who have been sealed' (v. 38). The *Testament of Isaac* 6:22 and 8:5–7 speak explicitly of 'the millennial banquet', while the *Testament of Jacob* 7:23–25 looks forward to eating the bread of life in the kingdom of God, receiving a portion from the tree of life, and becoming 'sons of our holy fathers, Abraham, Isaac, and Jacob in heaven forever'. Christian language is inserted into Jewish testaments in what may be some of the earliest implicit commentary on the wedding feast of the Lamb in the book of Revelation.

In light of all these passages, it is unclear why J. Priest (1992: 223) believes that intertestamental texts referring to the Messianic banquet are 'surprisingly few'. We would not expect them in the non-apocalyptic material, but most of the major apocalyptic texts contain at least one significant portrait of this hope. Earl Davis (1967: 38–39) is correct, however, that far more striking and frequent than explicit banquet texts are 'the lush materialistic themes' associated with the Messianic age. 'Long life and countless offspring are promised to those living in this period. The general productivity of the land is enormous, and as a broad symbol of this abounding fruitfulness, the yield of the vine is especially touted.' But what must be emphasized on any assessment of the Messianic banquet texts, as with the pseudepigraphal literature more generally, is how rarely any truly universal vision for the make-up of God's people appears. Far more common is the Jews' hope of vindication from *their* oppression, restoration to *their* paradise, the vanquishing of *their* enemies, and the re-establishment of a thoroughly nationalistic and perhaps even ethnocentric theocracy. With specific reference to dining, Sandra Shimoff (1996: 448) summarizes succinctly: '*Jews* are to eat their fill in the days of the Messiah' (italics mine). All this has emerged without even consulting the Dead Sea Scrolls, the most sectarian and boundary-setting corpus of all, to which we turn next. And even before we do, it is worth observing that nothing in these banquet texts even remotely resembles the distinctives of the Greek symposia (*contra* D. Smith 2003: 166–171).

Qumran and the Dead Sea Scrolls

Fascination with the Dead Sea Scrolls, discovered shortly after the Second World War, shows no signs of waning.[12] Despite a few challenges, it is still the very strong consensus that most of the non-biblical texts from Qumran reflect the Essene Jewish theology and practice of varying periods of time between the mid-second century BC and the mid-first century AD. The monastic sect on the shores of the Dead Sea was not identical in every respect to communities of Essenes who lived in distinct neighbourhoods in urban centres, but there is substantial overlap in beliefs among the various groups. While the Essenes at times pursued certain practices and fixated on disturbing trends of the larger Jewish world in extremist fashion, it is increasingly recognized that their perspectives reflected one logical outgrowth of Old Testament religion and simply applied Pharisaic concerns for purity and holiness more extensively, in what the Qumran sectarians believed were consistent outgrowths of those concerns (see, e.g., Hempel 1997). Not least because of the significant Essene quarter in Jerusalem, it is likely that Jesus came into contact with this group and that his behaviour in places reflects a conscious reaction to it (see esp. Flusser 1988).

As with the Apocrypha and the pseudepigrapha, we can touch on only some of the most significant and representative texts. A major theme throughout the Qumran literature remains the preoccupation for ritual cleanliness in countless situations (see esp. Newton 1985).

[12] For state-of-the-art overviews of scholarship, see VanderKam and Flint (2002) as well as Schiffman and VanderKam (2000).

Naturally, meal times would be an especially important occasion for purity. Hartmut Stegemann (1998: 191–192) sums up the sect's demands:

> Admitted to the Essenes' community meals were only full members who were free of handicaps – no women, and no minors. Also excluded from participation, however, were full members who temporarily found themselves in a condition of ritual uncleanness – for example, after sexual relations, or after the death of a family member – or who, on grounds of misconduct, had to keep their distance from the ritual community for some days, weeks, months, or even years. Until they were readmitted, they had to say their obligatory prayers privately and take their meals in the circle of their families. Thus, they temporarily lost the advantages of the community board, nor was any replacement forthcoming from that community.

The classic text that lays out the majority of these responsibilities appears in the *Manual of Discipline* (1QS 6:3b–8a). Here we read of a very hierarchically organized communal meal, requiring a quorum of ten men, led by a priest, with everyone seated according to his rank. Each is asked for his counsel according to that rank. Before dining or drinking new wine, the priest blessed the food and/or drink, and there always had to be someone present who could interpret the Law, because reading and explaining sections of Torah accompanied the meal. The *Manual* (1QS 6:15–23) proceeds to highlight the process by which probationers could eventually partake of the meal and by which those being punished were excluded.[13] 1QS 5:13 has already explained that participants must be in a state of ritual purity, while 4Q513 and 4Q514 likewise insist on purification baths before anyone partakes of the communal meal. Just as the unrighteous may not eat their meal, neither may they sell their food to the Gentiles (CD 12:5) or eat any impure food themselves (CD 12:10),[14] including that which has been touched by a Gentile (4QMMT 6–11).

A number of debates surround the description of Qumran's basic communal meal. Most have assumed that this was the main daily

---

[13] These injunctions form part of a much larger body of probationary requirements (on which see Sutcliffe 1960) and penalties resulting in temporary or permanent exclusion from the community for various offences (on which see esp. Weinfeld 1986; cf. Schiffman 1983: 155–190).

[14] On the exclusionary nature of the Damascus Document (CD) more generally, see esp. Christiansen 1998.

meal, at dinnertime, so that ritual purity in dining remained a daily preoccupation. Given the penalty code that excluded various kinds of people from this meal, there may have been two kinds of dinners: the 'pure meal' for members in good standing and a separate, presumably smaller repast for probationers and those being temporarily disciplined (Sanders 2000: 21). After noting this possibility, however, E. P. Sanders (2000: 22) decides that the simplest and thus most attractive explanation is that the pure meal outlined in the *Manual of Discipline* referred only to the special meals that accompanied the various seasonal festivals (noting especially the references to firstfruits and new wine). But even Sanders (2000: 23) concedes that the daily meals were still probably eaten in a state of purity, and that the sectarians 'may have been almost unique in requiring some degree of purity before all meals' (against the view that the Pharisees did as well). The former claim is probably true; the latter may not be (see esp. Neusner 1982; cf. Ringgren 1993: 220).

On any of these readings, Per Bilde's summaries (1998: 162, 163) seem solid. The common meal 'seems to have had a crucial position as possibly the most tangible expression, not only of the communal character of the group but also of its "purity" and its genuine "priestly" stamp, in other words, of its collective identity.' Moreover, 'it is difficult to imagine a more forceful and usable expression of social fellowship, and, at the same time, a stronger expression of social identity.' Here is the extreme example of a group that is not trying to influence others for the better by rubbing shoulders with them, but wants to separate from outsiders at almost all costs, fearing pollution by them (cf. Schiffman 1983: 173).[15]

Whether or not the communal meal in the *Manual of Discipline* is restricted to festivals, it is certainly the case that the Qumran literature contains extensive legislation for celebrating the various Jewish feasts, including who can partake, what they can eat, when and under what conditions. A key source for these injunctions is the famous *Temple Scroll* (see esp. sections 194–217).[16] Laws of clean and unclean foods and people are enumerated here at length. Among many items that could be cited, we read that blemished animals are reserved for unclean people (209.4 [52:10]); clean and unclean people can eat together what is not sacrificed in the temple (209.4 [52:5]); and foreign

---

[15] Davies (1999: 161) unpacks this in one specific instance: 'To eat with an outsider or a lapsed member was a highly serious offence, because it was to eat or drink an uncleanness, *which then crept into the human sanctuary* and defiled it.'

[16] On which see Crawford 2000: 49–57, with respect to the festival calendar.

women married by Israelites must wait seven years before eating pure food or the peace offering (217.1 [63:10]). But regulations about the necessary states of purity for celebrating festive (and other) meals dot even the smaller, more recently translated fragments. Thus we read of post-partum women not being allowed to eat sacred food (4Q266 2:10); of not taking the food of another participant (4Q270:10); and of not eating the produce from the garden or the harvest from the threshing floor until a priest has blessed it (4Q271:10).

The intriguing 4QMMT ('Some of the Works of the Law') allows the blind and deaf who are otherwise ritually clean to eat the pure food of the community (4Q394:1), but lepers cannot eat the food because they are perpetually defiled (4Q396:5). In the Damascus sect, however, the blind, lame, deaf, feeble-minded and under-age are all among those not permitted even to enter the community. In general, the Essenes established four levels of holiness for space, persons and food. With respect to people, priests were the holiest, then came the pure Israelites, then the impure Israelites (definitions debated), and last the Gentiles. With respect to food, the priestly sacrifices were the holiest, the other temple sacrifices came second, the pure food of the community was third, and other food last. Separation from impure food, a category considerably broader than just refraining from eating the animals forbidden in the Levitical dietary laws, now becomes the responsibility not just of the priesthood but of every member of the community. As Hannah Harrington (1997: 127) concludes, this requires 'a stringent lifestyle with regard to ritual purity of the whole people of Israel'.

Separation from impure people of course extended to every walk of life and not just eating. Even more so than with the Apocrypha and pseudepigrapha, one reads the corpus of the Dead Sea Scrolls and encounters warnings to separate from sin and sinners at every turn. 4Q266 is an entire short 'excommunication text' (Eisenman and Wise 1992: 212) that uses the explicit language of literal Old Testament boundary markers as an analogy to the rules of the sect which must not be transgressed if membership is to be retained (e.g., frag. 1, l. 18). The *Manual of Discipline* (1QS 5:10b–11a) demands that a member of the sect 'should swear by the covenant to be segregated from all the men of injustice who walk along the path of wickedness'.[17] The

---

[17] Knibb (1987: 109–110) remarks, 'the demand for separation was no doubt based on a desire to avoid contamination through contact with outsiders, who were regarded as unclean; but in making this demand the community was merely appropriating to itself the priestly and levitical ideals of the Old Testament. The regulations of columns V–VII appear to suggest that separation did not exclude all contact with outsiders.'

pešarîm (Old Testament commentaries of a sort) regularly contemporize the prophecies they treat by identifying evil characters with the 'man of lies' or 'wicked priest': *Jewish* arch-enemies of their day. The *Damascus Document* (CD 6:14–20) insists that its followers 'keep apart from the sons of the pit' (i.e. everyone outside their community!); 'to abstain from wicked wealth which defiles' (including the wealth of the temple, since it has been corrupted!); 'to separate unclean from clean'; 'to keep the sabbath day according to its exact interpretation, and the festivals and the day of fasting'; 'to set apart holy portions according to their exact interpretation'; and so on. Interestingly, none of this cancels out the complementary command, found in this very passage, 'for each to love his brother like himself; to strengthen the hand of the poor, the needy and the foreigner,' and 'for each to seek the peace of his brother' (6:20b – 7:1a). Still, as we have seen elsewhere, the brother, poor and foreigner are scarcely universal in their scope, especially as all the rest of *Judaism* is considered impure and thus wicked (cf. also 4Q418 81:2).[18] Here is important background information, too, for understanding the use of 'sinners' or 'wicked' in the Gospels. The terms certainly include the morally reprobate, but can also refer to a portion of Israel deemed ritually impure (on which, see esp. Dunn 1992). In this case, that portion proves quite sizeable!

Even the hymns of praise written by the Qumran sectarians, which one might expect to be somewhat more upbeat, regularly intone the dangers of sin and sinners (see 1QH 7:21–23; 10:10–11, 31–36; 12:7–21; 13:22c–25; 14:19–22; 15:3c; 18:22c–26, 29c–30a; 20:25–28; 21:8–9; 24:4–6; and 25:5).[19] One particularly intriguing passage seems to apply Psalm 41:9 in much the same way as the Gospels do: '[All who have ea]ten my bread have lifted their heel against me, and all those joined to my Council have mocked me with wicked lips' (1QH 13:23b–24). It would appear that the author, perhaps the Teacher of Righteousness and founder of the Qumran sect, is feeling betrayed by all those about him. Svend Holm-Nielsen (1960: 106–107) comments, 'The expression means obviously "to have fellowship (at table) with". It surprises me that no one has decided that it should refer to the mealtime fellowship in Qumran!' Dining would seem a likely original

[18] Elgvin (2000: 244) comments on this document, also known as 4QInstruction, that it 'reflects a community which saw itself as God's eternal plant, the men of God's pleasure, different from faithless Israel'.

[19] On imagery of physical nourishment in the *Hodayoth*, see Holm-Nielsen 1960: 286.

referent for the outburst, and a lament about dinnertime behaviour would certainly heighten the sense of treachery against the speaker.

As with our survey of the pseudepigrapha, we conclude our overview of the Dead Sea Scrolls with another look at the Messianic banquet. In the *Rule of the Congregation* (1QSa), the scene is sketched of the end of days, when the Messiah(s) of Israel[20] arrive(s) and enter(s) into the community, and all the heads of the clans will sit according to their rank. 'And [when] they gather [at the tab]le of community [or to drink the n]ew wine, and the table of the community is prepared [and the] new wine [is mixed] for drinking, [no-one should stretch out] his hand to the first-fruit of the bread and of [the new wine] before the priest, for [he is the one who bl]esses' the wine and the bread. 'Afterwar[ds,] the Messiah of Israel [shall str]etch out his hands towards the bread. [And afterwards, they shall ble]ss all the congregation of the community, each [one according to] his dignity. And in accordance with this precept one shall act at each me[al, when] at least ten me[n are gat]hered' (col. 2, ll. 17–22).

On the one hand, this is clearly a special, future meal, not to be equated with the regular communal meals of the sect, since a Messiah is explicitly present. On the other hand, the final line quoted suggests that the daily meals were to be viewed as foreshadowings of the coming, great eschatological banquet.[21] Huge amounts of ink have been spilled debating whether any of these meals were viewed as sacral or sacramental, in the sense of actually imparting grace or holiness of some kind. Those who think they were then often see key background here for Christ's Last Supper.[22] Today the tide seems to have turned in favour of a non-sacramental interpretation. Early on, J. P. M. van der Ploeg (1957) observed that none of the four major kinds of cultic meals that sociologists of religion identify – involving special foods not otherwise normally eaten; explicitly celebrating a covenant; accompanying an animal sacrifice; or offered specifically to a god – fit what was practised at Qumran.[23] There has also been a shift from an initial assessment that the sectarians looked solely to the imminent future for the arrival of the Messianic age to a perspective that sees them imagining themselves already to be living in the dawn

---

[20] As is well known, various Qumran texts suggest the expectation of two Messiahs, one priestly and one royal, while other passages may anticipate just one.

[21] See, e.g., Knibb (1987: 154), although this point is debated.

[22] The classic study was Kuhn 1957. Cf. also Pryke 1966.

[23] For a more recent summary of what seems now to be a majority opinion, see Schiffman 1989: 55–64.

of the new age, even if an identifiable Messiah (or two) was not quite yet apparent (see already Schiffman 1979).[24]

Nothing here suggests that the sectarians expected anything other than a literal fulfilment of their eschatological expectation. The larger context of the *Rule of the Congregation* involves preparation for the end-time conflagration (col. 1, ll. 21–28), described in glorious detail in the *War Scroll* (1QM). One of the main reasons for the Qumranians' withdrawal into the wilderness was to form the truly righteous remnant of God's people and spur his apocalyptic intervention to redress the horrible injustices of the present age, an intervention for which no other segment of Judaism was, in their opinion, properly preparing.[25] For D. Smith (1991) to speak of this banquet as mythological, therefore, and not as something the sectarians expected literally to happen in their midst, badly misreads the evidence.

Particularly significant as we draw near to our survey of Greco-Roman symposia is that the Jewish eschatological feast was one important ancient Mediterranean banquet in which participants remained seated rather than reclining. Since the latter was an unvarying hallmark of the symposium form, it is unlikely that the Essenes at Qumran were borrowing any features from that culturally foreign practice. As Lawrence Schiffman (1989: 56) elaborates,

> the eschatological banquet is to be eaten seated, as opposed to the tannaitic usage of reclining at formal meals. Indeed, reclining was the Greco-Roman pattern, whereas the biblical tradition was one of sitting. The Messianic banquet, in keeping with the approach of the sect, would embody the traditions of Israel, not those of the Hellenistic pagans.

The sole description of Essene meals in Josephus confirms this impression. There, the first-century Jewish historian describes a very simple, almost austere meal: the assembly gathering after bathing in cold water, dressed in linen cloths, taking their seats in silence, being served a single course of food. Prayer begins and ends the meal. 'No clamour or disturbance ever pollutes their dwelling; they speak in turn, each making way for his neighbour.' Josephus concludes by noting that outsiders think the rite 'some awful mystery', whereas it is

---

[24] Cf. the change of mind reflected in Priest (1992: 228–229), reversing his position of thirty years earlier (Priest 1963).

[25] For Qumran's eschatology and Messianism more generally, see esp. Evans and Flint 1997.

in fact due to their sobriety and limited provisions (*Bellum Judaicum* 2.128–133). One could scarcely imagine a stronger contrast with the symposium form, which so often degenerated into debauchery.

A final Jewish meal from the Second Temple period merits brief attention here. The Essene-like sect near Alexandria in Egypt known as the Therapeutae receives some treatment in Philo. In *De Vita Contemplativa* 34–39 Philo discusses their culinary traditions and a common meal comprising only bread and salt, sometimes with hyssop, and spring water. Diners consumed just enough to keep from hunger and thirst. Philo then contrasts at length the simple, quiet cheerfulness of their festive meals with the gluttony, drunkenness and noise of the banquets of the Gentiles (sections 40–63, esp. 40–47).[26] Clearly Smith has overstated his case when he argues that the symposium format was ubiquitous in the ancient Mediterranean world from 200 BC to AD 200 (see above, p. 21).[27]

A recent summary of the Essenes' passion for purity forms an apt recapitulation of their theology of meals as well. Bilha Nitzan (2000: 145) writes:

> we may conclude that the quest for holiness was the essence of the religious ideology and existence of the Qumran community. By its isolation from any impurity and evil, including those of the earthly Temple, and by its cultic rituals of atonement-seeking which substituted for the Temple worship, the Community fostered the consciousness of an holy congregation. Spiritual holiness, attained by strict devotion to the Law and by conscious maintenance of cleanness from any physical and ethical impurity, was considered an alternative means for atonement. It was this attempt for the acceptance of spiritual holiness as an appropriate cultic means which was the focus of the Qumran liturgy.

Whether or not we label the Qumran meals explicitly cultic, it is clear that their participants were consumed by the desire to remain pure by the avoidance of everything impure. No thought was given to the possibility that holiness itself might rub off on and cleanse that which was unclean.

Second Temple Judaism more generally, of course, did countenance

---

[26] For an excellent analysis highlighting this contrast, see Seland 1996.

[27] Indeed, even among Greco-Roman sources, the more ascetic meals of Iambulus' Utopia provide closer parallels to Qumran and the Therapeutae than do the symposia. See Mendels 1979.

that possibility under limited circumstances. Contact with certain holy things could make clean the common, just as defilement could make the ritually pure impure. Later rabbinic teachings, beginning (in codified form) with the Mishnah, but with oral traditions clearly predating it, would discuss these matters at length. Virtually a third of that dictionary-sized document would treat 'hallowed things' and 'cleannesses', in the fifth and sixth of its major divisions respectively (Danby 1933: x). But meals remained primarily a time for insiders to have fellowship with one another; for the most part they were not viewed as an occasion for what we would today call 'outreach'. As Bruce Chilton summarizes (1992: 473), 'meals ... were principal expressions within Judaism of what constituted purity. One ate what was acceptable with those people deemed acceptable. To eat in that manner could more truly be said to create a sphere of purity than merely to express such purity.' Despite superficial parallels, we will observe a fundamentally different model as we turn to the Greco-Roman symposium meal.

Greco-Roman symposia

Today we think of a symposium as a mini-conference in which various speakers gather to present and discuss their opinions on a particular topic. In ancient Greece and Rome, it was much more than that: a two-part banquet that began with an elaborate meal, followed by a 'drinking party' with various forms of entertainment (e.g. music, dancing, or sex) and including discussions of themes ranging from the serious to the banal. Walter Burkert (1991: 7) provides an accurate and thorough definition:

> The symposium is an organization of all-male groups, aristocratic and egalitarian at the same time, which affirm their identity through ceremonialized drinking. Prolonged drinking is separate from the meal proper; there is wine mixed in a krater for equal distribution; the participants, adorned with wreaths, lie on couches. The symposium has private, political, and cultural dimensions: it is the place of *euphrosyne* [good cheer], of music, poetry, and other forms of entertainment; it is bound up with sexuality, especially homosexuality; it guarantees the social control of the *polis* [city] by the aristocrats. It is a dominating social form in Greek civilization from Homer onwards, and well beyond the Hellenistic period.

Fundamental to such gatherings was a fairly homogeneous group-ing of participants. Dinner guests were the friends or relatives of the host (Athenaeus, *Deipnosophistai* 8.363). Women did occasionally attend with men, but the practice was frowned upon because it put them under suspicion of being courtesans: the sexual attendants to the men who, along with young adolescent boys similarly abused, more commonly frequented these gatherings. More typically, women (and even children) had their own symposia (though without the sexual element and same level of drinking) in groups defined by age and friendship (cf. Herodotus 1.172).[28] Thus when Burkert speaks of symposia as 'egalitarian', he is referring to equality *among peers*, not, for the most part, across social classes.

Special banqueting halls or large rooms were reserved for the symposia, and the practice of reclining on cushions that were placed next to a square-shaped U arrangement of tables (the *triclinium*) developed as a sign of the leisure and luxury of the meal. This arrangement also allowed guests to be seated according to rank, with each place designating a certain degree of honour. In the pre-classical period, the banquet seems to have evolved from a daily communal meal among members of a small village, along with special gatherings of soldiers preparing to go to battle (Pantel 1999: 39). Eventually, symposia were celebrated for the periodic gatherings of charitable foundations, religious cults, civic and business associations, trade guilds, patrons wooing their clients, philosophical collegia and funerary societies (Klinghardt 1996: 35–40). The objective of com-mensality remained central to all these forms (Pantel 1999: 56). Indeed, as Nicholas Fisher (1988a: 1167) summarizes, 'in few societies have celebrations of shared eating and drinking been so highly valued, so idealized and stylized, so widely practiced at many levels, and so significantly used as occasions for philosophical, political, and moral discussions and their reflections in poetic and prose literature.'

The key documents from classical Greece reflecting symposia are those of Plato and Xenophon. Plato's work entitled *Symposium* established the standard in the late fifth century BC (see Lamb 1975: 77). As with so many of Plato's writings, it focused on the activities of Socrates, in this case at a particular banquet hosted by one Agathon (174A–B). Participants first washed themselves to prepare for the occasion (175A). After the dinner itself, the transition to the sym-posium proper was indicated by a libation and a chant to the resident

---

[28] Both references come from Cooper and Morris 1990: 79.

god (176A). Guidelines were established so that people would then drink enough to serve their pleasure but not so much as to become 'tipsy' (176E). It was also recommended that the typical flute girl be dismissed, indicating that the more characteristic entertainment (at best light-hearted; at worst bawdy) would be replaced by more serious philosophical discourse (176E). Problems with ranking the guests were discussed and resolved (177E), and later a president over the proceedings was appointed (213E). The bulk of the symposium's conversation involved Socrates' discourse and dialogues with the celebrants over the nature of love (beginning in 199D).

Midway through the festivities, an uninvited guest by the name of Alcibiades crashed the party, causing the celebrants to debate whether or not to preserve the social homogeneity of the event, but eventually he was welcomed in (212D). This practice of 'party crashing' would later become common, particularly when invited guests would in turn bring uninvited friends of theirs, leading symposiasts to establish rules to deal with the arrival of such people and how to behave toward them (Klinghardt 1996: 84–97). Near the end of this particular symposium, as 'Agathon was getting up in order to seat himself by Socrates', 'suddenly a great crowd of revelers arrived at the door, which they found just opened for some one who was going out. They marched straight into the party and seated themselves: the whole place was in an uproar and, losing all order, they were forced to drink a vast amount of wine' (223B)! With this, several of the original guests began to leave and the gathering quickly broke up.

A generation later, in the early fourth century BC, Xenophon would pen his own *Symposium*, purporting to have been present at a different banquet with Socrates forty years earlier and apparently wanting to set the record straight that the lofty and sober discourse of most of Plato's narrative was more idealized than historical (Todd 1979: 530). Again, mostly historical personages are described, though there is no guarantee that the dialogue reflects anything more than what Xenophon wanted it to, several decades later. Still, the format and customs of the symposium, meshing as they largely do with the many other reports and portraits of similar celebrations, are likely to reflect historical practice.

Here participants prepared for the meal either with exercise and a rub-down or with a bath. Autolycus, the son of the host, Callias, sat at his father's side; 'the others, of course, reclined' (1.8). The feast began in silence, until it was interrupted by Philip the buffoon (or jester), who would ultimately provide some of the entertainment (1.11–13). After the meal, again a libation was poured and a hymn sung to a god. A man from Syracuse had been hired to provide merriment, along with a flute girl, a dancing acrobat and a handsome young zither player (2.1). Socrates praised the feast as 'a perfect dinner', 'above criticism', with 'delightful sights and sounds' (2.2). Callias then proposed to bring in perfumes for the diners to please their sense of smell as well, but Socrates rejected this idea as befitting women but not men (2.3–4). The discussion turned to the kind of knowledge in which one could take the most pride; one guest boasted that he could recite the whole of Homer's *Iliad* and *Odyssey* by heart (3.5)! Competition ensued as to who could hold forth most persuasively on the topic of righteousness (4.1); this comprises the bulk of the symposium. Eventually a young man and his courtesan were advancing in their romantic overtures to each other, so that 'the banqueters, seeing them in each other's embrace and obviously leaving for the bridal couch,' swore if they were unmarried that they would find themselves wives, 'and those who were already married mounted horse and rode off to their wives that they might enjoy them. As for Socrates and the others who had lingered behind, they went out with Callias to join Lycon and his son in their walk.' Xenophon closes his book with the laconic line, 'So broke up the banquet held that evening' (9.7).

As the Hellenistic period inaugurated by Alexander the Great unfolded, a new kind of banquet developed: various kings gave extravagant parties for their citizens as a show of their power and in hopes of winning the affections of their townspeople. The Macedonian rulers who succeeded Alexander often gained a reputation for debauchery as well. Athenaeus, for example, described how Demetrios I of Macedon and Lysimachos of Thrace each assaulted the other over the excesses of their respective royal courts, complete with prostitutes, lavish dishes, excessive drunkenness and dirty jokes (*Deipnosophistai* 614a–615a). Athenaeus likewise claims that Antiochus IV (Epiphanes) hosted thirty days of public games at the oracle of Daphne in Syrian Antioch, with successive days of 1,000 and 1,500 *triclinia* at which the people could feast and with public fountains flowing with wine (*Deipn.* 194c–195f).[29] Little wonder that orthodox Jews protested, though of course religious persecution played an even more central role in their revolt.

---

[29] Both references come from Fisher 1988a.

By the first century, so many symposia had degenerated into showcases of gluttony and drunkenness that satires were written about them. The most detailed and famous of these is Petronius' *Satyricon* on the banquet hosted by one Trimalchio. Luxurious treatment, drunkenness and quarrelling begin already in the bath-house (28); the dinner itself features an endless supply of the most exotic delicacies (31 *et passim*); the slaves who serve the meals are physically abused (34); the enormous wealth of the host is repeatedly stressed (37 *et passim*); guests tell extravagant and incredible tales of their travels and feats of heroism (38 and elsewhere); so much food is provided that no one can begin to sample it all (39–44) and some diners get sick (47); while similar quantities of wine are served, leading to the grossest of excess (beginning in 51). The entertainment again involves acrobats (53) and dancers (70), but it also includes presents for each of the guests (57). Throughout the proceedings the discourse remains banal at best and insulting at worst. Petronius brings the evening to a close in his penultimate paragraph:

> The thing was becoming perfectly sickening, when Trimalchio, now deep in the most vile drunkenness, had a new set of performers, some trumpeters, brought into the dining-room, propped himself on a heap of cushions, and stretched himself on his death-bed, saying, 'Imagine that I am dead. Play something pretty.' The trumpeters broke into a loud funeral march. One man especially, a slave of the undertaker who was the most decent man in the party, blew such a mighty blast that the whole neighbour-hood was roused. So the watch, who were patrolling the streets close by, thought Trimalchio's house was alight, and suddenly burst in the door and proceeded with water and axes to do their duty in creating a disturbance. My friends and I seized this most welcome opportunity, outwitted Agamemnon [who had secured for them their invitation to this party], and took to our heels as quickly as if there were a real fire (78).[30]

A similar, though considerably abbreviated, account appears in Juvenal's second-century AD *Satire*, part five, entitled 'How Clients are Entertained', while Martial's first-century *Epigrams*, section 60, contains the oft-quoted parody of unequal treatment when superiors did condescend to entertain their social inferiors:

[30] For an analysis of the *Satyricon* by a New Testament scholar, with comments on its relevance to that field, see Pervo 1985.

Since I am asked to dinner, no longer, as before, a purchased guest, why is not the same dinner served to me as to you? You take oysters fattened in the Lucrine lake, I suck a mussel though [*sic*] a hole in the shell; you get mushrooms, I take hog funguses; you tackle turbot, but I brill. Golden with fat, a turtle-dove gorges you with its bloated rump; there is set before me a magpie that has died in its cage. Why do I dine without you although, Ponticus, I am dining with you? The dole has gone: let us have the benefit of that; let us eat the same fare.

Of course, all these parodies exaggerate, perhaps even drastically, the typical conditions of a symposium. But their prevalence and popularity attest to the reality of at least some excess, common enough to draw the mockery and ire of the satirists.[31]

As with all topics of 'Greco-Roman' background to the New Testament, we must be careful that we do not blur the distinctions between the two cultures hyphenated in the adjective. On the one hand, one recent summary of the Roman *cena* applies reasonably aptly to the Greek symposium as well: from one's eating habits one could determine a person's morality, piety, sociability, efforts for war or peace, parentage and friendships. One who refused to participate in a *cena* when invited could be socially and politically marginalized. Good citizens would not act this way or they would be accused of avarice. And the economic function of the meal was to redistribute riches to a certain extent, permitting those with superfluous possessions to share a little at least with fellow citizens (Dupont 1999: esp. 59, 63). Furthermore, in at least some Roman circles there seems to have been concern to cross over social boundaries, though not in the sense of the rich inviting the truly poor. It certainly became more acceptable in Roman settings for wives to attend banquets with their husbands, though others would inevitably look down on them when they did. The Greek predilection for pederasty frequently gave way to more heterosexual lovemaking. And Augustus attempted, with varying degrees of success, several reforms geared to reduce the extravagance and immorality involved (Fisher 1988b). Already in the Julian era, Cicero had remarked that the Roman *convivium* was a better term than the Greek symposium, 'because it implies a communion of life', that characterized the Roman practice, rather than just drinking (and eating) together (*De Senectute* 8.45). Yet he also

---

[31] It may likewise reflect the depth of the conviction that properly conducted symposia formed a central index of civilized behaviour (Paul 1991).

acknowledged that it might have been the older age of his companions and himself that led them to moderate and temper their excesses, rather than anything inherent in the form of the party (8.44). In the mid-first century, Statius had a brief but generally positive description of the *convivia* put on by the emperor for his citizens (*Silvae* 1.6), while in the early second century Pliny the younger, the Roman governor of Bithynia, declared that he attempted not to make class distinctions among those whom he invited to meals (*Letters* 2.6.3).

At about this same time Plutarch was writing his *Moralia*, including nine volumes of 'Table Talk' that present and discuss key questions that had particularly occupied the symposiasts over the years. The most relevant for our concerns are whether philosophy is a fitting topic for conversation at a drinking party (1.612E); whether the host should arrange the placement of the guests or leave them to seat themselves (1.615D: the ease with which he concludes for the former suggests it was not much in debate); why places at banquets acquired honour (1.619); why it is customary to invite many guests to a wedding supper (4.666); why large numbers of invitations to ordinary banquets become more problematic (5.678); on the appropriateness of flute girls' music for after-dinner entertainment (7.710); what kinds of entertainment are most appropriate more generally (7.710–711); and whether it is good to deliberate over wine (7.714: yes, so long as people do not get too drunk).

What may we conclude about the symposia? With occasional exceptions they were reserved for the aristocratic elite (Garnsey 1999: 10, unpacked in 113–127). Those who violated the norms were often ostracized, except within a small middle class (Schultz 1993: 34). By the time we reach the decades immediately before and during the New Testament period, the symposia had declined in prevalence and significance in the predominantly Greek portions of the empire, while being revived a little in the more Roman areas (Garnsey 1999: 130–131). At the same time, Roman 'snobbery' toward non-Romans often outdid Greek exclusivity, so that whatever crossing of class lines may have occurred certainly did not extend to the foreigner (Balsdon 1979 *passim*). Meanwhile, vase paintings and other artifacts that occasionally depict Greek symposiasts in foreign attire have been shown to portray native Greeks in borrowed garb, not actual guests from other nationalities (M. Miller 1991).

However much other variety there may have been in the proceedings, the key element that distinguished the symposium from any other meal was the fixed period of after-dinner drinking. This period reflected the Greeks' fascination with wine more generally. A game, called the *kottabos*, was even played to see how accurately guests could spit their wine and hit various targets. Even when participants did not become totally inebriated, drinking and merriment remained the primary purposes of most symposia. Elevated philosophical discourse proved to be the exception and not the rule.[32]

Conclusions

This chapter has traversed a vast terrain in time and culture. Without merely repeating the conclusions from the end of each of its sub-sections, we may make the following generalizations. Even more so than in the Old Testament, intertestamental Judaism viewed meal-times as important occasions for drawing boundaries. Dining created an intimate setting in which one nurtured friendship with the right kind of people, eating the right kind of food. The Dead Sea Scrolls reflect just how exclusive one sect of Judaism was prepared to become, but the Qumran sectarians merely elaborated on principles amply documented already in the Apocrypha and pseudepigrapha; indeed, in the Old Testament itself. Fundamental among those principles was the notion that unclean people and objects constantly threatened to corrupt God's holy, elect nation and individuals within it. Like literal physical disease, we may think of ritual impurity as contagious. The idea of a godly person's holiness rubbing off on and transforming an unclean or unholy person scarcely seems to have been countenanced.

Of course, Second Temple Judaism had its assimilationists, especially among the aristocracy, who embraced cultural forms of the dominant Hellenistic world in which they lived, but their 'decadence' simply reinforced the standard conviction that putting pure and impure people together merely corrupted the pure. Already toward the end of the biblical period, the *marzēaḥ* denounced so roundly in Amos, along with the Babylonian and Persian royal banquets of Esther and Daniel, in part resembled the form and decadence of the later Hellenistic symposia (Burkert 1991: 9–17). Greco-Roman sympathizers among the Jewish aristocracy would continue to indulge in symposiac practices throughout the intertestamental period, leading to the warnings in the literature of this era, particularly in Sirach. But the vast majority of Jews would probably never have had occasion

---

[32] For all the points in this paragraph, see esp. Lissarrague 1990.

even to wrestle with the decision of whether or not to attend such banquets; they would never have been invited.

Thus, despite superficial similarities between the feasts of ancient Judaism and the symposia of Greece and Rome (stressed throughout Klinghardt 1996 and D. Smith 2003), the main impression one receives as one reads the primary literature on these two traditions is the sense of two reasonably distinct worlds. Burkert (1991: 8) rightly speaks of 'more contrasts than parallels' (cf. also Feeley-Harnik 1981: 71–106). Shimoff has surveyed the extent to which Hellenistic and rabbinic Jews assimilated to Greek cultural practices, especially in banqueting, and notes degrees of 'capitulation' in different times and places. But with respect to pre-rabbinic Judaism within the land of Israel – the background most relevant for interpreting Jesus – she observes (1996: 443–444):

> The affluent Jews in hellenistic Eretz Israel had aspirations of forming an elite aristocracy, and adopted many of the more innocent Greco-Roman practices (e.g., names, clothing style, etc.). But the Greco-Roman banquet was rooted in idolatry, and was marked by flagrant hedonism. Whatever else might be said about these banquets, it is clear that they were not appropriate expressions of traditional Jewish religious values. The Greco-Roman banquet thus represented an important boundary condition, the limiting case of how far a Jew might go in accepting, adopting, or adapting hellenistic cultural practices.
>
> In a sense, then, if we want to appreciate the true extent of hellenization among Jews in Eretz Israel, and how the rabbis reacted to hellenization, Greco-Roman banquets are of special significance; no other hellenistic practice was at once so culturally-attractive and so religiously-reprehensible.

Three other points make it unlikely that any of the Jewish meals commended in the literature we have surveyed adopted significant elements of the Greco-Roman symposium. The first is the central role of 'breaking bread' in Jewish meals, a feature that will be treated when it appears again in the Gospels (see below, pp. 105, 124–125). Klaus Berger (1993: 97) notes that the expression 'to break bread' does not occur outside of biblical Greek, not even in Philo or Josephus. Breaking bread to begin a dinner formed an important responsibility for the father of a home in Jewish circles, whereas it played no significant role in the Greco-Roman meal. This feature alone keeps numerous Jewish and Christian meals distinct from their pagan counterparts. None of the symposia surveyed above included a discrete scene involving the breaking of bread, so in those accounts in the Gospels where bread *is* central, strong counterbalancing evidence will have to be marshalled to make the idea probable that a symposium is being depicted.

Second, even as late as the rabbinic literature, when greater assimilation to Hellenistic practices did at times occur, Israel Abrahams (1967: 55) observes that 'the Rabbis would have been chary of intercourse with ['persons of immoral life, men of proved dishonesty or followers of suspected and degrading occupations'] at all times, but especially at meals.' At least some of the participants in symposia would regularly have fallen into these categories, especially whenever *sexual* intercourse formed part of the merriment. Thus the Talmud declares that the pure-minded in Jerusalem would not sit for a meal unless they knew who their table companions would be, particularly out of concern 'that the meal not degenerate into mere eating and drinking' (*b. Sanhedrin* 23a). Most Jews would not readily have accepted invitations to Greco-Roman-style banquets at all. Even if on occasion they recognized the need to invite to their own meals persons not otherwise deemed fully acceptable, they would assuredly not have attended meals hosted by those other people in *their* homes (Abrahams 1967: 56).

Third, the one feature of the symposium that seems to have been widely borrowed throughout the ancient Mediterranean world – *reclining* to eat – for that very reason cannot demonstrate that a particular meal was a formal banquet, much less a symposium *per se.* Hugo Blümner (1966: 203) stresses that even at ordinary Greek meals, heads of households regularly reclined,[33] so the mere reference to reclining in an account about a meal cannot mark it off as a more sumptuous feast, much less a symposium. Precisely because such Greek customs *did* permeate Second Temple Judaism, we may not infer any particular kind of meal simply from a reference to diners reclining. Jewish experts concur. In describing 'home and family', in his co-edited volume on *The Jewish People in the First Century*, Shmuel Safrai (1976: 736) observes that the *triclinium* couches for reclining were 'used for festive banquets, as well as for regular meals and also for the reception of honoured guests'. But even then, 'the

---

[33] The wife customarily sat at her husband's feet, with the children around the table in chairs. When there were guests, the wife and children usually dined separately. If a woman reclined next to a man at table it suggested she was a courtesan.

more usual seat was a chair.' David Noy (1998: 138) adds that 'reclining' often became synonymous with 'dining', so that at times we may not even infer an actual posture from the use of the term. To record that a group of Jews reclined at table may therefore tell us little more than that they gathered for a meal. To conclude anything further about the nature of that meal could quickly outrun the evidence. All these remain crucial qualifications to keep in mind as we turn to our next subset of ancient Jewish dining practices: the meals of Jesus and their participants, as reported in the New Testament Gospels.

Chapter Four

Jesus the consummate party animal?

Jesus' eating with sinners in the Gospels I: Material not distinctive to Luke

J. D. Crossan has provocatively described Jesus as the consummate party animal.[1] By this he appears to mean Jesus' love of associating with a broad cross-section of people, but particularly the outcast of Jewish society, in the context of festive banquets. Like Sanders, Crossan (1994: 66–74) does not highlight Jesus' calls for repentance but focuses on an 'unbrokered kingdom' and a 'radical egalitarianism' that he believes Jesus is establishing among his followers and supporters. Because Crossan (1991; 1994) largely excludes singly attested Gospel material from his database of authentic Jesus tradition, it is natural to use his label for Jesus in question form as a title for this chapter, which contains discussions of all the multiply attested Synoptic pericopae on our theme (along with three passages peculiar to either Matthew or John).

Primed with all the historical background of chapters 2 and 3, we may at last turn to the New Testament Gospels to discover their contribution to our topic of Jesus, sinners, and table fellowship. For the sake of avoiding one giant chapter, we have grouped the texts into two segments. First will appear material found in Mark, Q, or John: some of it paralleled elsewhere and some not. This will leave the distinctively Lukan texts for our next chapter. While somewhat artificial, this grouping allows us to examine certain claims about the uniquely Lukan material separately. It also conveniently divides the Gospel texts roughly in half. We begin with the so-called triple tradition: texts found in all three Synoptic Gospels.

---

[1] I have heard him use this expression in several public addresses but am not aware of a printed occurrence of it.

Levi's party: Mark 2:13–17 and parallels

The account of the calling of Levi is usually classified as a pronouncement story or, in more recent literature, a chreia. Dennis Smith (2003: 227–230) views these as wholesale creations of the early church. Far more standard, however, is the form-critical approach that recognizes the pronouncement with which this kind of story climaxes as the most stable part of the tradition, even if individual details vary in the build-up to the climax.[2] One would thus expect verse 17, containing Jesus' little proverb about the sick rather than the healthy needing a physician, to be the most authentic core of the passage. While clearly it could be used to summarize numerous situations, there is nothing inappropriate or historically implausible about its use in this particular context.

The introduction in verse 13 parallels Mark 1:16, in which Jesus likewise walked beside the Sea of Galilee. Now he is doing it 'again' (*palin*). Since the former passage introduced Jesus calling several of his first disciples, we are not surprised to find him summoning another individual to follow him here.[3] As we saw in chapter 1, a tax collector like Levi (v. 14) is likely to have been a Jewish middleman between the Roman government and the Galilean populace. Translations like 'toll collector' or 'revenue contractor' capture the nature of his responsibilities better (cf. above, pp. 23–24). The specific verb with which Mark summarizes Jesus' call to Levi to 'follow' is *akolouthei*. In the Gospels *akoloutheō* is used 'only of Jesus' disciples, never of those who oppose him' (Edwards 2002: 81), so we expect this call to be heeded, as in fact it is.

If the information in John 1:35–51 has a historical basis, as many commentators believe (see Blomberg 2001: 80–85), then several of the disciples called in Mark had some prior exposure to Jesus during the period of time when his ministry overlapped with that of John the Baptist. We might muse that the same was true of Levi, but this is not information Mark wants to communicate. The impression remains of an instantaneous response to Jesus' call. Likewise, other events must have intervened after Levi left his tax business, but the next paragraph (vv. 15–17) moves without additional comment to a subsequent dinner involving Levi and Jesus.

---

[2] For this approach in general, see esp. Hultgren 1979; on this specific passage see esp. Vledder 1997: 204–212.

[3] Decker (2001: 71) notes that *palin* in contexts like this 'marks a seam between two pericopes and, along with the geographical notation, serves to introduce the second, referring back to the previous pericope'.

Despite most English translations' attempts to interpret the text by the addition of names, the original Greek at the beginning of verse 15 reads merely, 'And it came about when he was reclining in his house ...' Who is eating in whose home here? Many commentators have wanted to argue that this must be Jesus' house, since Jesus is the nearer (implied) antecedent to the pronoun 'he'. Moreover, Jesus appears to act as a host in subsequent verses by leading the dialogue. This interpretation requires Luke 5:29 to reflect mistaken redaction, because Luke explicitly identifies the banquet hall as Levi's. But neither is this the most probable interpretation of Mark. No other evidence in any of the Gospels suggests that Jesus had a home of his own during his great Galilean ministry in which he could throw such parties. Rather, his itinerant homelessness is emphasized (see esp. Matt. 8:18–20 par.). More tellingly, this view overlooks the culture of reciprocity in which an invitation to discipleship by Jesus would naturally lead Levi to want to do something special for his new master in return (see esp. May 1993).

Verse 15 also includes the first reference to 'tax collectors and sinners' in the Gospels. This odd combination does not necessarily mean that tax collectors and sinners are two separate categories; the Semitic as well as Greek constructions 'A + B' could either generalize or particularize (Marcus 2000: 226). In other words, the one noun could form a subset of the other. From our analysis in chapter 1, we could expect 'sinners' here to be a narrower term than one referring to all those thought ritually impure by the Pharisees (i.e. the *'am-hā-'āreṣ*) but broader than one denoting the most morally wicked in Jewish society. Nevertheless, depending on the specific ways in which Levi exercised his toll collecting, he might have been viewed as particularly corrupt above and beyond the general immorality ascribed to his profession by Jews living under Roman occupation.[4]

The verbs for dining in verse 15 come from the roots *katakeimai* and *synanakeimai*, respectively. The first refers simply to 'reclining'; the second, to 'reclining together with' someone. Depending on how wealthy Levi was and how much he had assimilated to Greco-Roman customs, he might well have wanted to host a symposium here. On the other hand, Louw and Nida (1988: 251) note that both *anakeimai* and *katakeimai* often refer just to eating, without any reference to posture at all (and recall above, pp. 95–96). And if no

---

[4] Marcus (2000: 226) notes that Mark 7:21–22 may give the best insight into who Mark thought such sinners were. The sins listed here are primarily those of immoral or unethical behaviour, but it is going too far to deny any element of ritual impurity at all.

reclining on couches were implied here, then this would certainly not be a symposium.

The 'many who followed Jesus' probably refer to Levi's friends, perhaps even fellow tax collectors, because Mark has introduced only a handful of Jesus' disciples thus far. The last clause of verse 15 in the Greek reads literally, 'for there were many, and they were following him.' But the 'and' reflects Markan paratactic style, which can be more smoothly rendered by the relative pronoun 'who' (Guelich 1989: 102). The imperfect tense for 'they were following' could suggest ongoing past action and some measure of commitment to Jesus over a period of time. If such a significant period has elapsed between verses 14 and 15, Jesus may well have gathered other followers, from among Levi's friends and acquaintances, even if not as part of the inner core of twelve. Alternatively, the imperfect tense may point to the 'remoteness' of the action (cf. Decker 2001: 107), relegated to the parenthetical clause as it is. But the very meaning of the verb requires at least some interval of time for one person to establish himself or herself as 'following' someone else. R. T. France (2002: 134) notes that verse 15b is a typical Markan 'piece of extra verbiage . . . heightening the scandal of Jesus' disreputable entourage', while the repetition of the verb 'follow' suggests 'a degree of enthusiasm for Jesus similar to that which led Levi to leave the *telōnion*' (i.e., his tax collector's station).

Another interval of time may be implied between verses 15 and 16. The one portion of this passage most often alleged to be historically implausible is the claim that the Pharisees and scribes 'saw' Jesus eating at this banquet. But *idontes*, as with the English verb 'seeing', could mean simply 'finding out'. Word could have spread after the party and the Pharisaic criticism come at a later time (e.g. Morris 1992: 221). On the other hand, it is not as impossible as some claim for the Jewish leaders to have been present on this occasion. Observers could have watched in an open courtyard even if they were not invited guests (Gundry 1993: 129), or open doors to a banquet hall could have permitted certain uninvited attendees to gather around the perimeter of the room (Love 1995: 201). But the fact that the leaders questioned the disciples about Jesus' behaviour, rather than addressing Christ himself, may well suggest a separate venue altogether.

Still one more break in time may be implied between verses 16 and 17. An interval must have elapsed for the disciples to report their conversation with Jesus' critics back to the master himself. Then Jesus replies by citing the proverb that forms the focal point of this passage. Many have found irony here, understanding 'the righteous' to mean the 'self-righteous' or 'those who think they are righteous but are not'. Yet Jesus may just be adopting their self-estimation for the sake of making his point (see esp. France 1985: 168). This interpretation fits the use of 'sinners' as well. Jesus is welcoming those who, by the conventions of his world, are seen as sinful, whether they are or not according to *God's* moral law, so it would make sense for him also to use 'righteous' as referring to the conventional estimation of the Jewish leaders.

We have already seen the increasing invective against people deemed flagrant sinners within the intertestamental literature. Neither was the early church known for its high tolerance of 'sinners', so there is no difficulty demonstrating discontinuity with antecedent Judaism and with subsequent Christianity (cf. Marcus 2000: 227). At the same time, the banquet theme provides continuity with past Jewish meals and future Christian ones, so that authenticity appears probable by the double similarity and dissimilarity criterion. William Lane (1974: 106; cf. also Witherington 2001: 123) notes that the specific reference to Jesus calling Levi and his colleagues suggests that 'the basis of table-fellowship was messianic forgiveness, and the meal itself was an anticipation of the messianic banquet.' We have already seen that this is a quite different trajectory from that which led to the Greco-Roman symposium. Of course, only a Messianic figure eating with outcasts appears explicitly here; more elements of Isaiah 25:6–9 will emerge in later Gospels texts. But it is hard to imagine such a celebration in Israel not also including wine, while Jesus' fellowship with these unlikely table companions surely reflected God's welcome and their rejoicing and celebrating, additional features characteristic of the eschatological banquet. While only Luke 5:32 specifically adds the reference to Jesus' proverb that he was calling people 'to repentance', it is difficult to see Mark 2:17 with Jesus' 'call' to 'sinners' meaning anything different Thus while 'Sanders is surely right that no one could object to the repentance of sinners,' France (2002: 136) correctly adds that 'what they found unacceptable was the breach of social and religious convention into which that mission led Jesus.'

The parallel passage in Matthew (9:9–13) contains two notable changes. Levi is now named Matthew (vv. 9–10),[5] while verse 13 adds

---

[5] Hagner (1993: 238) finds it unlikely that Matthew could have substituted his name for Levi were they not the same person.

the quotation of Hosea 6:6. Otherwise the texts run very closely parallel, with Matthew smoothing out Mark and omitting a little of his redundancy.[6] But the central theme and climax of the pericope remain identical; nothing needs to be modified concerning our conclusions from Mark's account about Jesus and his partners in table fellowship.

The third version of this story in the Synoptic Gospels (Luke 5:27–32) also parallels Mark reasonably carefully. As we have already noted, Luke makes explicit that it was Levi's and not Jesus' house in which the banquet occurred. Indeed, Luke emphasizes that it was a 'great banquet' rather than merely a 'dinner' which Levi hosted (v. 29). Luke also makes explicit that, when Levi left his tax collector's booth to follow Jesus, he 'left everything' (v. 28). Again as already noted, the closing proverb in verse 32 explicitly adds 'to repentance' to the summary of Jesus' call. But all of these modifications can be seen as merely making explicit what is already implicit in Mark; none of Luke's changes alters the conclusions we have already made about this incident, any more than did Matthew's editing. One could of course argue that, if it emerged that Luke consistently turned Jesus' Jewish meals into Greco-Roman symposia, then his reference to a 'great banquet' here would fit that redactional tendency (e.g. Green 1997: 244). But that line of reasoning presumes a trajectory yet to be demonstrated (see below, ch. 5), while even sumptuous banquets in Jewish contexts did not necessarily adopt the symposium format (see above, pp. 94–96).

Jesus thus defies the conventions of his world by his intimate association with a group of people deemed traitorous and corrupt in his society. Still, he does not condone their sinful lifestyles but calls them to repentance, transformation and discipleship. A catena of quotations captures the correct balance in interpreting this episode in Jesus' life: 'It is a story about saving grace, for there are no penalties, and no demands, except to follow Jesus' (Hooker 1991: 94). Or, more expansively, 'It may also entail summoning them to repentance in the moral sense of that term. What is nonetheless striking is that Jesus appears to not require repentance *in advance* of having table fellowship with sinners and tax collectors' (Witherington 2001: 123, italics mine). Perhaps most strikingly of all, 'Jesus is not defiled by his contact with impurity but instead vanquishes it through the eschatological power active in him' (Marcus 2000: 231). We might thus speak

---

[6] For the essential historicity of the passage, as well as Matthew's distinctive redactional contributions, see Davies and Allison (1991: 97–106).

of holiness for Jesus, rather than sin, being that which he views as 'contagious' (cf. also Borg 1984: 135).

Feasting in the wilderness: Mark 6:30–44 and parallels

The only other passage in the triple tradition involving Jesus and meals (apart from the Last Supper itself) is the feeding of the five thousand. Here even the Fourth Gospel presents a parallel (6:1–15). It is generally assumed that John is substantially independent of Mark and that these two accounts together provide a window into the earliest understanding of Jesus' miraculous feedings.

Mark alone introduces the event with the allusion to the crowds being like 'sheep without a shepherd' (Mark 6:34). Probably he is thinking of the laments throughout Ezekiel 34 that God's people in the sixth century BC lacked godly leaders. But this chapter of Old Testament prophecy is regularly viewed as predicting a coming Messianic replacement who will rule Israel properly. Thus at least Mark sees in the feeding miracle probable Messianic significance (see e.g. Edwards 2002: 191). The repeated references to the location as a remote or desert place (vv. 32, 35) conjure up memories of the Israelites wandering in the wilderness, especially when it turns out that Jesus' miracle involves abundant bread for the hungry. One cannot help but think of God's provision of manna in olden times (Exodus 16) and the Jewish tradition of the Messiah coming as a new Moses, once again bringing an abundance of bread in the wilderness (a point brought out explicitly in John's 'Bread of Life' discourse in John 6:26–59; recall *2 Baruch* 29:5–8).

The disciples' plan to send the crowds away to purchase food in the surrounding villages and countryside (vv. 35–36) does not seem very realistic, given the size of the multitude. Nevertheless, it is the only option they can imagine. Jesus, however, will give them a spectacular alternative. The supplies of bread and fish, minuscule as they are, will suffice to feed the crowds with ample leftovers. That the meal consists of loaves and fishes rather than bread and wine (v. 38) makes a foreshadowing of the Eucharist here unlikely. Instead, one thinks again of *2 Baruch* 29 and the consumption of the great fish Leviathan as part of the Messianic banquet (v. 4; cf. Marcus 2000: 410). Utopian texts in the Greco-Roman world likewise envisioned special meals with abundant food (Pervo 1994: 177–182). In addition, Lane (1974: 230, n. 103) points out the very similar language of blessing and breaking bread in Acts 27:35 (the scene with Paul and the pagan sailors on his ill-fated voyage to Rome). At least at the original historical level of Acts one can scarcely imagine this meal as a Eucharistic celebration, because it is not a Christian meal of any kind. Returning to the five thousand, then:

> it is appropriate to see in the feeding of the multitude a fresh affirmation of the promise that the Messiah will feast with men in the wilderness (Isa. 25:6–9). The austerity of the meal, however, is more reminiscent of the manna in the wilderness than of the rich fare promised for the eschatological banquet. Moreover, the absence of an enduring relationship between Jesus and the people indicates that the fellowship which they shared was essentially that which exists between a host and his guests. The meal was eschatological to the degree that the people experienced rest in the wilderness and were nurtured by the faithful Shepherd of Israel, but it pointed beyond itself to an uninterrupted fellowship in the Kingdom of God.
>
> (Lane 1974: 232–233)

Robert Gundry (1993: 328) further notes that the disciples are not described as eating with the crowds, but only in Mark 7:2 after a later sea crossing. This is another reason for not viewing the feeding of the five thousand as an anticipation of the Lord's Supper; one would otherwise expect the disciples to share in the meal at this juncture. Moreover, 'The bread of the Lord's Supper is not notable for being left over at all, let alone in abundance' (Gundry 1993: 333).

Intriguingly, only Mark describes the crowds as sitting down in symposia (*symposia*) in verse 39. This word occurs in the New Testament only here, and it need not retain its technical sense. Standard lexica define it just as a 'common meal' (e.g. Bauer 2000: 959; Balz and Schneider 1993: 289). Lane (1974: 229, n. 99) thinks that 'the text denotes a group of people eating a fellowship meal together,' similar to the Hebrew *ḥăbûrôt*. Marcus (2000: 419) finds a traditional linkage with the Passover, which had come to be celebrated in symposium style. But the primary allusion is to the departure from Egypt; the imagery points forward to the hope for a new exodus by a renewed Israel in the spirit of Qumran. Moreover, there is 'a progression in the transformation of the people from an *ochlos* or disorganized crowd (6:34) to the *symposion* or table fellowship (6:39) to a *prasia* or organized group (6:40)' (cf. also Bolyki 1998: 94–97).

Once again the verbs for reclining – *anaklinai* in verse 39 and *anapiptein* in verse 40 – could suggest a banquet but need not. Given that the setting is out of doors in a remote place, we are certainly not to imagine people reclining on couches. The verbs again refer simply to sharing a meal.

Mark 6:40 contains a second New Testament *hapax* by depicting the groups of hundreds and fifties as *prasiai*. The term literally denotes a garden plot (France 2002: 267). To the extent that such numerical groupings do suggest a more formal meal, the allusion is probably again to the Messianic banquet (Edwards 2002: 192). The references to hundreds and fifties in fact point our attention back to similar arrangements made for the Israelites in the wilderness (cf. esp. Exod. 18:25; Num. 31:14; and, among the Essenes, 1QS 2:21–22 and CD 13:1), a motif we have already seen lies behind the imagery of this account. The presence of green grass in verse 39, finally, proves unusual in a wilderness setting. Of course, this could simply reflect springtime after heavy winter rains, the one time of the year when the desert 'bloomed', but it is likewise possible that Mark is alluding to eschatological abundance.

The blessing of the food and the breaking of the loaves (v. 41) form the standard start of a Jewish meal. Jesus thus plays the role of host to this giant crowd. We also recall how breaking bread did not play a significant role in Greco-Roman meals, including symposia (see above, pp. 94–95). The switch from the aorist tenses, with the verbs for 'taking', 'looking', 'blessing', and 'breaking', to the imperfect *edidou* ('he kept on giving'), along with the astonishing quantity of leftovers (v. 43), stresses the lavish nature of this meal (cf. R. Young 1994: 114) despite the fact that only bread and fish appear on the menu. But these are not yet the rich meats and fine wines of the eschatological banquet itself, merely a foretaste (Witherington 2001: 218). The feeding of the five thousand further calls to mind the smaller-scale miracle story of Elisha feeding one hundred men with twenty hand-sized loaves, in which a reference to leftovers again appears (2 Kgs 4:42–44). So Jesus is being presented not only as a new Moses but also as a new Elisha.[7]

What is regularly overlooked in this account is that the multitude will have almost certainly come from a wide cross-section of Galilean society. Just as a sizeable majority eked out a marginal existence, so

---

[7] Cf. France 2002: 260; Guelich 1989: 341. See also Marcus (2000: 407), although one does not have to choose between this miracle and the supernatural provision of the manna as sole or even primary background.

too the simple farmers, fishermen, and homemakers of the province would have made up the largest portion of this crowd. Thus, by Pharisaic standards, one must describe this gathering as ritually impure (Edwards 2002: 193). The desert location, moreover, implies that there is no possibility of being selective with the guest list, that some deemed as undesirables are present, and that there can be no seating plan and certainly no facility for handwashing or other cleansing rites. Pharisaic purists would have objected on multiple counts (Poon 2003: 228). As Wilson Poon (2003: 226) reiterates, 'The good news of God's unconditional acceptance of sinners is *materially fulfilled* by Jesus' table fellowship with all kinds of "undesirables" without regard to the meal conventions of the Pharisees.' Once again, 'the abundant provision at these shared meals is symbolic of the *joy* of God's *uncalculating* forgiveness, and a pointer to the eschatological *messianic banquet.*'

The parallel account in Matthew (14:13–21) substantially abbreviates Mark's detail, but no obviously theological differences emerge to shed a significantly different light on the meaning of the episode. The most notable omission is the arrangement of the people into their various groups. An allusion to the feeding of the Israelites in the desert of old nevertheless remains clear. David Garland (1993: 155) represents most commentators when he observes that the miracle 'recalls the exodus theme (as the first redeemer, so the last; *Qoheleth Rabba* 1:9), where Israel is fed in the wilderness (Exod. 16; Pss. 78:18–30; 81:17; 105:40)'. As in Mark, 'the abundance may signify the presence of the messianic age and salvation.' Davies and Allison (1991: 480) think the passage is first of all a gift miracle, teaching about the compassionate Christ and his physical provisions for needy people. Nevertheless, they recognize the foreshadowing of the Messianic banquet, the identification of a new Moses, and the allusion back to 2 Kings 4:42–44 as important secondary themes.

Davies and Allison also see a foreshadowing of the Eucharist, but Matthew introduces no changes to his sources to make such an interpretation any more probable here than in Mark. With Craig Keener (1999: 402), it is better to conclude that the foreshadowing of the Messianic banquet forms the primary purpose of the text, while an important subordinate point involves Christology: 'In the context of other attempted signs-workers in the wilderness in Jesus' day, his sign in the wilderness involves a clear messianic statement.' The verb *chortazein* with the sense of 'to completely satisfy', while common to Mark 6:42 and Matthew 14:20, has already been used earlier in

Matthew in a non-Markan passage with obvious eschatological associations (Matt. 5:6) (Hagner 1993: 418). Even Andrew Overman (1996: 217), who argues unpersuasively for a liturgical and ecclesial setting for the feeding narratives, nevertheless agrees that both Matthew and Mark contain eschatological elements that tie in with the heavenly banquet and meal (218–219).

The Lukan parallel (Luke 9:10–17) diverges from Mark a little more than Matthew did. Even where the two texts contain similar information, there is less verbal parallelism, suggesting greater influence of the oral tradition on Luke's form.[8] Still, no truly noticeable theological distinctives emerge in Luke's version. The third evangelist specifies the location of the feeding as near Bethsaida (v. 10). Instead of referring to Jesus' compassion, he describes him welcoming the crowds, and Luke adds that Jesus was speaking about the kingdom of God (v. 11). In the portion of the text most relevant to the debate over Luke's use of symposia forms, verses 14b–15 refer twice to reclining by the verb *kataklinō*, which again has no necessary bearing on whether this scene is depicted as a formal banquet or not.

More tellingly, Luke, who according to some is most interested in creating symposia involving Jesus (see below, ch. 5), makes no reference to the organization of the crowds, does not even use the word *symposia*, even when he finds it in his Markan source, and describes the divisions of the people simply as 'companies' (*klisias*). But this is a much more ordinary word for groups of people eating, coming as it does from the *klinō* word group for reclining, than either *symposia* or *prasiai*. Darrell Bock (1994: 832) notes that the term can denote any group that is reclining, though it certainly can refer to reclining for a meal. Luke describes these clusters of diners only with the number 'fifties' (v. 14), leading some to think that the parallel to the arrangement of the Israelites in the wilderness has also been diluted (Bock 1994: 831; Fitzmyer 1981: 757). But the allusion to the overall provision of the manna remains clear enough that a conscious reminiscence of the wilderness wanderings seems to have been preserved.

Once again, the heterogeneous make-up of the crowd comes to the fore, especially when we recall Luke's particular interest in sinners and outcasts. Joel Green's observations are worth citing at length:

---

[8] For the need to incorporate this element alongside literary dependence in studies of Synoptic parallels, see esp. Dunn 2003.

Once the boundary-setting and boundary-maintaining function of meals is recalled, the failure of Jesus and his disciples either to observe this role or otherwise to encourage the crowds to observe practices affiliated with it is startling. Here are thousands of people, an undifferentiated mass of people, some undoubtedly unclean, others clean, some more faithful regarding the law, others less so. The food itself – is it clean? Has it been properly prepared? Have tithes been paid on it? Where is the water for washing in preparation for the table? Such concerns are so lacking from this scene that we might miss the extraordinary character of this meal, extraordinary precisely because these concerns are so completely absent ... Again, Luke's narration underscores the degree to which God's benefaction is without limits.

(Green 1997: 365)

Again, too, the passage reflects a partial fulfilment of the Messianic banquet prophecies, in which case 'in some way the messianic age must have begun' (R. Stein 1992: 275). Christology again complements eschatology. Jesus resembles a prophet like Elijah or Elisha and the last prophet like Moses, precisely the two kinds of figures who appear in the transfiguration narrative, juxtaposed in Luke much more closely to this feeding miracle (Luke 9:28–36) than in Mark or Matthew, because of Luke's omission of Jesus' theological and geographical withdrawal from Galilee (Mark 7:1 – 8:26 par.) (Bovon 2002: 359).

Almost nothing relevant to our interests in Jesus' table fellowship changes when we turn to the Fourth Gospel's account (John 6:1–15). One can distinguish between a historical core and theological overlay (see Blomberg 1986: 338), but at neither level does any reference to a symposium or any kind of division of the five thousand appear. The practice of reclining is referred to twice, by the verbs *anapiptō* and *anakeimai*. Again the words by themselves prove nothing about the nature of the meal. Interestingly, the TNIV can even translate the latter as 'sit down', though a posture of reclining may in fact be implied. But without the possibility of using couches or cushions in the wilderness, it is difficult to assert this with any confidence.

A repeat miracle: Mark 8:1–10 and parallel

The feeding of the four thousand is often viewed as a doublet of the multiplication of the loaves for the five thousand.[9] From Mark's perspective, however, the two incidents are clearly distinct, inasmuch as Mark 8:1 indicates that 'another large crowd gathered'. The Greek uses the adverb *palin* ('again').[10] The dialogue in 8:14–21 will also refer back to both episodes as separate.[11] As we will see below, there are reasons for viewing the episodes as distinct at the level of the historical Jesus, too.

Although the crowd is slightly smaller, the situation that triggers this second feeding miracle appears more severe. Verse 2 explains that the multitudes have already been with Christ for three days and had nothing to eat. Jesus again exhibits compassion for the crowds, this time not because they resemble sheep without a shepherd but because of the length of time they have been with him and their lack of food. On this occasion, if he sends them away hungry they may faint on the road, and some of them have come from a long distance (v. 3).

The obtuseness of the disciples proves striking (v. 4), since they have seen their master deal with such a situation before. But the point may be that they think Jesus is asking *them* to replicate the earlier miracle (vv. 4–5). Once again Jesus gives the command for the crowds to recline (from *anapiptō*), but once again this may mean nothing more than to 'sit down' (v. 6). Nothing else in the passage calls to mind any Greek symposium background.

On the other hand, the feeding in the wilderness will again stir up memories of Moses with the Israelites of old and the manna that God provided (see esp. Marcus 2000: 483–485). All of the observations about the probable uncleanness of many in the crowds that we made with reference to the five thousand apply equally strongly here. Indeed, it is likely that this feeding took place in predominantly Gentile territory. At the end of the passage, Jesus and the disciples cross over the Sea of Galilee to the region of Dalmanutha (v. 10). No

[9] Even as conservative a commentator as Hagner (1995: 450) seems content with this theory: 'Although it is of course not impossible that there were two similar, miraculous feedings, the data surveyed above seem more consistent with the hypothesis of one original event that came to be transmitted in two different versions, each with its own symbolism.'

[10] France (2002: 307) notes that '*Palin* underlines Mark's belief that this was a sequel to an earlier and similar event, and alerts the reader to compare and contrast the two stories.'

[11] Edwards (2002: 228) has a good list of the differences between the feedings of the five thousand and the four thousand.

such site has ever been discovered, but the parallel in Matthew (Matt. 15:39) refers to Magadan, a variant of Magdala, on the western shore of the sea. It is possible that both names developed from an original Migdalnunya, meaning 'fish tower' (Blomberg 1992: 247). Jesus would then have fed the four thousand somewhere to the east of the Sea of Galilee in Gentile territory. The distinction in the locations of the two feeding miracles, combined with the obscurity of the geographical references, supports the conviction that both were separate events in which Jesus was actually involved.

The probable symbolism of the numbers of baskets left over supports these conclusions. In Mark 6:43 the disciples collected twelve basketfuls (a standard Jewish number, given the twelve tribes of Israel), while in 8:8 they pick up seven basketfuls (a standard Jewish number for universal realities). Even the distinct words for basket in the two passages denote characteristic Jewish lunch bags and common Gentile shopping baskets, respectively (see Blomberg 1992: 245–246). As Ben Witherington (2001: 235–236) summarizes,

> Very clearly the first feeding indicates Jesus manifesting himself to Israel as the new Moses, but in Mark 8 there is no allusion to Moses or David ... It is true that both stories take place in an isolated or deserted location, an allusion perhaps to manna in the wilderness, but as Hurtado points out, at v. 3 it is stressed that some have come from far off, a phrase often used to speak of Gentile foreigners from distant lands (Isa. 60:4; Jer. 46:27; and material found only in the Greek version of Jer. 26:27 and 38:10).
>
> The emphasis in Mark 8 is quite clearly on Jesus feeding Gentiles, though of course the audience is mixed since it also involves some of the disciples.

The lack of any reference to arranging the crowds according to the judicial groupings of Moses' Israel also fits the hypothesis that the four thousand were primarily Gentiles, the five thousand mostly Jews (Gundry 1993: 394).[12]

The two feeding miracles are nevertheless sufficiently similar to suggest that, if the former conjured up notions of the eschatological

---

[12] That some of them had come from a long distance 'fits entirely with the austere and rugged geography of the Decapolis, which has fewer towns and settlements than does the west side of the lake. It is no place to be without provisions' (Edwards 2002: 230).

banquet, so would the latter. To the extent that Gentiles come more to the fore in the second miracle story, the Old Testament theme of foreigners partaking in the Messianic banquet is magnified. But even for those who play down Gentile connections and stress Israelite typology (see esp. Marcus 2000: 489), the foreshadowing of the eschatological banquet remains transparent. Robert Guelich's mediating position (1989: 409) seems soundest: 'While not intended to provide an exclusively gentile [sic] Feeding set in contrast to an earlier exclusively Jewish Feeding, the literary and geographical setting of this Feeding bears witness to the breaking down of the boundaries between Jews and Gentiles rooted in Jesus' ministry.'

As with the miracle for the five thousand, Matthew (15:32–39) offers few, if any, theological distinctives. Again he abbreviates his Markan source, though this time less drastically. He also rearranges the sequence of a few details, so that one wonders if oral tradition has influenced his structure. Perhaps the most significant change, while affecting only one word, comes in verse 33 with the emphatic first-person plural pronoun: 'where are *we* to get bread enough . . .?' This may confirm our suggestion with respect to Mark that the disciples are not forgetting Jesus' ability to work a miracle under these circumstances but thinking that he is now asking *them* to do it, just as he earlier commissioned them to replicate his ministry in other respects (Matt. 10:1–8).

Davies and Allison (1991: 562) reverse the standard interpretation of the symbolism, thinking that the feeding of the four thousand focuses more on the fulfilment of promises to Israel. A key plank in support of this claim is the distinctive reference in Matthew 15:31 to the praise of 'the God of Israel'. While this could indicate that the crowds were made up mostly of Israelites, it seems a redundant expression for a Jewish-Christian writer addressing a Jewish-Christian audience. But if the point is that even Gentiles blessed a God they were not known for worshipping, then the language makes very good sense. Also less convincing are both Keener's view that the disciples simply missed the significance of the miracles in general[13] and the more common suggestion that the change in verb to a form of *eucharisteō* for Jesus' thanksgiving (v. 36) implies a conscious foreshadowing of the Eucharist (e.g. Montague 1989: 176). At most

---

[13] Keener (1999: 419): 'Perhaps they see him too often in his "ordinary" humanness to expect miracles from him *all* the time. Despite Jesus' earlier feeding miracle, they assume again that they must procure bread by purely natural means (15:33).'

this may reflect Matthean overlay, but it is not likely to form part of Jesus' original meaning.[14]

How not to win friends and influence people: Matthew 8:11–12 and parallel

We turn now from Markan texts to Q-material. Though brief, this passage proves central in understanding Jesus' perspectives on the future eschatological banquet. In Matthew, Christ's sayings come as a climax to the account of the healing of the centurion's servant (Matt. 8:5–13). Already in verse 10 he has praised the faith of this Roman commander who believed Jesus could speak a word at a distance and effect the desired healing. Thus Jesus declares the centurion's faith greater than that of anyone in Israel! When Jesus then proceeds to promise that 'many will come from the east and the west, and will take their places at the feast with Abraham, Isaac and Jacob in the kingdom of heaven' (v. 11), the contrast must almost certainly involve Gentiles. Noting that almost all ancient and modern exegetes make this assumption, Davies and Allison (1991: 27) give six reasons for disputing it:

(1) 'Gentiles are not explicitly named.'
(2) Verse 11 alludes to Psalm 107:3 and the gathering of dispersed Jews from each point of the compass.
(3) East and west in fact are frequently associated in Jewish literature with the return from the diaspora.
(4) In the Old Testament, 'the coming of the Gentiles to Israel is never conceived of as a judgment upon Israel,' as in the Matthean text.
(5) Only Jews are referred to as the sons of the kingdom who are thrown out (v. 12).
(6) Finally, none of the Old Testament texts speaking of the pilgrimage of the nations to Zion is cited.

We may make the following response to these points:

(1) The centurion whose faith is praised is almost certainly a Gentile, especially in light of Jesus' compliment in verse 10.

---

[14] Schnackenburg (2002: 153) does not even find it as one of Matthew's purposes, while allowing it as a possible Markan meaning.

(2) This suggests that Jesus is expanding the Old Testament diaspora language, just as many other New Testament texts generalize from the exclusively Jewish contexts of various Scriptural quotations to more universal ones.

(3) Jesus does not explicitly claim that the coming of the Gentiles is itself the judgment upon Israel; the two components are simply juxtaposed.

(4) The more natural contrast in verse 12 is between certain (not all) Jews being excluded and certain (not all) Gentiles being accepted.

(5) The passage is a very short one, which does not explicitly cite the eschatological banquet of Isaiah 25 either, but an allusion certainly seems present.

(6) Finally, while it is true that Isaiah 25 makes no mention of people streaming from all parts of the world to Zion, the text does refer to the presence of 'all peoples' (v. 6).

Thus the contrast in Jesus' proclamation cannot be simply between privileged and unprivileged Jews but must compare unbelieving Jews with believing Gentiles (*contra* Davies and Allison 1991: 28). Keener (1999: 270), following Gundry (1982: 145), clinches the argument: 'Because no one questioned whether Diaspora Jews as a whole would inherit the kingdom, they would make little sense in "an example of surprising inclusion in contrast with surprising exclusion" ... Whereas we can affirm that Jesus very probably meant Gentiles, that *Matthew* means the Gentiles is clear: Rome was the great power that lay to the west, and Matthew had earlier illustrated the coming of pagans from the east (2:1).'[15]

The verb for taking one's place at table in verse 11 comes from *anaklinō*. As we have seen before, while this verb can refer to reclining, it need not, and even when it does, it does not necessarily suggest a banquet. Nevertheless, this context obviously does allude to the eschatological banquet. Given Jesus' presence at the meals that foreshadowed this feast, it seems fair to infer that he would imagine himself present at this final banquet as well, thus turning the occasion into the more specific Messianic

---

[15] Overman (1996: 118), while stressing that only certain Jews are replaced, nevertheless acknowledges that some of the replacements will include Gentiles, even if he hastens to add that 'this does not mean for Matthew that therefore traditional Jews and historical Israel are out.'

banquet.[16] Certainly, Jesus' imagery of people coming from all corners of the world (presumably to Israel) and joining the Jewish patriarchs sufficiently alludes to Isaiah 25 for us to assume conscious dependence. Indeed, Jesus' words dovetail 'with the prophecy of the pilgrimage of the peoples to Zion (Isa. 2:2–3 = Isa. 60:3–4; Jer. 3:17; Mic. 4:1–2; Zech. 8:20–22; etc.) and of the festival meal on God's mountain (Isa. 25:6–8)' (Schnackenburg 2002: 82). Again, however, the Messianic banquet proves different enough conceptually from the Greco-Roman symposium that no allusion to the latter need be present.

The 'subjects of the kingdom' (v. 12) reads more literally 'sons of the kingdom' and refers to some who thought they would obtain their eschatological inheritance merely by their Jewish ethnicity. The Semitic expression 'sons of' can sometimes mean 'those destined for' (Keener 1999: 269), a rendering that fits the self-understanding of these complacent Jews well. But the second half of verse 12 makes it clear that a fate quite different from what they expect awaits those who presume upon God's favour. They will be thrown into the 'outer darkness', where people will weep and gnash their teeth. This is language used throughout the Gospels, and especially in Matthew, to refer to eternal punishment or hell (cf. Matt. 13:42; 22:13; 24:51; 25:30; Luke 13:28). This 'great reversal' would have shocked and no doubt angered Jesus' original audience. 'Until this point, such a banquet was thought to be a strictly Jewish affair (cf. Zeller), with the Gentiles at best receiving the overflow from the blessings to the Jews. The Gentiles would indeed make their pilgrimage to Jerusalem at the end (cf. Isa. 2:2–3), but mainly as witnesses of God's blessing of Israel, not as direct participants in it' (Hagner 1993: 205). As Donald Hagner continues, 'But now with the coming of the Messiah, that exclusivism is turned on its head in an apparent reversal of salvation-history. It is the Gentiles who are being called from the ends of the earth (*contra* Davies–Allison; cf. France, Luz).'

The Lukan context of Jesus' sayings proves entirely different (Luke 13:22–30; cf. esp. vv. 28–29). Jesus is passing through towns and villages on his way to Jerusalem (v. 22) and is responding to the

---

[16] Cf. Morris (1992: 195): 'The saved, in the end, will come from all over the earth, which clearly means that many Gentiles will be included. It may be significant the words here used of Gentiles are similar to Old Testament passages referring to Jews (e.g. Ps. 107:3; Isa. 43:5–6; 49:12) . . . One way first-century Jews had of referring to the coming bliss was to speak of the messianic banquet, an occasion of festivity in the world to come. To recline with the patriarchs was to feast in leisurely manner in the very best company.'

question of whether only a few people will be saved (v. 23). For the reader familiar with Matthew, Jesus' response in Luke reads like a pastiche of sayings scattered about various Matthean contexts. Much critical scholarship, of course, has assumed each of these to be independent logia most likely from Q. The reference to the narrow door (v. 24) reminds one of Christ's similar teaching in the Sermon on the Mount (Matt. 7:22–23). But the theme of not being able to enter, leading to Jesus' response that he does not know the people on his doorstep calling him Lord (v. 25), more closely resembles the parable of the ten bridesmaids (Matt. 25:1–13). Verses 26–27 appear to expand on the latter Matthean parallel, while verse 30 seems to reflect a 'wandering logion', also found in Matthew 19:30, 20:16 and Mark 10:31.

In between verses 27 and 30 appears the saying on the coming banquet, with considerable verbal parallelism to Matthew 8:11–12. The references to weeping and gnashing of teeth, to the names of the patriarchs, to the phrase 'in the kingdom', and to the fate of being cast out exhibit the greatest parallelism. But the order of the two main parts of the passage is reversed, with Matthew 8:11 corresponding more to Luke 13:29 and Matthew 8:12 more closely resembling Luke 13:28. Indeed, one can divide this teaching further into (a) people coming from east and west; (b) joining the patriarchs; (c) some people being cast out; and (d) the weeping and gnashing of teeth. This sequence, corresponding to Matthew's order, then becomes (d), (b), (c), and (a) in Luke. This much variation in wording and sequence, even granted the verbal parallelism that remains, suggests the possibility of two separate teachings of Jesus on two distinct occasions. That Matthew and Luke have in fact placed this material in two entirely different contexts supports this hypothesis. As Bock (1996: 1230) elaborates on Luke 13:22–30 overall, 'Despite conceptual parallels [to various texts in Matthew and Mark], this passage is an independent tradition that Luke alone has or that represents the combining of various materials from Jesus' ministry.' But for those who argue that Luke has arranged this material or who trace it back only to Q, Bock adds, 'But why must Luke be the source of such a synthesis? Could not Jesus be working with his own imagery in a creative way like any expressive teacher (Godet 1875: 2.126)?'[17]

Once more, the verb for sitting at table (v. 29) comes from *anaklinō*. Against I. H. Marshall (1978: 568), the term by itself need

---

[17] Alternatively, Bock continues, 'If an anthology of national images from Jesus' ministry is present, then Luke has briefly summarized Jesus' teaching in one place.'

not refer to reclining at a meal, nor does it necessarily indicate that the heavenly banquet is pictured. But the conceptual parallels which Marshall musters (Isa. 25:6; 65:13; Ezek. 32:4; 39:17–20; *1 Enoch* 62:14; *2 Baruch* 29:4; *4 Ezra* 6:49; *2 Enoch* 42:5; Luke 14:15; Matt. 22:2–14; Mark 14:25; and Rev. 19:9) certainly suggest that the end-times celebration to which so many Jews looked forward is being depicted here. But beyond this simple verb, nothing points to any symposium setting.

Green (1997: 532) thus speaks for many by summarizing: 'Ironically, some who claim Abraham as father will be forbidden access to Abraham's table, not because they have miscalculated their family tree but because status among those being saved is not inherited.' Again, 'Jesus thus insinuates how some from Israel might be excluded from the kingdom banquet. Opposing God's prophets, they oppose God's purpose; opposing God's purpose, they fail to comprehend who Jesus is and the nature of his divine mission (foretold by "all the prophets", 24:27; Acts 3:18, 24; 10:43); consequently, they do not reorient their hearts and lives around the word of God and, in this way, they demonstrate that they are not children of Abraham after all' (Green 1997: 533). Perhaps because there are no Gentiles like the centurion present in Luke's context, John Nolland (1993a: 735) reverses conventional wisdom by claiming that, 'while Matthew applies the text to the gathering in of the Gentiles, Luke seems to stay with its original reference to the eschatological gathering of Israel.' But given the overall structure of Luke's travel narrative (9:51 – 18:34), showing God's plan of salvation moving forward despite Jesus' coming execution and God's judgment on that act of rebellion with a grand reversal of outcasts replacing hypocrites in the centre of God's kingdom (Shirock 1993: 15–29), it is more likely that Luke sees Gentiles flocking to join God's people. To be fair to Nolland, he too goes on to note that 'in the full Lukan context we will find anticipated the inclusion of the Gentiles in the salvation purposes of God.'

A glutton and a drunkard: Matthew 11:19 and parallel

Both Matthew 11:19 and its Lukan counterpart (Luke 7:34) belong to Jesus' conclusion to the little parable of the children in the market-place. The two versions (Matt. 11:16–19; Luke 7:31–35) are extremely similar throughout the entire account, especially after the introductory questions. Both Gospels also place this parable in the context of

Jesus' witness concerning John (Matt. 11:7–15; Luke 7:24–30), which in turn follows immediately after Jesus has replied to messengers coming from the imprisoned Baptist (Matt. 11:2–6; Luke 7:18–23). The most notable differences in these larger contexts are that only Matthew contains verses 12–15, with their treatments of the time from John the Baptist 'until now', the kingdom suffering violence, the prophets and the Law prophesying until John, and John representing an Elijah figure. Luke, on the other hand, in place of these sayings uniquely includes the parenthetical verses 29–30, which refer to all the people (*laos*), and tax collectors in particular, justifying God, in contrast with the rejection of Jesus by Pharisees and scribes.[18] While the parenthetical comments obviously reflect Luke's clarifications as narrator, the fact that he refers back to contrasting responses to the ministries of John and Jesus suggests these are observations firmly rooted in the tradition. No later Christian is likely to have created such portraits that highlight the centrality of response to John, almost at the expense of Jesus. Verses 29–30 likewise create a tight link between the material on the Baptist and the parable, just as Matthew does with his different insertions.

I have elsewhere encapsulated the three main points of the parable proper: on the nature of the rejection of John, the nature of the rejection of Jesus, and the vindication of God's wisdom represented by both of his spokesmen (Blomberg 1990: 210). Robert Stein (1992: 232–233) unpacks the first two of these points as follows:

> The rejection of the gospel message is not due to the form of its presentation. John preached the gospel while living an ascetic life-style (Luke 5:33a). Jesus preached the gospel in the joy of the kingdom's arrival, but both were rejected (5:33b–35). Neither satisfied the wishes of this generation because their message was the same. Both preached a message of repentance (cf. 3:3, 8 and 5:32; 13:3, 5) and both offered salvation to the outcasts (cf. 3:12–14 with 4:18; 5:27–32; 7:22).

At the same time,

> The difference between the form of Jesus' message and of John's message was striking. John understood the coming of God's kingdom as requiring repentance and portrayed this via his fasting;

---

[18] Bock (1996: 676–677) has a good defence of understanding vv. 29–30 as Luke's parenthetical comment as narrator rather than the continuation of Jesus' words.

Jesus saw the coming of God's kingdom as a time of great celebration and portrayed this by the analogy of a wedding feast (5:33–34). Both are valid expressions of different aspects of God's kingdom, and if either is totally ignored, an unbalanced portrayal will result.

(R. Stein 1992: 233)[19]

Jesus is no doubt creating caricatures of reactions to John and himself, but each takes its point of departure from genuine tendencies in the behaviour of each man – John's self-denial and Jesus' 'partying'. The language about John 'not eating or drinking' versus Jesus 'eating and drinking' obviously cannot be taken too literally (Matt. 11:18–19). John did not deny himself all foodstuffs, and the 'problem' with Jesus was the manner and settings in which he ate and drank. Perhaps Luke is trying to clarify precisely this when he adds that John came eating 'no bread' and drinking 'no wine' (Luke 7:33), though bread and wine can be stock terms for food in general (Fitzmyer 1981: 680–681). It is possible that the Baptist literally drank no wine (Luke 1:14) but unlikely that he ate no bread (Davies and Allison 1991: 253). On the other hand, Marshall (1978: 301) thinks that Jesus means John did abstain from normal forms of food (cf. Mark 1:6 pars.), while Bovon (2002: 287) remarks, 'If *artos* does not simply mean food (thus indicating sparing intake), as often in the Hebrew Bible, then it means that John, as Mark 1 intimates, eats only raw foods unprepared by human hands. His dietary intake was in any case more ascetic than the Law of Moses commanded, so that his lifestyle attracted criticism.'

On the other hand, if the longer Lukan form is more original, later abbreviated by Matthew, then perhaps the implication of Luke 7:34 is that the Son of Man came eating *bread* and drinking *wine*. At least those who accused him of being a drunkard (Luke 7:34; Matt. 11:19) obviously believed he drank a fermented beverage and drank too much! Freyne (2000: 271–286) thinks Jesus is being associated with Dionysiac cultists, who were known in Galilee, as tiled portraits in the ruins of Sepphoris have demonstrated, while the vilification of Jesus depended on a caricature and thus is not to be taken literally. It is to be taken seriously, however, as others' perceptions of him (*contra* Morris 1992: 285, who thinks he is merely being accused of not

---

[19] Cf. Kee 1996: 383: The parable reflects on John and Jesus and their contemporaries' reactions to different modes of sharing in the common life, 'either by ascetic restraint' or 'by joyous participation'.

adopting an ascetic lifestyle). Both *phagos* and *oinopotēs* appear in the New Testament only in this parable. The same combination is found in Deuteronomy 21:20 and Proverbs 23:20–21. The former context proves intriguing, since there 'a glutton and a drunkard' alludes to the rebellious son whose misbehaviour created a capital offence (Keener 1999: 342). The caricature of Jesus 'was perhaps caused by [his] frequent attendance at banquets' (Hagner 1993: 310). The reference in the parable to piping (or playing the flute) (Matt. 11:17; Luke 7:32) suggests that one of the children's proposals was to 'play wedding'. This immediately makes one think both of Jesus' parables involving wedding banquets (esp. Matt. 22:1–14; 25:1–13) and of his actual attendance at the wedding in Cana (John 2:1–11).

If 'a glutton and a drunkard' is something of a caricature, what do we say about the parallel charge of being 'a friend of tax collectors and sinners'? Here it would seem the language is more straightforward, because such friendship has been securely established in other passages already, apart from any parabolic or metaphorical context.[20] The two charges in Matthew 11:19b/Luke 7:34b are simply juxtaposed without a connective conjunction. The grammar alone, therefore, does not prove that Jesus' scandalous friendship is directly tied to his customs at table, but with the numerous examples in parabolic and non-parabolic narratives throughout the Gospels of Jesus' table fellowship with sinners, the link is almost certainly implied here too. We do not have to choose between D. Smith (2003), Corley (1993b), and others who see merely an unjustified slander, and the majority who assert that Jesus did indeed fraternize with the outcasts and despised of his world. A genuine pattern of behaviour can be unfairly exaggerated. As Rudolf Schnackenburg (2002: 107) explains, 'Underlying the reproach are Jesus' meals with "tax collectors and sinners"' (see 9:10). The crass expressions used reflect denunciations in leading Jewish circles and are actually traceable to Jesus' days on earth.'

Despite the variation between 'deeds' and 'children', the closing lines in both versions of the parable agree that God's wisdom is justified. Thus both John's and Jesus' messages, once allowances is made for the caricatures, reflect God's true plans for his people. The

---

[20] Davies and Allison (1991: 264) thus think that 'glutton and drunkard' stands in synthetic parallelism with 'friend of toll-collectors and sinners'. The first phrase has maligned Jesus' well-known habit of holding festive table fellowship, while the second phrase, not in strict synonymous parallelism, refers to the genuinely disreputable company with whom he was typically imagined to associate.

use of this kind of more generalizable proverb ('wisdom is justified by her deeds/children') serves rhetorically to deflect tension away from the immediate controversy by appealing to a shared history and cultural values. Thus Jesus employs a 'soft word that turns away wrath' (Shantz 2001: 259). Placed in the larger context of Jesus' justification of John, the parable makes at best an implicit Christological claim but points at least as much to the Baptist as to Jesus himself. These features can only enhance the case for authenticity (on which see further Blomberg 1990: 208–210).

The referents of our text once again include the coming Messianic banquet. 'The uncomprehending generation could not understand that Jesus was signaling the in-breaking of the eschatological time of salvation: that his meals with sinners presaged the eschatological banquet ... of those who have received God's grace and forgiveness at the time of his eschatological visitation. The harsh judgment upon Jesus here expressed is not likely to have been formulated in the later church' (Nolland 1989: 346). Or, with Green (1997: 303–304):

> The existence of two such widely divergent appraisals of the ministries of John and Jesus points to the inherent ambiguity of their ministry practices. By those who are aligned with the world system that supports and is supported by 'this generation,' they will be interpreted one way. Within that system Jesus has no claim to holiness, but as a companion of sinners and toll collectors he has distinguished himself as one of their company, and John is relegated to the status of a demoniac. But for those who visualize the world through the lens of allegiance to God and God's purpose, the characteristic practices of John and Jesus are understood along vastly different lines. Now they are regarded as manifestations of the divine purpose at work in the world.[21]

Tax collectors and prostitutes: Matthew 21:31–32

These two verses form the conclusion to the parable of the two sons, a passage unique to Matthew, though in some senses a skeletal equivalent of Luke's fuller parable of the prodigal (Luke 15:11–32).

---

[21] On the charge that John had a demon, see Keener (1999: 342), who thinks this could suggest a 'prophetic' madness or a familiar spirit; and Garland (1993: 129), who thinks the accusation came because 'only supernatural beings can exist without food or water.'

In context, the Jewish leaders have just challenged Jesus to identify the source of his authority, and he has replied by forcing them to answer the question of the source of the Baptist's authority (Matt. 21:23–27). Further reference to John appears explicitly in verse 32. To the extent that verses 31–32 form even a partial conceptual parallel to Luke 7:29–30, a brief discussion of their significance is apposite here. As in Luke 7, tax collectors are becoming right with God because of the ministry of John, but the Jewish leadership is rejecting God's overtures through his spokesman. But whereas Luke 7:29 speaks of 'all the people, even the tax collectors', Matthew 21:31 refers more pointedly to 'the tax collectors and the prostitutes'. The objection that such a slogan need not always refer to literal prostitutes (or literal tax collectors for that matter) is well taken, though we need not deny that representatives of those two 'professions' did in fact form a significant portion of the 'riff-raff' entering the kingdom (thus both with and against Corley 1993b; 2002). After all, we will see that it is most likely that Luke 7:36–50 does describe at least one literal prostitute who became a follower of Jesus (see below, 'A sinner in the city' in ch. 5).

The use of the verb *proagō* in Matthew 21:31 supports the authenticity of this saying; literally, the tax collectors and prostitutes 'go before you' into the kingdom. Nothing here requires the permanent exclusion of the Jewish leaders; they simply have not yet made the appropriate response. At this late date in Jesus' ministry, to leave such an open-ended possibility of repentance for Jesus' antagonists cuts against the grain of their general response and is not likely to have been invented by a later writer.[22] That the application refers to John directly, but to Jesus at best indirectly, likewise supports authenticity. John came in 'the way of righteousness' (v. 32), an apt summary of his ministry, and the 'tax collectors and prostitutes' believed him, even though the Jewish leaders did not. Again Jesus is indirectly defending himself by implicitly aligning himself with John, but explicitly highlighting only the various responses people made to the Baptist.

The other significant detail made more explicit in the parable of the two sons than in the parable of the children in the marketplace is that a person's appropriate response, synonymous with entering the

---

[22] For a fuller discussion of the authenticity of these verses and the parable in which they appear, see Blomberg 1990: 184–186. For a more recent assessment of the passage as an integral whole, particularly against its Semitic and rabbinic backdrops, see Langley 1996: 228–243.

kingdom of God, is to 'repent' and 'believe' (v. 32). While these two verbs do not appear in the parable of the children in the marketplace, they capture the correct reaction to both John and Jesus required there. Accepting the proposals to play either 'wedding' or 'funeral' would have meant to align oneself with either the teaching of John or the proclamation of Jesus, each of which fundamentally involved repentance, especially in Matthew's Gospel (cf. 3:2 and 4:17). Sanders' claims (see above, p. 25) thus again seem overstated. While neither the parable of the children in the marketplace nor the story of the two sons spells out in detail what discipleship involves, each clearly recognizes that an obedient response is required. The change of heart by the son who first refused to work in his father's vineyard is even described as repenting (though from *metamelomai*[23] rather than *metanoeō*) (v. 29). Jesus is not simply associating with the sinners or outcasts of his world and making no demands of them. If they would have an ongoing relationship with him, they must respond to him positively with repentance and faith. At the same time, it is clear that Jesus does not view their past or present behaviour as any barrier to beginning an association with them. Both parables function, as Howard Kee (1996: 381) puts it, describing the children in the marketplace, as 'a direct challenge to the widespread concern among Jews of this period for maintenance of ritual and ethnic purity'.

The joy of new wine: John 2:1–11

Among non-Lukan sources, only John remains. Two passages unique to the Fourth Gospel impinge on our theme of Jesus at meals. The first is the famous miracle story of changing water into wine in Cana. While not found in the first three Gospels, this passage nevertheless proves strikingly similar to Jesus' Synoptic parable (or metaphor) about new wineskins for new wine (Mark 2:22 pars.). The miracle thus admirably satisfies the criterion of coherence with teaching generally recognized to be authentic elsewhere (cf. further Blomberg 1986: 333–337). Jesus' enjoying festive food and drink likewise meshes with the core truth underlying the caricature just discussed

---

[23] The choice of this rarer verb may be due to the imagery of the parable: the son is deciding to do what his father asked him to do after all, rather than converting to a new belief and/or lifestyle. When *metamelomai* differs from *metanoeō*, it does so by having a less overtly theological sense. Thus Louw and Nida (1988: 373) define *metamelomai* as 'to change one's mind about something, with the probable implication of regret'. But, when applied to sin, such change closely mirrors repentance.

in the parable of the children in the marketplace.[24] The clearest redactional or theological overlay in the passage comes at the end, when John describes this miracle as the first of Jesus' signs (*sēmeia*) – the standard expression in the Fourth Gospel for Jesus' mighty deeds – but the historicity of the core miracle itself is unaffected by this label.[25]

The only part of any actual banquet implied (or presupposed) during this wedding feast (*gamos*: v. 2) is wine drinking. Precisely because the host runs out of this beverage, Jesus intervenes miraculously to provide new and better wine (*oinos*: v. 3). This is the first and only passage in the Gospels outside the Last Supper narratives that makes explicit mention of people drinking wine (though such is obviously presupposed by the epithet 'drunkard' or 'wine-bibber' in Luke 7:34 par.). Inasmuch as it is the distinct segment involving wine drinking that turns a banquet into a symposium, if ever there were a case for symposium imagery in the Gospels, it would be here. As it turns out, though, wine drinking is the only dimension of this kind of feast alluded to at all! Given wine's standard role in Jewish weddings over the centuries, its presence here hardly demonstrates that this feast was fashioned along the lines of the more distinctive Greco-Roman symposia. The presence of a master of ceremonies (v. 8) could be viewed as analogous to the person selected to preside over symposium proceedings (see above, p. 88), but precisely who is implied by this *architriklinos* is uncertain. The expression may have been coined on the basis of stories of feasting in Esther, but many ancient weddings had this kind of official (cf. Aus 1988: 15–17), so again there is no need to resort to seeing the influence of any backgrounds other than Jewish ones.

Unlike other texts discussed thus far, there are no references to any notorious sinners present on this occasion, nor even to those who are ritually impure. At the same time, verse 6 stands out in a narrative otherwise so brief that the actual miracle itself is never even described.[26] John must see some significance in the fact that the water turned into wine had been contained in six stone jars used for

[24] For further discussion of the authenticity of the passage, see Blomberg 2001: 85–87.

[25] Cf. Kollmann (1990: 206–208), who finds this story only slightly redacted by John, taken over from the putative signs-source but supplemented particularly by vv. 11–12.

[26] Kruse (2003: 94) observes that 'By saying "the servants who had drawn the water knew" [where the wine had come from: v. 9], the evangelist seems to suggest that what they drew from the stone jars was only water. If this was the case, the miracle occurred as they carried what they had drawn to the master of the banquet.'

ceremonial washing.[27] If the imagery of the little parable of the wineskins may guide us at all, then presumably the Fourth Evangelist, and apparently even Jesus himself, believed that the old 'water' of Judaism was being transformed into the 'new wine' of the kingdom age Jesus was inaugurating (cf. Blomberg 1997: 225). So again there is at least implicit support for the idea that Jesus is unconcerned with and even deliberately overturning the purity rituals surrounding meals in his culture (cf. esp. Keener 2003: 509–513).

A meal of reinstatement: John 21:1–14

At first glance, it may appear strange to include this passage in a study of Jesus' table fellowship. No 'sinners' are present, in the sense in which that term is used in the other main passages in the Gospels on our theme, and, while the account depicts the miraculous provision of food comparable to the feedings of the five thousand and four thousand and to the miraculous provision of drink in John 2, the incident from elsewhere in the Gospels that most closely parallels this one is the miraculous fish catch of Luke 5:1–11. There, no account of anyone eating with anyone else appears at all!

On the other hand, the very next passage in John (21:15–23) focuses on the reinstatement of Peter, who has proved to be a notorious sinner of a very different kind: in his threefold denial of Christ (cf. John 18:15–18, 25–27). And, differing from the miracle of Luke 5, Jesus does here actually eat with his disciples. So it is not surprising that most treatments of Jesus' meals do give this passage at least brief attention (cf. Bolyki 1998: 163–165).

The question with which Jesus addresses his followers in verse 5 is often translated 'haven't you any fish?' But the term rendered fish is *prosphagion* – a New Testament *hapax* – more literally, 'something to eat'. Obviously in this context it must refer to fish, but even with this initial question, Jesus may be hinting at the fact that he plans to dine with the disciples. Unique, too, is the fact that Jesus has already prepared a charcoal fire with some fish on it (v. 9), an even clearer indication that he is planning for table fellowship. That Jesus has bread waiting with the fish makes one think of the previous feeding miracles when a few loaves of bread and a couple of fish were

---

[27] Interestingly, archaeologists have confirmed the use of precisely such jars; see Reich 1995. More generally, on Khirbet-Qana as the accurate site for ancient Cana, along with the possible significance of the city as a rival in importance to Capernaum, see Richardson 2002.

multiplied to provide for the crowds (cf. Kruse 2003: 390). The same is true of the language in verse 13 of Jesus taking the bread and giving it to them, especially with the shift to the historical present *didōsin*, reminiscent of the switch to the imperfect tense *edidou* in the earlier feeding miracles (see above, p. 105). The emphasis in each case is on the ongoing nature of the giving.

Verse 12 portrays Jesus inviting the disciples to 'come and have breakfast' with him. The verb here is *aristēsate*, which could refer to either the first or the second meal of the day: that is, what we would call breakfast and lunch, respectively. But if the disciples have been out all night fishing, then this meal must almost certainly be breakfast. Any attempt to argue for John portraying this encounter as a symposium, perhaps in light of the dialogue that followed the meal (vv. 15–23), founders on the fact that Greco-Roman symposia normally took place at an evening dinner, occasionally at a midday lunch that was more ample than most, but never at breakfast. Some would find a Eucharistic allusion here (e.g. Lindars 1972: 632), especially given the fact that fish was occasionally substituted for wine in the early church's celebration of the Lord's Supper. But if John intends such significance, he certainly does not spell it out, and the Eucharistic substitution is not attested until a considerably later date (cf. further Keener 2003: 1231).

More likely, we are meant to think back to John's account of the feeding of the five thousand (6:1–15). The word used for fish in 21:9, 10, and 13 is *opsarion*, found nowhere else in the New Testament except in John 6:9 and 11. As with *prosphagion* in verse 5, the word in and of itself does not necessarily mean 'fish'. Bauer's lexicon notes that it is a diminutive of *opson*, one meaning of which can be 'cooked food eaten with bread' (Bauer 2000: 746). But again, in this particular context, fish are obviously in view. Despite countless attempts to allegorize the number of fish (153; 21:11), the quantity is probably accurate and just meant to point to the abundance of God's provision (again as in the earlier feeding miracles; Keener 2003: 1231–1233).

All the points we made about inclusiveness and lack of concern for ritual purity in the earlier feeding miracles therefore apply here as well, even if the 'crowd' is much smaller. It is easy to forget the diverse backgrounds of Jesus' various disciples, while the reinstatement of Peter that occupies verses 15–23 clearly deals with the restoration of a repentant sinner (cf. Peter's bitter weeping in Mark 14:72). Intriguingly, while Peter's sorrow does not appear in John's account of the denial, only John refers to a charcoal fire in the high priest's courtyard

(18:18). The word he employs is *anthrakia*, precisely the term reappearing here in 21:9 (and nowhere else in the New Testament). Couple this with Jesus' threefold pronouncements over Peter in verses 15, 16, and 17, and the deliberate allusion back to his earlier denial seems virtually certain (see further Blomberg 2001: 277–278). Jesus does not automatically reinstate Peter without first belabouring the point concerning Peter's love for his master; it is thus not unreasonable to see Christ as insisting that his chief apostle publicly affirm his repentance. But the reinstatement that follows this affirmation proceeds immediately; no period of penance or probation intervenes first.

It is, of course, easy to dismiss the authenticity of this passage, because of both the presence of the miraculous and its location as a 'post-resurrection' narrative. Many scholars believe that the passage merely forms a doublet of Luke 5:1–11: an alternative account of only one original tradition. Tellingly, however, many of these same scholars believe John's version is the more original, largely because the disciples do not at first recognize Jesus (while also often arguing that this is a misplaced pre-resurrection narrative; see, classically, Bultmann 1971: 705). But the two passages scarcely need be pitted against one another. Each is intelligible in its own context.[28]

Summary and conclusion

In banqueting with Levi, Jesus has shown himself unwilling to follow his culture's traditions about not associating with the ritually impure and the morally wicked. But Jesus does not simply transgress boundaries; he clearly calls Levi and his associates to follow him in discipleship. Luke's account merely makes explicit what is already implicit in Matthew and Mark: these tax collectors must repent. In the miracles of feeding the five thousand and the four thousand, the very size of the crowds and the remote wilderness conditions make it virtually certain that Pharisaic cleanliness laws could not be followed. A diverse, heterogeneous group of those interested in Jesus' message is clearly portrayed. The likelihood that the first feeding miracle involved a primarily Jewish audience and the second a primarily Gentile crowd heightens the emphasis on diversity. In neither miracle, however, is the focus so much on discipleship as on Christology. Jesus demonstrates himself to be both a new and greater Moses and a new

---

[28] For more on the authenticity of vv. 1–14, including the larger question of whether ch. 21 forms an integral part of the Gospel overall, see Blomberg 2001: 272–277.

and greater Elisha. The spectacular provisions of literal bread are meant to point more deeply to the one who could provide spiritual nourishment (as made explicit in Jesus' 'Bread of Life' discourse in John 6). While no explicit commands to repent appear, the implications remain obvious. Jesus is now God's eschatological agent, who must be followed.

With the healing of the centurion's servant, the contrast between the shocking faithlessness of Israel and the surprising faithfulness of a Gentile reaches a zenith. Yet again, Jesus is not welcoming an outsider simply for the sake of promoting diversity among his followers. It is this Roman commander's faith which has so endeared him to Christ. Jesus thus uses the contrast as a springboard to depict a similar heterogeneity in the guest list for the coming Messianic banquet. The little parable of the children in the marketplace alludes to the apparently prevailing criticism of Jesus as 'a glutton and a drunkard'. As also in the parable of the two sons, key Jewish leaders do not accept Jesus' message when one would have expected them to do so, while the riff-raff even within Judaism, symbolized by 'tax collectors and sinners/prostitutes', are flocking into the kingdom. Jesus remains unconcerned with the criticism he receives for associating with these outcasts, even in the intimacy of table fellowship, but again the people with whom he mingles do not remain outsiders. They are becoming his disciples, thus demonstrating repentance, even if that precise term is not used.

The wedding in Cana affords no obvious opportunity for Jesus to break down any social barriers. But his miraculous provision of new wine clearly demonstrates his willingness to celebrate, even to some excess, on an understandably joyous occasion. At the same time, as in the feeding miracles, he points to himself as the one who in his ministry offers a new and greater elixir. The choice of water from Jewish jars for purification to be the object of his transformation suggests a deliberate contrast with the cleanliness rituals of his day. The miraculous fish catch of John 21 harks back again to the feeding miracles, as well as to the closely parallel miracle of Luke 5:1–11. Here no purity laws are broken, but at least one notorious 'sinner' is present: Peter, who vehemently denied Christ three times after equally strenuously promising never to do any such thing. To the degree that the other disciples had also fled and abandoned Christ, the entire little gathering may be viewed as needing the kind of reinstatement and recommissioning which Jesus gives Peter. As one of the resurrection appearances, this account also presents profound Christology. Jesus' pre-crucifixion claims have been vindicated; he alone can provide the spiritual nurture to bring people to God. The need for repentance and discipleship remains present, even if more implicit than stated in so many words.

It is not impossible that one or more of these accounts, particularly as written up by the respective evangelists, is intended to reflect elements of a Greco-Roman symposium. The various words for reclining at table can certainly be used in that context. As a tax collector, Levi could well have been Hellenized, and the sumptuous banquet he prepared could easily have followed non-Jewish models. In Mark's account of the feeding of the five thousand, the very Greek word for symposium explicitly appears. The caricature of calling Christ 'a glutton and a drunkard' would certainly fit well if he had sometimes attended symposia, even if he had not himself over-indulged. On the other hand, none of these features proves that the symposium model was ever adopted in the meals under investigation. The fact that Luke, the most Hellenistic of the evangelists, does not pursue symposium imagery in the feeding of the five thousand speaks against the word having that meaning in Mark. The feeding of the four thousand contains no language in either of its Synoptic versions of dividing people into such 'companies'. The eschatological banquet predicted in Jesus' response to the centurion, the account of the wedding at Cana, and the post-resurrection breakfast narrative altogether lack any elements that would support the symposium hypothesis.

Instead, the unifying theme that emerges from the passages surveyed in this chapter is one that may be called 'contagious holiness'. Jesus regularly associates with the various sorts of sinners on whom the most pious in his culture frowned, but his association is never an end in itself. Implicitly or explicitly, he is calling people to change their ways and follow him as their master. But unlike so many in his world (and unlike so many cultures throughout the history of the world), he does not assume that he will be defiled by associating with corrupt people. Rather, his purity can rub off on them and change them for the better. Cleanliness, he believes, is even more 'catching' than uncleanness; morality more influential than immorality.

Even under the older criteria of authenticity, the majority of commentators rightly recognized the probability that at least a core of Jesus' teachings and actions in these passages was authentic.[29] Our

---

[29] So e.g., even from a fairly rigorous tradition-critical approach, as in Kollmann 1990: 190–238. Even more confidently, cf. Bolyki 1998: 68–118.

texts describe behaviour sufficiently different from both the prevailing Judaism and subsequent church practice that they satisfy the older dissimilarity criterion. They appear in the triple tradition, the double tradition, and in texts unique to Matthew, John, and, as we will see in the next chapter, especially Luke, thus thoroughly satisfying the criterion of multiple attestation. They mesh well with Jesus' kingdom teaching elsewhere and so fulfil the criterion of coherence. Because Jesus' table fellowship with sinners does not consistently reflect Greco-Roman symposia, the more recent challenges to the traditional scholarly consensus on the authenticity of these texts fails.

On the improved and more helpful double similarity and dissimilarity criterion, these texts fare even better. Despite dissimilarity from Judaism and early Christianity, they fit in well in an early first-century Jewish milieu conversant with the debates about what and who are ritually impure. And while the primitive church was not known for any common practice of table fellowship with outcasts, the debates over associating with Gentiles who did not become Jews first in order to follow Jesus, along with the entire practice of celebrating the Lord's Supper, demonstrate points of continuity with early Christian behaviour too. On either set of criteria, then, we may remain confident that Jesus' table fellowship with sinners reflects an important historical core of the canonical Gospel tradition.

To end with the question with which this chapter began, was Jesus a party animal? Not in the sense we usually mean by the expression: someone who simply loves to eat, drink and enjoy other forms of entertainment with friends just for the immense pleasure of it. There were always kingdom purposes involved in Jesus' presence at banquets and other special meals. Yet it remains striking how willing he was to socialize, even in the intimacy of table fellowship, with anyone and everyone for the sake of accomplishing his mission. In chapter 6, we will turn to the issue of how to apply his practice in today's world. Meanwhile, it remains to be seen if this trend continues in the uniquely Lukan texts, especially since many commentators have treated them as a distinctive subset of the Gospel passages on our topic (see above, p. 22). We turn to this task in chapter 5.

Chapter Five

Pervasive purity

Jesus' eating with sinners in the Gospels II:
Material distinctive to Luke

Introduction

Craig McMahan (1987: 118–119) identifies five common characteristics of what he calls 'type-scenes of meals with outcasts' involving
Jesus in the Gospel of Luke:

(1) Jesus or his representatives eat with those who in some sense are
considered second-class citizens in Israel.
(2) These outcasts regularly respond to Jesus' message with joy.
(3) Pharisees and scribes, by way of contrast, equally commonly
grumble and complain about Jesus' behaviour.
(4) The episodes are consistently introduced by calls to discipleship.
(5) Finally, the scenes regularly conclude with a statement of Jesus'
mission and redemptive purpose in order to refute the objections raised against his behaviour.

After our survey of the other strata of the Gospel tradition apart from
distinctively Lukan material, none of these five characteristics causes
surprise. Each has been seen one or more times in the texts surveyed in
chapter 4, an observation which should predispose us not to assume
that Luke is presenting wholly unusual or incompatible narratives in
the material peculiar to his Gospel. McMahan (1987: 131) goes on,
however, to claim that 'Eating with outcasts is defended as the
quintessence of Jesus' mission ... only those who can share Jesus'
joy expressed in his feasting with repentant outcasts, can recognize,
[*sic*] who he is and perceive the nature of his mission.' It would be an
overstatement to claim that the texts studied thus far demonstrate
Jesus' table fellowship with sinners as the most central aspect of Jesus'
ministry. Whether Luke elevates it to that level remains to be seen. We
will survey the relevant passages in a straightforward, sequential order

according to their appearance in the third Gospel, with a view not only to this question but also to the others that have occupied previous chapters.

A 'sinner in the city': Luke 7:36–50

For many critics, the Lukan account of the woman who anoints Jesus is simply a redactional development of the anointing of Jesus during the last week of his life, as depicted in the other three Gospels (Mark 14:3–11 pars.). It would thus not belong in this chapter at all. Still, Luke clearly believes it to be a separate incident. The setting is different (the home of Simon, the Pharisee), as is the nature of the woman who approaches Jesus (one 'in that town who lived a sinful life': v. 37). The subsequent controversy, spanning verses 39–50 and involving Simon's criticism of Christ, Jesus' parabolic reply, and the pronouncement of salvation upon the woman, is entirely unparalleled in the other canonical accounts, which focus on one of Jesus' female followers symbolically preparing him for his coming death and burial. The striking similarities, most notably the use of an alabaster jar of perfume, could suggest that the two divergent accounts have influenced one another in some small ways, but there are no compelling reasons for not treating Luke 7:36–50 as primarily a separate incident. As John Nolland (1989: 352) elaborates,

> Despite the similarities there is not sufficient reason for identifying the Lukan and the Bethany anointings. Nevertheless, the degree of similarity appears in the case of the Johannine account to have led to a transfer of motifs from the one episode to the other, and it is possible though by no means certain that some of the language affinities between the Lukan and the Markan accounts have a similar cause.[1]

The meal Jesus attends is unspecified. The Greek states merely that he was invited by Simon, 'so that he might eat with him'. That this is a 'dinner' is a natural, though not necessary, inference. Since Simon is a Pharisee and Pharisees frequently invited guests of honour to larger lunchtime meals after Sabbath morning worship services, perhaps we are meant to envision that kind of a banquet here (Bock

---

[1] See further Blomberg 1990: 184–185. Marshall (1978: 304–307) offers a good survey of the various tradition-critical options.

1994: 694).[2] The verb for reclining in verse 36 is once again *kataklinō*. As elsewhere, this reference alone hardly demonstrates that the meal had taken the character of a symposium (*contra* Bovon 2002: 290; and Green 1997: 306). A dinner hosted by a leading Jew for an honoured guest could nevertheless suggest at least one of the Jewish forms of banqueting, while nothing entirely excludes one of the more Greco-Roman forms. First-century Israel was Hellenized to varying degrees; without further information we simply have no way of knowing the nature of this meal. If the banquet does involve the customary couches on which diners would recline, their posture (with legs extended perpendicular to the tables) would explain how the woman had easy access to Jesus' feet (R. Stein 1992: 236). More importantly, the Pharisee's overture to Jesus suggests the absence of any hostility, at least at the outset. Luke, in fact, is the Gospel writer who includes the greatest number of comparatively positive references to Pharisees concerning their relationship with Jesus.[3]

The presence of a woman deemed sinful raises all the questions of ritual impurity for which we have seen Jesus' lack of concern elsewhere (Green 1997: 307). The woman need not be a prostitute. 'The other possibilities are that she is the wife of someone with a dishonorable occupation ... a woman in debt, or an adulteress' (Bock 1994: 695). Barbara Reid (1995: 43) expands the list of possibilities to include someone ill, disabled, or in regular contact with Gentiles. Clearly the woman is not a formal courtesan, as commonly encountered in Greco-Roman symposia. No self-respecting Pharisee would arrange that form of entertainment (Love 1995: 206). Reid (1995: 44) further notes that the woman comes to the banquet neither as a participant nor doing any of the things for which courtesans at banquets were known, such as drinking, reclining, dancing, playing music, or the like. Nor does Luke employ any of the standard terms for a professional prostitute, such as *pornē*, *koinē*, *pankoinē*, or *hetaira* (Reid 1995: 44–45). The Greek of verse 37a is in fact more ambiguous than the TNIV suggests ('a woman in that town who lived a sinful life'),

[2] R. Stein (1992: 235–236) notes that it was quite common to invite a visiting rabbi or teacher to the Sabbath meal after he had taught in the synagogue, and he cross-references Mark 1:29–31.

[3] Cf. Green (1997: 307–308), who notes that the variegated approach to Pharisees in Luke, the initial invitation by Simon labelling him a prophet, and Jesus' direct address to him (calling him by name and attempting to teach him rather than condemning him) all combine to contradict the notion that Luke is drawing a stereotypically negative portrait of the Pharisee. For a more specialized study of Luke and the Pharisees, cf. Ziesler 1979.

reading merely 'in the city a sinner'. This leaves open the possibility that the woman is viewed by the city simply as in some sense sinful. With all of these caveats, the most common reason for a woman to be so stigmatized would be that she was in fact a harlot (Bovon 2002: 293; Green 1997: 309).

Why does this woman appear where Jesus is dining at all? Is her attendance at this meal even historically credible? Those inclined to see a symposium here would liken her to the stock figure of an uninvited guest (cf. above, p. 88). But uninvited guests were separate from the courtesans and prostitutes, playing different roles: engaging in dialogue or providing entertainment. Presumably, this woman had prior knowledge that Jesus would be present (Kilgallen 1998: 108). The aorist participle *epignousa* in verse 37 could point in this direction. If she had also had a previous positive encounter with Jesus, her appearance, while no doubt shocking to Simon and the other guests, could hardly be declared improbable. We have already seen, in our discussion of Levi's banquet, that open doors provided access to courtyards or to special banqueting rooms, enabling other onlookers to view the festivities (see above, p. 100). The use of an alabaster jar of perfume by definition makes this a luxurious anointing. So the woman either is quite wealthy (seldom the case with first-century prostitutes) or is making an enormous sacrifice.

The woman's actions, narrated in verse 38, need not be viewed as inherently erotic, but the observers would have viewed them at best as culturally inappropriate (Bovon 2002: 295) and at worst as so sexually suggestive as to be shameful. Reid (1995: 45) points out that loose hair did not in and of itself link a woman with prostitution, and if she were unmarried it produced no stigma at all. But Simon's response, in verse 39, clearly implies that her behaviour here gave the assembly reason to disapprove of it.[4]

The Pharisee's reaction, therefore, remains natural, especially if Jesus had prophetic insight. Surely he would recognize this woman as a 'sinner'. In this instance, Jesus' fellowship obviously goes beyond a casual association with the ritually impure to a scandalous intimacy with the profoundly immoral. That the woman is actually touching

---

[4] R. Stein (1992: 236) notes that 'letting down one's hair in public was shameful and even afforded a ground for divorce,' while Green (1997: 310) determines that 'Letting her hair down in this setting would have been on a par with appearing topless in public, for example. She would have appeared to be fondling Jesus' feet, like a prostitute or slave girl accustomed to providing sexual favors.'

Jesus specifically in the ways described in verse 38 merely magnifies the offence. Luke's use of verb forms stresses the repeated, ongoing nature of each stage of the woman's actions. She was standing 'weeping' (*klaiousa*: an ongoing present-tense participle); she 'began to wet his feet' (indicating that she continued to do so); and she was kissing him (the imperfect *katephilei*, indicating ongoing past action) (cf. further Bovon 2002: 294). The anointing is likewise described in the imperfect tense (*ēleiphen*).[5] Though somewhat speculative, Nolland's summary (1989: 354–355) presents one plausible sequence of events:

> The accidental fall of tears on feet begins a chain reaction: with nothing at hand to remove the offending tears, the woman makes use of her let-down hair; the intimate proximity thereby created leads to a release of affectionate gratitude expressed in kissing the feet which have just been cleaned from the dust of journey in this unique and probably unintended manner; and the anointing perfume, no doubt intended for the head (since only this has a place in Jewish custom) but finding no ready access thereto, is spent upon that part of Jesus' body with which the woman has already made intimate contact.[6]

In verse 40 Jesus reverses roles with the Pharisee and acts as teacher rather than guest. 'As the host must descend from the position of teacher (in the first scene) to student (in the second), Jesus gradually gains back his contested authority' (Bovon 2002: 291). The three prongs of the parable with which Jesus confronts Simon prove transparent:

> (1) Like the man owing fifty denarii, those who take their spiritual condition for granted and are not aware of having been forgiven of numerous gross wickednesses should not despise those who have been redeemed from a more pathetic state. (2) Like the debtor owing five hundred denarii, those who recognize they have much for which to be thankful will naturally respond in generous expressions of love for Jesus. (3) Like the creditor, God forgives

---

[5] Cf. also Bock (1994: 697), who concludes that 'the impression is that each step took some time.' The present tense of 'touching' in v. 39 functions similarly. The other possibility is that the switch from the expected aorist to the less common imperfect tense in historical narrative 'foregrounds' the actions so described for emphasis (cf. Porter 1992: 23). Clearly these verbs reflect the most 'outrageous' of the woman's actions.

[6] Similarly, Marshall 1978: 308–309.

both categories of sinners and allows them to begin again with a clean slate.

(Blomberg 1990: 185–186)

The authenticity of the parable (vv. 41–42), like that of the entire episode, is supported by the fact that both debtors are forgiven so that no ultimate condemnation, even for the Pharisee, plays any role.

After Simon renders the obvious verdict as to who would be more grateful (v. 43),[7] Jesus turns to the unwelcome woman. The upshot of verses 44–46 is that Jesus proclaims to Simon that 'She did *more* than that which you did *not* do' (Bovon 2002: 291). These gestures of kindness – providing water for his feet, offering a welcoming kiss, and anointing his head – were scarcely mandatory but would have extended a natural courtesy (cf. R. Stein 1992: 237).

Despite centuries of debate among Catholic and Protestant interpreters over verse 47, there is now widespread agreement among scholars of both communities that the causal clause, 'for she loved much', must modify the verb 'tell' rather than 'have been forgiven' (see Blomberg 1990: 185). In other words, Jesus is not pronouncing God's forgiveness on the woman because of the love just poured out on him. After all, verse 50 makes it clear that her faith, rather than the act of anointing Jesus, has saved her. But it is her outward show of gratitude which now enables Jesus to declare publicly that she has trusted in him. As with Levi, some level of transformation has already occurred in her heart prior to the banquet scene. John Kilgallen (1985; 1998; 1999; 2001) has repeatedly argued for the possibility that she came to repentance already under the ministry of John the Baptist.[8] The twofold use of the perfect tense with the verb 'forgiven' in verses 47 and 48 supports this suggestion. The woman appears already in a state of forgiveness when Jesus pronounces these words over her (cf. Bock 1994: 703; more generally, Kilgallen 2001). Kilgallen (1985) defends the link with John because of the nearby inclusion in Luke 7 of verses 29–30, which point back to the Baptist. He further notes the distinction between the woman's prior faith and Jesus' direct assurance on this occasion that her sins had been forgiven, a clear advance from her earlier understanding of her own state (Kilgallen 1999). Another intriguing possibility stems from Jesus' declaration in verse 50. The refrain 'Your faith has saved

---

[7] Verse 43 shows that Simon realizes he has been caught in a trap and answers reluctantly (Marshall 1978: 311).

[8] Cf. also Moritz 1996: 54–55.

you' appears three other times in the Gospels, in each case with individuals for whom Jesus has also provided physical healing (Mark 5:34 pars; Mark 10:52 pars; Luke 17:19). It is not impossible that Jesus had already also healed this woman of some malady, but obviously we cannot be sure (see further Blomberg 1994b).

In verse 49, the other guests are described as the *synanakeimenoi*: literally, those reclining together. As with all the other terms for reclining surveyed, nothing about the term itself requires a symposium format. There is the slightest hint of an ongoing discussion in the debate over who Jesus is, given his claim to forgive sins. But instead of making us think of a symposium, this comment more quickly makes us think of the aftermath of the healing of the paralytic, which in Luke appears in 5:17–26 (see specifically v. 21). No meal was involved at all on that occasion. Whether or not a prior physical healing, or even any other kind of previous encounter with Jesus or John, can be inferred from verse 50, the kind of salvation implied almost certainly remains holistic. 'Faith is seen when there is no break in the pattern of divine initiative and human response by means of which a restored relationship to God is established. The woman leaves Jesus a whole and rescued creature: she departs into peace' (Nolland 1989: 362).

That Jesus tolerated such seemingly scandalous behaviour, and even affirmed the woman exercising it, strongly supports historical authenticity even by the older dissimilarity criterion. The similarities with Mark 2:1–12 and parallels enable the passage to satisfy the criterion of multiple attestation. As already noted, the lack of any harsher criticism of the Pharisee makes this episode fit the newer double similarity and dissimilarity criterion as well. The forgiveness of both debtors reflects extraordinary grace, characteristic of the ministry of Jesus. With Green (1997: 308), 'This account is open-ended at the beginning and the end. The woman's actions assume some encounter with Jesus prior to the onset of this scene, and the narrative anticipates some form of response on the part of Simon to Jesus' remarks to him concerning the woman.' Perhaps we cannot be quite as confident as this, but both prongs of Green's affirmation remain probable. Yet neither reflects the way the story would probably have been invented if made up out of whole cloth by the early church. Even within the New Testament period, primitive Christian congregations gained no sterling reputation for lavishing undeserved favour on either the notoriously sinful or their legalistic critics.

More clearly than in some of the passages already surveyed, the 'sinner' with whom Jesus shares table fellowship here falls more into Sanders' 'notoriously wicked' category. But, as in all of the previous passages studied, Jesus' association does not form an end in itself but is clearly bound up with the process of sinners coming to faith. In this passage, it seems to be presupposed; even if not, Jesus explicitly declares it to be present by the end of the account. Thus Jesus is scarcely currying favour with the wicked apart from calling them to repentance. 'It is not enough to say that the woman (instead of Simon) properly received Jesus as a guest. She comes to him and wishes to follow him. This is illustrated in her action, in which the body becomes a means of expression not only of faith (v. 50) but also of love (v. 47a). Such close fellowship with Jesus is otherwise seldom narrated' (Bovon 2002: 298). Far from being corrupted by this woman or her scandalous actions, Jesus has imparted some of his holiness to her (whether first at an earlier encounter or simply on this occasion). Purity, rather than impurity, is what is being passed from the one person to the other, and this holiness involves the entire person, not in degrees or gradations as elsewhere in Judaism (Moritz 1996: 57).

Hospitality versus holiness: Luke 10:38–42

No formal meal appears in this passage, yet the kind of hospitality described presupposes the offer of overnight lodging and evening dinner. Thus most surveys of our theme include a discussion of this text (e.g. Bolyki 1998: 116–118); it merits our brief attention here too. The expression 'opened her home' in verse 38 renders the Greek *hypedexato*, more literally implying that Martha 'welcomed' Jesus. Given the context of verse 40, she would naturally have been concerned to provide Jesus a nice meal. Interestingly, only Martha functions as the subject of the welcoming, as if perhaps she were the older of the two sisters and thus the rightful hostess.

Verse 39 introduces Mary into the narrative for the first time. The verb for sitting, *parakathezomai*, can mean to 'sit beside' (Bauer 2000: 764), but when modified by *tous podas* must refer to sitting 'at his feet'. Luke describes Mary as also listening to Jesus' words. This is the sum total of what we are told here about this woman. Nevertheless, it is reasonable to infer from her posture in this context that Luke wants to depict her as a disciple learning from her rabbi, a role normally forbidden to women in Israel at that time (see e.g. Spencer 1985: 58).

On the other hand, it goes far beyond anything the text declares to infer full-fledged egalitarianism among Jesus' followers.[9]

Verse 40 returns to Martha's perspective. She was 'distracted': from *perispaō*, meaning to be pulled away, to have one's attention directed from one thing to another, or to be quite busy and over-burdened (Bauer 2000: 804). But what are the preparations that are distracting Martha? In a novel reading of the text, Warren Carter (1996: 269) thinks that the serving (*diakonia*) that distracts her most likely implies involvement in 'Jesus' eschatological mission and participating in the community of the disciples of Jesus'. Carter (1996: 274–275) appeals to the use of *diakonia* in Acts 6 and elsewhere, which frequently involves leadership ministries of various sorts. He thus concludes (279) that our passage warns against the danger that 'leaders may be so energetically engaged in ministry that they, like Martha, are distracted from ministry's source.' If Carter is right, then there is no reference, even implicitly, to a meal in this passage, and the text proves irrelevant for our concerns. It likewise becomes inappropriate to use it in support of a symposium hypo-thesis. On the conventional assumption that verse 40b refers to preparations for a meal, one might argue that a two-part banquet is in view, with Jesus stressing the importance of the conversation/teaching over the communal dining. But even this perspective diverges significantly from conventional symposia, in which the wine drinking remained central and the dialogue secondary.

Verse 41 contains the first of the two most important textual variants in these verses. The question is whether to read a form of the verb *thorybazō* or one from *tyrbazō*. Both terms refer to being troubled, though the latter seems somewhat stronger, suggesting disturbance or agitation (Bauer 2000: 458). The external evidence supports the former, which may have been felt to be too weak a term by a few later scribes. The more difficult of the textual variants involves verse 42. Should the longer version that reads 'but few things are needed – or only one' (as in the TNIV) be preferred to the shorter text 'only one thing is needed' (TNIV mg)? Lionel North (1997) takes the longer version to be original and suggests that it meant Mary was close, or better, very close (i.e., to pursuing the proper priority). But the external evidence seems strong enough to follow the UBSGNT[4] and prefer the shorter reading, which perhaps, in the minds of later tradents, cried out for clarification. On this evaluation of the

---

[9] For details see Blomberg 2005 and the references there cited.

evidence, the better part must refer to learning the word of God from Jesus. That 'it will not be taken away from her' (v. 42) suggests the eternal permanence of spiritual nourishment versus the transience of arrangements for even such basics of earthly existence as food consumption. The TNIV leaves untranslated the *gar* ('because' or 'for') at the beginning of verse 42b. Kilgallen (1992), believing a clause to have been omitted by ellipsis here, renders the meaning, 'No, I'm not concerned by Mary's leaving you, Martha,' *for* she has chosen the better part.

The upshot of all these exegetical decisions surrounding verses 40–42 is that, even if Jesus *is* dining with these women, proper meal etiquette is furthest from his mind. What counts is doing God's will, which in the larger context of Luke 10:25–42 is depicted as loving God and neighbour, just as in the Great Commandment of Mark 12:28–34 and parallels. The Good Samaritan illustrates love of neighbour; Mary's devotion to Jesus depicts love of God (cf. Wall 1989: 28).

While the Jesus Seminar colours this entire passage black, believing it to be a 'clamp-down' on 'women managers' (Taussig 1991), this verdict assumes an egalitarianism elsewhere in Jesus' ministry that has not been demonstrated. In fact, against the background of the day, while falling short of proving that he would have interchanged all gender roles indiscriminately, Jesus' actions nevertheless remain counterculturally affirming of women (e.g., Wilkins 2001: 100). This perspective speaks strongly for the authenticity of the passage by either the older or newer criterion of dissimilarity. Even though it is not the focus of the text, that Jesus implicitly eats in such a familiar fashion with both women furthers the theme of his breaking down boundaries with supposed second-class citizens. Mary and Martha are in no way described as morally impure, though one or the other could easily have been ritually impure because of her monthly period. Beyond these observations, little emerges here to support any hypothesis about the nature of Jesus' table fellowship and particularly little to support the view that his feasts adopted the style of symposia.

A meal turned sour: Luke 11:37–54

Many would partition or subdivide this passage and parcel out various components to Q. Luke here presents a similar but briefer compilation of Jesus' woes against selected Pharisees than the more famous invective of Matthew 23:1–36. On the other hand, as with

Luke 7:36–50 and its supposed parallels, Luke envisions an entirely different context for this account than do his sources. Yet his setting for Jesus' harsh critique proves just as appropriate as Matthew's. It is inconceivable that Jesus clashed with certain Pharisees only once or twice during his ministry. That he should repeat some of the same kinds of charges against them is in fact precisely what we would expect of any consistent itinerant teacher. Bock (1996: 1106–1108) notes that the debate over handwashing and kosher food in Mark 7:1–23 and parallels in some ways contains even greater similarities to Luke 11:37–54, and yet few people treat them as genuine historical or literary parallels. It is better that we consider this passage as uniquely Lukan material and treat it as a unity in its own right.

As in the Luke 7 text, a Pharisee invites Jesus to eat with him (11:37), though this time Luke does not record his name. In contrast to the earlier passage, here it is the Pharisee who initiates an implied criticism of Jesus' behaviour by expressing surprise that he did not perform the customary ritual handwashing before the meal. But Jesus quickly replies with an even more scathing critique. Green's perceptive observations (1997: 470) merit extensive citation:

> The fact that a Pharisee would even invite Jesus to dinner suggests a certain openness to him, though we should also recognize that the extension of hospitality might itself serve as a test. The extension and acceptance of an invitation signaled the abeyance of hostility, a social contract whereby host and guest were to act with honor toward one another. This would require, for example, that Jesus prepare for the meal in the way prescribed by the Pharisees and that he withhold any negative (insulting) valuations of the host or his treatment in the home of the host; to perform otherwise would signal a breach in the implicit social contract. Unlike the parallel scene in 7:36–50, in this account no evidence is brought forward to suggest that Jesus has been snubbed. To the contrary, the cryptic form of Luke's narration – Jesus 'went in and took his place at table' – at first masks what the Pharisee cannot miss: Jesus snubbed his host by failing to wash before the meal. Even then the Pharisee maintains social propriety, for he does not call attention to his guest's behavior, in spite of its aberrant quality.

Only the last of these observations outruns the evidence, inasmuch as we are not told in what form the Pharisee expressed his surprise.

Interestingly, the word for eating in verse 37 comes from the verb *aristaō*, the very word for having breakfast that John 21:12 and 15 employed. Reasonably well-to-do Jews, like this Pharisee, typically ate twice on weekdays: 'a light meal in mid-morning (*ariston*), and a main meal in the late afternoon (*deipnon*); a snack meal might also be taken before starting the day's work ... Three meals were eaten on the Sabbath, the principal one being held about midday after the synagogue service ... The use of the word *ariston* ... suggests, but does not demand that the earlier meal ... a Sabbath meal may well be meant' (Marshall 1978: 493–494). The word for reclining in this case comes from *anapiptō*, which should be taken literally if this is a Sabbath meal. If it refers to breakfast, then the posture would be simply to sit at a table. In neither instance is a full-blown symposium required; in the latter case, it would be excluded.

Pharisaic objection about Jesus' failure to wash his hands reflects oral Torah, not any written requirement of the Hebrew Scriptures. It was of course ceremonial rather than hygienic legislation (R. Stein 1992: 340). The verb for wash in verse 38 is *ebaptisthē*, the same root which when used elsewhere in the New Testament normally refers to the baptism or immersion of people in water. But the expression could be used more broadly to refer to the dipping or dunking of other objects in various solutions (Bauer 2000: 164–165). Roger Booth (1986: 189–203) discusses in detail the various practices that this Pharisee may have hoped Jesus had followed. The picture is not entirely congruent with the discussion in Mark 7:1–23 and parallel, but whatever the details, Jesus has failed to adopt the etiquette of his host, even temporarily, so the Pharisee can only assume that Jesus' involvement with the crowds left him consistently impure (Nolland 1993a: 663).

That the Pharisee 'notices' that Jesus does not wash suggests in this context literal observation, even though the verb *idōn* can imply merely coming to know about a matter. If, as we would suspect, the bowls for handwashing were passed around the tables, Jesus may well have deliberately handed them on without using them.[10] While elsewhere, on occasion, Jesus seems to be able to discern people's unspoken thoughts, the most natural interpretation of the transition in verses 38–39 is that the Pharisee expressed his surprise in some outward fashion, leading Christ to reply as Luke describes. The word for surprise can also be translated 'marvelled' or 'was astonished'

[10] C. Evans (1990: 503) notes this possibility, along with the alternative that Jesus 'neglected a bowl standing ready' for handwashing.

(from *thaumazō*), suggesting almost shock. As it turns out, Jesus retorts with equally strong words.

The contrast in verses 39–41 between external and internal purity mirrors Jesus' declaration in Mark 7:20–23 and parallel that only what comes from inside a person can make that person unclean. Luke 11:41 proves particularly difficult to translate, reading literally 'give alms for what is within and behold everything is clean for you.' While many commentators have tried to play down the force of Mark 7:19b ('in saying this, Jesus declared all foods clean'), the similar context here makes it hard to argue that it is merely a later Markan belief and not part of Jesus' intention all along to set the stage for superseding the kosher laws (on this text see further Blomberg 1999: 135–136). Jesus' subsequent berating of his host and various other guests ranges widely, far beyond the issue of ritual cleanliness, and the other topics need not detain us here. There is a slight hint of a dialogue formed with verse 45 intruding as an objection from scribes or lawyers present for the meal. But that is the sole extent of anything resembling the interactive form of a symposium discussion. Clearly Jesus' words are not designed to start a conversation but to unleash a critique and lament which simply leave his audience angry and ready to mount a counter-attack.

On the other hand, E. S. Steele (1984) has argued vigorously that this banquet *does* represent a symposium. He correctly observes that a symposium involved a host, a chief guest, and various other invitees. The host was notable for his wealth and/or wisdom; the chief guest, at least for his wisdom. Other invitees typically came from the social elite. The format of the banquet often produced a gradual reversal of the honour or identity of various guests and an explicit *fait divers* as the point of departure for speeches and debate. All of these characteristics appear in Luke 11; Steele notes that others have found them in chapters 7 and 14 as well. By withholding reference to the lawyers until verse 45 and to other scribes and Pharisees until verse 54, the impression of a discussion with several participants taking turns is heightened. The *fait divers*, in Steele's opinion, is the host's unspoken amazement at Jesus' failure to wash his hands. To his credit Steele recognizes that Luke scarcely focuses on the meal, makes no reference to the central role of wine drinking, and lacks the customary speeches from each of the principal participants. Thus Steele speaks of a 'modified Hellenistic symposium' here. Still, with so many elements unique to the symposium absent altogether – a clear separation of meal and discussion, the invocation of the gods, the pouring of the libation at the transition between the two parts of the festivities, levity and other forms of entertainment, and even the presence of courtesans – it is difficult to see how Luke's portrait must represent a symposium at all. All of the elements present that Steele stresses were common to numerous forms of banqueting in the ancient Mediterranean world, including distinctively Jewish celebrations, as we have seen throughout our survey thus far.

What does remain clear is Jesus' radical challenge to the Pharisaic conventions of ritual purity as well as to their hospitality practices more generally. Yet in verse 39, Luke describes as 'the Lord' the person whose behaviour was deemed deviant by all those around him. Here again the guest plays the role of host or master, complete with the right to declare whose behaviour does or does not produce impurity. Jesus has dramatically turned the tables on his critics, setting the stage for declaring all foods clean every bit as much as in Mark 7.[11]

For the second time in Luke, we see Jesus' willingness to eat not just with the outcast or stigmatized of his world but also with the religious leaders. As in his previous encounter, such meals lead to confrontation rather than to acquiescence with Pharisaic standards, a pattern that will recur at least once more, in chapter 14. That Jesus even accepts the invitation to the Pharisee's home in the first place shows that Luke is not portraying their interaction with unrelentingly dark strokes. Such divergence from characteristic redactional tendencies bespeaks authenticity.[12] So also does Jesus' characteristic challenge to the confining strictures of Pharisaic conceptions of purity (contrast, e.g., Fitzmyer 1985: 944). The so-called modifications of the symposium format prove drastic enough to suggest a parody of that genre, a pattern that will emerge explicitly in Luke 14:1–24, to which we turn next.

---

[11] Cf. Green (1997: 470–471) 'Jesus' deviant behavior might have led to his negative valuation, a possibility Luke circumvents by referring to Jesus as "Lord" and by reasserting Jesus' capacity and mission, prophesied by Simeon, to make known the inner thoughts of others (2:35). In a remarkable turn of events, then, the one whose behavior seems deviant is acknowledged to Luke's audience as Lord, and the Lord classifies those whose behaviors apparently have not transgressed the boundaries of socio-religious propriety as "fools".'

[12] While Luke is the one Synoptist not to portray Jesus' encounters with the Jewish leaders as uniformly hostile, a sizeable majority of them still describe significant conflict. For the entire spectrum of scholarly perspectives on the Jews in Luke-Acts, see Tyson 1988.

A cagey host and a rude guest: Luke 14:1–24

For the third time in Luke's Gospel Jesus finds himself invited to a Pharisee's home for a meal. This 'prominent' Pharisee is more literally 'one of the rulers[13] [*archontōn*] of the Pharisees'. For the first time Luke tells us explicitly that this was a Sabbath meal. Typically, when one of the Gospel writers mentions the Sabbath in connection with Jesus' activity, it sets the stage for some conflict with Pharisaic legal tradition. Indeed, this is precisely what transpires here. Little wonder that verse 1 describes Christ as being 'carefully watched' (*paratēroumenoi*). Verses 2–6 indeed generate a significant conflict, as Jesus encounters a man suffering from dropsy, whom he proceeds to heal despite the Pharisaic interpretation of work on the Sabbath, which this action violated.

Bock (1996: 1256–1257) thinks that the sick man was deliberately planted here as a trap. He notes that the use of *idou* (behold) to indicate surprise could suggest the possibility that the man has just walked in. The account, however, gives no other indication that he was not already there, in which case the surprise of *idou* would be that such a person attends the meal at all. Either way, 'combined with the presence of the "watching eyes" of the Jewish leadership (14:1), this verse suggests a trap, especially since 11:54 indicates that after the last meal the leadership determined to catch Jesus. A set-up is likely.' A leader among the Pharisees would probably own more than an ordinary Pharisee, who sometimes occupied no higher a socio-economic bracket than what we would call the lower middle class. The Sabbath meal, likewise, would afford an occasion for a more elegant banquet than most other Jewish meals. Nevertheless, it is interesting that the only expression Luke employs to describe this meal is 'to eat bread' (*phagein arton*: v. 1): the one feature noticeably absent from synopses of symposia. And for once there is not even a single word in the text that could be translated 'reclining'.

Nevertheless, because of the status of the host, 'we may assume that those who join [Jesus] at the table are likewise persons of high status in the community. Meals, after all, were used to advertise and reinforce social hierarchy' (Green 1997: 545). Indeed, all the other table companions may have well been Pharisees. Is it historically

---

[13] Marshall (1978: 578) notes that the *archontes* 'may refer to rulers who belonged to the Pharisaic party ... or rulers of the synagogue ... or to leading men among the Pharisees ... The objection that the Pharisees did not have leaders ... is met by reference to Jos. *Vita* 21.'

credible for Jesus to have been invited to join such an exclusive group? Green (1997: 546) thinks so on three counts: (1) 'Jesus is a pilgrim journeying to Jerusalem' and this form of Sabbath hospitality might be actually expected. (2) Jesus has been in the habit of both attending and preaching in the synagogues and has developed a reputation as a teacher in those contexts. (3) As we have previously noted, Luke portrays Pharisees with a variegated brush, not simply as uniformly hostile to Christ.

The presence of the dropsical man could 'constitute a vivid parable of Jesus' socially elite, Pharisaical table companions. Just as in front of Jesus stood a man who had dropsy, so, around the table, sat persons whose disorder was no less self-detrimental. As Jesus moves to heal the one, so with regard to the others is diagnosis pronounced and the prospect of help extended' (Green 1997: 547). Willi Braun (1995: 41) proposes a more intriguing connection. The man appears to be present 'neither as an "uninvited guest" (aklētos), a stock figure in ancient literary symposia, nor only to evoke the "beggar near the banquet" image, though he helpfully does that, but as a hapless literary figure whose brief cameo role is a physical, visual representation of an ethos of craving desire.' Dropsy, of course, was the disease in which people who drank too much and became bloated, ironically, still felt parched with thirst.

While nothing in verses 1–6 suggests a symposium, verse 7 does refer to Jesus observing how the invited guests chose the best seats for themselves, which suggests a formal seating arrangement according to rank or honour.[14] The little parable that begins in verse 8 forbids such self-arrogation and does use one of the verbs for reclining (kataklinō). Verse 10 similarly employs anapiptō, which as we have repeatedly seen need not even mean 'recline', much less demonstrate the presence of a symposium. But the context of a formal Sabbath meal probably would have involved couches and a posture of reclining. In the parable, the setting is explicitly one of a wedding feast (gamos), which, as we saw in the context of John 2:1–11 (above, p. 123), hardly necessitated the symposium format. Jesus' teaching, in contrast with those who immediately grabbed the best seats, enjoined the guests to humble themselves, take the place of least honour and let the host exalt them should he so choose. 'Standard patterns of reciprocity and concern for those of our own standing are overturned here' (Nolland 1993a: 751). If Luke thinks Jesus is attending

---

[14] The middle voice in the verb, exelegonto, may show that the guests chose seats for themselves (Bock 1996: 1262).

a symposium, then Jesus is subverting its very genius with his commands.

Verses 12–14 narrate Jesus' second 'mini-parable'. Here he refers to the custom of giving a lunch or dinner, using the terms *ariston* and *deipnon* respectively. The first normally refers to breakfast although it can mean a small lunch. The latter typically describes an evening dinner, though it can depict a main meal during midday (see above, p. 141). It would appear that Jesus intends to apply his principle to any context of sharing a meal with others.[15] Thus Jesus is scarcely focusing simply on a symposium or any other particular kind of banquet or special meal. Yet it is true that the kind of instruction Jesus imparts through this series of parables would fit well into a Hellenistic symposium. Jesus' countercultural perspective would prove most poignant in precisely such a context. Here one thinks of the occasional banquet described in the ancient Mediterranean world in which wealthy persons invited the comparatively poor as a charitable gift for them. Joseph Fitzmyer (1985: 1046–1047) notes that similar advice is later attributed to Rabbi Simeon ben Azzai in *Leviticus Rabbah* 1 and that a comparable anonymous saying is recorded in *Aboth de Rabbi Nathan* 25.[16] In a Greco-Roman milieu, a striking parallel to verses 12–14 appears in the satires of Lucian, complete with his characterization of both poor and rich and the invitation to the poor, with post-mortem rewards and punishments for the various participants (Braun 1995: 58–60). Jesus' stark contrast between the two kinds of invitations of course depends on the Semitic figure of speech in which 'not X ... but Y ...' means 'Y much more than X' (Marshall 1978: 583). Jesus does not actually forbid people to invite their friends or others who can repay them, but invitations to meals should not be motivated by the hope of favours extended in return. The sting in the tale still hurts!

As in Luke 11:37–54, there is a one-verse interruption by another speaker (v. 15), which creates the barest hint of a dialogue form, but this hardly turns Luke's episode into a symposium. It is difficult to know what this speaker intends with his beatitude, praising the person 'who will eat at the feast in the kingdom of God'. A verbal link with verse 1 is created by the expression, 'to eat bread'. Marshall

[15] Cf. Bock (1996: 1265): 'All kinds of meals are in view since *ariston* indicates a late morning meal, while *deipnon* is the main late afternoon meal.'

[16] Because of the later dates of these teachings, Fitzmyer adds the rhetorical question, 'Are these rabbinical traditions possibly influenced by the early Christian tradition?'

(1978: 587) thinks the guest is offering a corrective to the implied restriction in Jesus' parables, thus stressing that '*all* who attain to the heavenly banquet will be blessed.' The underlying assumption of the comment may well be that the Pharisees too will be favoured at that table (Bock 1996: 1272). In any event this individual's outburst focuses attention squarely on the eschatological banquet.[17] With the twofold use of the expression 'to eat bread', it would appear that Luke is clearly distinguishing this feast from the symposium, in which bread played no central role (see above, pp. 94–95). For Luke as narrator, verse 15 does not present 'a pious remark of a fellow guest striving to save the evening by changing the topic and thereby rescuing the host from Jesus' implied criticism in vv. 12–14'. Rather, it forms Luke's transition and introduction to the third and longest parable (vv. 16–24). 'Jesus' answer will say, in effect, to this fellow guest, "You are right; but if invited, will you be among those to decline?"' (Fitzmyer 1985: 1054).

The parable of the great banquet mirrors the meal at which it was uttered in several respects. Once again, an obviously wealthy man has prepared a feast, invited honoured guests, and summoned them in a culturally appropriate fashion by sending his servants (vv. 16–17).[18] In this setting, however, the unthinkable occurs, as all the original invitees refuse and for very flimsy reasons at that (vv. 18–20). The rest of the parable matches Jesus' advice on whom to invite by showing the host intent on filling his banquet hall, even if with the riff-raff from town and countryside (vv. 21–23).[19] Braun (1995: 93) may have best envisioned what Jesus had in mind with his depiction: 'It may be that the final guests are drawn from the ranks of those people who live close to the city precincts because their livelihood depended on the city, but not within the city walls because the nature of their business was too naturally noxious, socially odious or religiously suspect.' Cemeteries, for example, were always located outside the city and undertakers came to be included among the *exopyleitoi*, that is, those who lived outside the gates. Tanners, too, normally plied their trade outside the city and probably lived there, nearby with drovers, squatters, and others involved in butchery. 'Along with these we might expect an assortment of refugee aliens, disenfranchised villagers, run-away

---

[17] R. Stein (1992: 392) thinks that the *Messianic* banquet and the resurrection of the righteous are explicitly intended, not just an eschatological feast.

[18] On the cultural aspects underlying the entire parable, see esp. Bailey 1980: 88–113.

[19] On the issue of whether Gentiles are explicitly in view by the second sending of the servant further afield, see Blomberg 1990: 235–236.

slaves, prostitutes, roving beggars', and various others living on the perimeter of the city (Braun 1995: 94).

Whatever details of the interpretation of the great banquet may be disputed, the parable clearly mirrors Jewish hopes for the eschatological feast; but the way to participate in that feast now runs through Jesus. Excuses for rejecting his offer of the kingdom prove exceedingly lame and even insulting (cf. Bock 1996: 1273). E. R. Wendland (1997: 172) notes the narrowing of focus in intertestamental Jewish depictions of this banquet. 'The vision of a universal gathering of distinct peoples of all kinds has definitely been lost – or worse, has been deliberately transformed to state the opposite of the plain prophetic intention.' One thinks especially of the Targum to Isaiah 25:6, in which Yahweh will make a meal for all peoples but, though they suppose it an honour, it will be a shame for the Gentiles leading to inescapable plagues. In the great banquet parable, Jesus thus has to restore the original meaning of the Messianic feast in the Hebrew Scriptures.

Once again, Jesus upends conventional social practice in the characteristically radical fashion that supports historicity. As Green (1997: 550) elaborates:

> Because the sharing of food is a 'delicate barometer' of social relations, when Jesus subverts conventional mealtime practices related to seating arrangements and invitations, he is doing far more than offering sage counsel for his table companions. Rather, he is toppling the familiar world of the ancient Mediterranean, overturning its socially constructed reality and replacing it with what must have been regarded as a scandalous alternative.

While it is often viewed as a symposium, Braun (1992; 1995) rightly labels our text an anti-symposium instead. If Luke has the Greco-Roman symposium in mind, he intends to critique it via 14:1–24. The original defenders of the symposium hypothesis seldom note how few elements distinctive to that form of feasting are present, and in fact they make little of their identification in their actual interpretations (Braun 1995: 136–144; see esp. 139).[20] Or, with Nolland (1993a: 745), if there is a connection with Greco-Roman dining, 'It is probably for the sake of contrasting typical symposium patterns with those that are worthy of, or to be practiced in relation to, the Kingdom of God'.

---

[20] The exemplar to whom most refer is de Meeus (1961).

Josephus can certainly describe festive Sabbath-day meals and hospitality without any reference to symposium forms (*Life* 54.279; *m. Shabbat* 4:1–2).

A scandalous summary: Luke 15:1–32

Luke 15 does not present a full-blown passage on Jesus eating with sinners. Nevertheless, the three parables that form the heart of this chapter are all introduced by Luke's observation that 'the tax collectors and "sinners" were all gathering around to hear [Jesus]. But the Pharisees and the teachers of the law muttered, "This man welcomes sinners, and eats with them" ' (vv. 1–2). Festive rejoicing, including meals, may be implied in the conclusions to the parables of the lost sheep and lost coin (vv. 6, 9), but if so Jesus scarcely makes this explicit. In the fuller, more famous parable of the prodigal son (vv. 11–32), feasting clearly plays a central role. It celebrates the return of the wayward younger son and affords the occasion for the older brother to display his resentment (vv. 22–24, 28–30).[21]

The complaint in 15:2 reminds Luke's readers of the similar objection by Pharisees and scribes in 5:30 to Jesus' intimate association over meals with 'tax collectors and "sinners" '. It also sets the stage for the fuller account of the conversion of a chief tax collector, Zacchaeus, and the grumbling that occurs in that context in 19:7. As before, the combination of tax collectors and sinners stands 'for the outcast, the irreligious, and the immoral; in this episode they flock to Jesus as they had to John the Baptist in 3:12–13, anxious to hear him – thus they are foils to the grumbling Pharisees and Scribes' (Fitzmyer 1985: 1075). And the imperfect tense with the verb for grumbling suggests prolonged, ongoing criticism (Fitzmyer 1985: 1076). Green (1997: 570) highlights the importance of this cast of characters, especially given their appearance in 7:29–30 as well, again reflecting opposite responses to Jesus' ministry: 'In fact, the present scene appears as a concrete illustration of the earlier characterization of toll collectors (and sinners) as persons who "justified God", and the Pharisees and legal experts as those who "rejected God's purpose for themselves".'

Several other grammatical touches help us nuance our understanding of verses 1–2. The periphrastic imperfect in verse 1 ('were drawing near') may well refer to 'general circumstances of Jesus' ministry rather than one particular incident' (Marshall 1978: 599; Nolland

---

[21] On the parables of this chapter, and particularly the prodigal son, see esp. the various works of Bailey (esp. 1976, 1992), now culminating in Bailey 2003.

1993a: 770). The verb for welcome (v. 2) is *prosdechomai*, which may denote more than simply entertaining guests. Elsewhere it is used in context of financial provision and social honour (cf. Rom. 16:2 and Phil. 2:29; so Marshall 1978: 599). In addition, the muttering or grumbling in verse 2 'associates the Pharisees and legal experts with those of the wilderness generation who complained against God's representatives, Moses and Aaron', and who were severely judged for doing so (Green 1997: 571).

More significantly, given that all three parables of this chapter explicitly describe repentance, it simply will not do to argue, with Sanders, that Jesus accepted sinners without demanding a changed life from them. Jesus' rationale for associating with the outcasts is simple: 'he wishes to draw them to God' (Bock 1996: 1299). More pointedly, while the Old Testament injunctions against associating with sinners were doubtless applied to Jesus' 'transgression', he ignores these restrictions to offer people salvation through repentance and faith. Yet he does not participate in their sinful behaviour (R. Stein 1992: 403). As has become a pattern in his ministry, it is the lifestyle of discipleship, purity, and doing God's will which Christ believes he can impart to others, rather than being contaminated by their impurity. Yet it remains striking that Jesus uses table fellowship as the setting for redrawing the religious boundaries of his world. 'Jesus thus behaves toward these outsiders, these unclean, contemptible persons of ignoble status, as though they were acceptable, as though they were his own kin' (Green 1997: 571). As he does so, many of them choose to follow him and indeed become kin, as new members in Christ's spiritual family.

Luke 15:1–2, of course, is universally recognized as Luke's redactional introduction to the triad of parables that follow. But almost equally broad is the consensus that finds the parables of lost sheep, coin and sons largely, if not entirely authentic, indeed at the very core of bedrock material about the historical Jesus (see further Blomberg 1990: 172–183). To the extent that the parables also presuppose joyous feasting with returned prodigals, the case is bolstered for the authenticity of this motif in Jesus' ministry more broadly. It is equally important to stress that the celebration with the fattened calf in the parable of the prodigal (vv. 22–25) is thoroughly Jewish and fully intelligible in an early first-century Galilean context. Not the slightest hint of a symposium format intrudes here.[22]

---

[22] On Jewish background, in addition to Bailey 2003 (noted above), see esp. B. Young 1998: 130–157. For a comparison with Greco-Roman teachings, on the topics broached here, see esp. Holgate 1999.

The extravagant celebration described in the parable of the prodigal does not as immediately conjure up memories of the long-awaited eschatological banquet as with several of the texts previously surveyed. Nevertheless, the imagery of the slaughter of one large special animal to be eaten recalls the role of Behemoth in *2 Baruch* 29. It is certainly not impossible, therefore, that Jesus may intend to hint at, even if not directly allude to, the coming Messianic feast. But the far more central point remains the inclusion of the outcasts who return to God. While Jesus does not accept them without looking for a change of heart, he clearly welcomes them without imposing any period of probation or penance, as other Jewish leaders were often wont to do. And the father's reaction to the prodigal son clashes entirely with the common Jewish custom of a parent 'cutting off' or disowning a wayward child, refusing ever to re-establish them within the family circles or to return to them the privileges entailed in family membership (see esp. Schnider 1977).

Zacchaeus short-changed? Luke 19:1–10

At last we come to the famous story of Zacchaeus,[23] known to Sunday school children primarily as the short man who climbed a sycamore tree to see Jesus. In the vicinity of Jericho (v. 1), a man appears who is described as a 'chief tax collector'. This term immediately distinguishes Zacchaeus from all other tax collectors referred to in the Gospels, in that he is an *architelōnēs*: that is, a ruler or leader of tax collectors. We should have inferred, therefore, that Zacchaeus would be wealthier than the rest, but Luke leaves

---

[23] The name Zacchaeus itself appears to be the Greek form of the Hebrew *zakkai*, meaning clean or innocent (Bock 1996: 1516). This does not, however, justify the thesis of Ravens (1991), who thinks that this is the third in a series of names in uniquely Lukan material where the name is significant for the character: Simon (Luke 7), whose name means hearing, which is what he must do to Jesus; Lazarus (Luke 16), the Grecized form of Eleazar meaning 'God helps'; and Zacchaeus here in Luke 19. Ravens takes all this to offer further support for the view that Zacchaeus is not converting here but merely vindicating his consistent behaviour (on which see further below, pp. 154–156). But everyone who encounters Jesus is supposed to listen to him, and Simon is a very common Hebrew name. Lazarus is a special case, because he is the only character in any parable in any of the Gospels to be given a name. And there are plenty of other characters, even in the peculiarly Lukan material, whose names are not significant for their characters in the narrative: e.g. Elizabeth, Mary the mother of Jesus, Martha and her sister Mary, etc. Finally, Zacchaeus is already well known as a name elsewhere.

nothing to chance, explicitly describing him as *plousios*, that is, rich.[24] 'More specifically, as a "ruler" in the Greco-Roman world Zacchaeus would have enjoyed relative power and privilege, though from the perspective of the Lukan narrative we would anticipate his opposing the mission of Jesus' (Green 1997: 668).

Luke offers no explanation for why Zacchaeus 'wanted to see who Jesus was' (v. 3), an intriguing omission, especially since he uses the imperfect tense of *zēteō* to suggest continual or ongoing seeking. Many view this merely as an expression of curiosity, but Fitzmyer (1985: 1223) asks, 'Or is there something more, a vague discernment of something special about this person who was passing through and of whom he had heard (4:14, 37)?' Mention of Zacchaeus' short stature may likewise represent a simple historical observation, but Mikeal Parsons (2001) mounts a fascinating case for taking this as part of Luke's uniformly derogatory or demeaning portrait that he paints of Zacchaeus prior to his conversion. Parsons' study demonstrates that unusually short height in the ancient Mediterranean world was one of numerous physical abnormalities that could lead to public ridicule. Climbing the tree, in his attempt to see Jesus, may well have further exposed Zacchaeus to shame in the eyes of onlookers, since they would view this as an undignified action for a well-to-do male ruler claiming status in the community (Green 1997: 669). Indeed, Green (1997: 670) thinks that the depiction 'is not simply that Zacchaeus cannot see over the crowd; rather, the crowd itself is present as an obstacle to him. On account of their negative assessment of Zacchaeus (cf. v. 7), the people refused him the privilege of seeing Jesus as he passed by.' The imperfect form of *dynamai*, stressing Zacchaeus' ongoing inability to see, could reinforce Green's intuitions here.[25] At any rate, one is struck by the lengths to which this potential rival to Christ goes to try to have an encounter with him. And although enough of the Jewish leaders have proved hostile to Jesus

---

[24] 'In English translations, Zacchaeus is usually referred to as a "chief toll collector", taking Luke's expression as a job description, a kind of "district manager" with other toll collectors working as his subordinates. The term itself is without parallel in contemporary Greek texts, so it is not clear that a job title is intended. By way of analogy with other Lukan texts, however, it is clear that Zacchaeus is thus presented as a person of advanced status, even if only among other toll collectors' (Green 1997: 668).

[25] Alternatively, because the clause in which this verb appears merely provides background information to explain why Zacchaeus had to climb the tree, perhaps the imperfect tense actually makes this action more remote (recall above, p. 100).

thus far in the Gospel narratives, tax collectors have repeatedly become his disciples. Thus Luke may intend for us to assume that verses 1–4 envision Zacchaeus as a 'seeker': one who has some positive image of Jesus already in mind, now wanting to get to know him better.

The question of what he would have said or done when Jesus passed by the tree in which he was perched nevertheless remains unanswered. After all, verse 5 describes Jesus taking the initiative in the conversation, doubtless shocking both the tax collector and the crowd with his command and prediction, 'Zacchaeus, come down immediately. I must stay at your house today.' Zacchaeus, however, responds immediately and gladly, complying with the request (v. 6). 'He welcomes Jesus into his home . . . and he does so with joy . . . since the coming of Jesus to share his home is a sign of fellowship and ultimately of forgiveness' (Marshall 1978: 697). The crowd, however, interprets the scene in diametrically opposite fashion (v. 7), for, from their perspective, 'to stay in such a person's home was tantamount to sharing in his sin' (Marshall 1978: 697).

As with Jesus' lodging with Mary and Martha, this text describes no explicit meal, yet the passage remains relevant for our theme and is discussed in all major treatments of it. If Jesus will stay at Zacchaeus' home, then he will spend the night there, and Zacchaeus must serve him dinner. The verb for Zacchaeus' welcome (*hypodechomai*), as we have seen already, suggests precisely such hospitality. The walk from Jericho to Jerusalem can then be completed the next day (cf. Nolland 1993b: 905).

We have already confronted the recurring refrain 'tax collectors and sinners' in the Gospels. Now we have one who is a chief tax collector at the same time called a 'sinner', not merely by a handful of Pharisaic leaders but by 'all the people' (v. 7). Little wonder Walter Pilgrim (1981: 129–130) finds this text paradigmatic for Luke's theology of salvation and stewardship alike. R. Stein (1992: 467) believes that Luke reveals to his readers what it was Zacchaeus sought so earnestly by describing what he received in verse 9, namely, salvation. He may well be correct.

The locations in which verses 7 and 8 take place remain unclear. One could imagine Zacchaeus 'welcoming' Jesus by greeting him effusively in the same public place where the crowd had gathered. The onlookers could then assume the two would proceed to his house, and the criticism of verse 7 might have begun at once. On this reading, even Zacchaeus' reply in verse 8 could still have been delivered out of doors before he returned to his home.[26] On the other hand, after Jesus' command that implies the request for lodging, or room and board as we might call it (Fitzmyer 1985: 1224), the welcome of verse 6 reads somewhat more naturally as describing the scene at Zacchaeus' residence. The means by which 'all the people' could have seen this are the same as with the Pharisees' criticism of Levi's feast (see above, p. 100). The 'seeing' could refer to a subsequent report and the people's reaction; or the crowds could have literally returned to Jericho and observed Zacchaeus' hospitality from outside an open courtyard. That Jesus demonstrated his remarkable willingness to associate with one deemed a flagrant sinner, even in the intimate context of table fellowship, makes verse 8 most likely to reflect Zacchaeus' repentant response to Christ's compassionate overtures. As Marshall (1978: 697) helpfully summarizes:

> The statement of Zacchaeus is to be understood as a reaction to the initiative of Jesus and to the objections of the crowd. In order that Jesus may be freed from the suspicion of consorting with a sinner he makes a public declaration of his intention to live a new life. In such a situation a declaration of intent was an adequate sign of repentance. At the same time, his action is to be seen as an expression of gratitude to Jesus for his gracious attitude to him, and as an example of the sort of change in life that should follow upon the reception of salvation.

With verse 8, however, a major interpretative problem that has generated extensive recent debate also emerges. While the traditional understanding of Zacchaeus' declaration is that he is renouncing his previously sinful lifestyle, promising to live in a godly way instead and to provide restitution for all those he has defrauded, a surprising number of recent scholars have argued that Zacchaeus' use of the present tense refers to his customary practice, so that his declaration is merely vindicating himself against the unjustified slander of verse 7. We will return to this debate after we have considered the rest of verses 8–10, since all three verses impinge on a solution.

The TNIV potentially overinterprets the grammatical markers of verse 8 with its rendering 'Here and now I give half of my

---

[26] Indeed, Bock (1996: 1519) notes five possibilities for the setting of v. 8: during or after dinner in Zacchaeus' house; at some other time with visitors present; during his conversation with Jesus before his conversion; immediately at the tree; or at a meal before other people.

possessions', inasmuch as the characteristic, ongoing nature of the present tense could even more plausibly be rendered 'I am continuing to give', or 'I customarily give'. In other words, there are no separate Greek words besides the verb itself corresponding to the TNIV's 'here and now'. On the other hand, the conditional clause in verse 8 ('if I have cheated anybody . . .') is a first-class condition. While such a clause can assume the truth of the condition merely for the sake of argument, it is hard to see how that ploy could prove meaningful in this context. More likely, then, this 'if' is semantically equivalent to a 'whomever', and Zacchaeus is acknowledging that he *has* swindled or defrauded[27] people whom he is now willing to repay, and to repay with substantial interest![28] The grammar thus makes it probable that Zacchaeus is acknowledging serious offence in his past behaviour and promising to change his ways from this time forward. The historical background briefly surveyed in chapter 1 (see above, pp. 23–24) certainly poses no problem for assuming that this 'chief' toll collector had lined his pockets, in part at least, by overcharging those under him, who in turn would have had to collect sums from the people well beyond what was legally required.

Jesus' climactic declaration in verse 9 strongly supports the interpretation that sees Zacchaeus converting on the spot. Otherwise, it would make less sense for Jesus to declare: '*Today* salvation has come to this house.' 'Son of Abraham' in verse 9 reminds us that Zacchaeus is still Jewish. Not all of Jesus' meals with outcasts point to the inclusion of the Gentiles. Here Jesus' lesson may be more that of inclusiveness within Israel. Just as God cares for the 'down and out' among his people, he likewise shows compassion to the 'up and out'. The grammar reinforces Jesus' emphasis, as the otherwise superfluous uses of both *autos* ('he himself') and *estin* ('is') demonstrate. Verse 9b thus literally reads, 'because also he *himself* a son of Abraham *is*.' Jesus is not always looking beyond the borders of Israel, but as Bruce Chilton has frequently stressed, he does regularly affirm that *all* Israel remains the object of God's salvific concerns (see esp. Chilton 2000).

---

[27] The Greek root is *sykophanteō*, which occurs only here and in Luke 3:14 in the New Testament. Bauer (2000: 955) defines it as 'to put pressure on someone for personal gain' or 'to secure something through intimidation'.

[28] Nolland (1993b: 906) observes that, 'The fourfold restitution is probably not the fulfillment of any legal requirement. In Jewish law restitution in connection with theft normally required only the addition of a fifth (Lev. 6:2–5) . . . Roman law required fourfold restoration in certain circumstances, particularly in cases of wrongful accusation in the courts.'

The proverb of verse 10, with which the passage concludes, while an apt summary of Lukan theology (see esp. Marshall 1988: 116–156), proves an equally fitting conclusion to this pericope. It need not be seen as a wandering saying secondarily attached here. Indeed, the very verb for seeking (*zēteō*) reiterates the diction of verse 3, in which Zacchaeus was seeking to see Jesus. As Robert O'Toole (1991) unpacks it, what began as Zacchaeus' quest to find Jesus ends up as the Son of Man's quest for lost people. Jesus' characteristic and distinctive use of the 'Son of Man' title further supports the authenticity of the saying, while the tightly knit outline of the passage (structured as either an ABA ring composition or a four-part [ABBA] chiasm [O'Toole 1991: 111, 113]) points to the integrity and thus the authenticity of the entire passage.[29]

A look back at the whole episode confirms the traditional interpretation that Zacchaeus is converting or repenting. In addition to the points already made, verse 8 would seem boastful if understood as Zacchaeus' typical behaviour. The expression translated 'possessions' can suggest 'what I have had all along' rather than just 'my current income'. 'I pay back' is better understood as a futuristic present (as the TNIV explicitly interprets by adding the word 'will'). All wealthy men in Luke's Gospel to date have been in need of salvation when they met Jesus, and the immediately preceding passages tying 18:9 – 19:10 together all describe individuals confronted with the offer of salvation for the first time (R. Stein 1992: 466–467).[30]

Although a meal *per se* is only implied, rather than explicitly narrated in this passage, the encounter between Jesus and Zacchaeus powerfully reinforces the pattern that has consistently unfolded in our study. Jesus so cares for those rightly or wrongly stigmatized by society that he ignores the conventional restrictions on intimately associating with them. He is willing to go to their homes. Indeed, here he insists on it. He shares in their food and lodging, but he never does so simply for inclusiveness' sake. A call to repentance is always implicit unless, as here, the individual in question takes the initiative to declare his change of heart and behaviour. Whereas the crowds see Jesus accepting the hospitality of a man whose wealth is ill-gotten as becoming a partner with him in his crimes (Derrett 1970: 281–282),

---

[29] Marshall (1978: 695–696) makes the historical observation concerning this account in general that 'the fact that Jericho was a likely post for a tax-collector means that the Zacchaeus story could well belong to this locality also.'

[30] For representative studies on each side of the debate in the secondary literature, see esp. Mitchell (1991) versus Hamm (1991).

Jesus believes that godly character and righteous living can be modelled and have a positive impact by rubbing off on others as they commit to change their ways. As for seeing a symposium here, even the implied meal is never described, and we are not even sure that the words of Zacchaeus and Christ took place at that meal! Beyond these barest of hints, nothing else of a symposium emerges at all. If one must look for analogies with other banquets, strictly Jewish backgrounds prove far more promising. The expression 'son of Abraham' in verse 9, of course, means a true Jew. But Jesus might be using that circumlocution to hint at the eschatological banquet when Abraham and all the patriarchs will participate (recall Matt. 8:11). Even if not, the language, like the imagery, reminds us that this passage is fully explicable in non-Hellenized Jewish terms.

Cleopas and company: Luke 24:13–35

The final uniquely Lukan text depicting Jesus at mealtime is the post-resurrection appearance of Christ to Cleopas and his anonymous companion[31] along the road to Emmaus, culminating in their breaking bread together when they reach the village. The passage begins as the two disciples are talking with each other about everything that has happened to Jesus (vv. 13–14). Christ then appears (v. 15), 'but they were kept from recognizing him' (v. 16). The dialogue with their Lord incognito spans verses 17–27, climaxing in verses 25–27, in which Jesus expounds representative parts of the Hebrew Scriptures to demonstrate that the sufferings of the Messiah fulfil biblical prophecy. But none of this larger setting directly impinges on our theme of Jesus, sinners, and table fellowship.

More relevant are verses 28–32. In verses 28–29 Jesus, still unrecognized, seems to want to travel further. But the disciples persuade him to stay with them, since 'it is nearly evening; the day is almost over' (v. 29). As with other accounts of overnight lodging, the hospitality they offer Jesus doubtless includes an evening meal. 'Jesus gave the two disciples the opportunity to practice hospitality to "a herald" of the gospel message. Luke may have intended for this to serve as a model of such hospitality' (R. Stein 1992: 612).

Verses 30–32 confirm this supposition, describing what happened at dinner. It has actually been suggested that the simpler midday meal is in view here, inasmuch as a typical dinner would have taken place

---

[31] Polaski (1999) makes an intriguing case for this disciple as Cleopas' wife.

after it was already evening and the day was entirely over (e.g. Bornhäuser, cited in Marshall 1978: 897). But the traditional interpretation seems more probable. The language of the invitation, which still had been made well in advance of the dinner itself, would have to be considerably exaggerated if referring to a lunch at noon or early afternoon. The day would then be nowhere close to being 'over'. The kind of hospitality extended here also reminds the reader of the contrasting accounts introduced in Genesis 18:3 and 19:2 with Abraham and Lot (Bock 1996: 1918).[32]

Verses 30–32 describe what happened at the meal itself. The language of taking bread, giving thanks, breaking it, and beginning to give it to the others harks back to the feeding miracles, even in the very specific parallel of switching to the imperfect tense for the verb 'give' (9:16). While many have heard an echo here of the Last Supper narrative (e.g. Fitzmyer 1985: 1560),[33] it is interesting that there (22:19) the simple aorist tense appears (*edōken*), rather than the imperfect (*epedidou*) as here (24:30). Also as in the feeding miracles, Luke's focus remains Christological. Disciples' eyes are opened to Jesus' identity just before he departs from them, and they would naturally think back to the ways in which he has just taught them that he has fulfilled Scripture (vv. 25–27). Green (1997: 849–850) notes that the feeding of the five thousand affords opportunity for a similar revelation. Prior to the feeding there are misconceptions about Christ's identity, including the possibility that he is just a prophet. Afterwards Peter acknowledges Jesus as the Messiah. The same sequence recurs in the larger context of Luke 24 here. In the Last Supper narrative, however, it is the significance of Christ's death, rather than his person, that the evangelist most highlights.

As at the earlier meals with Pharisees or tax collectors, while Jesus is the guest at table, he assumes the role of host or *paterfamilias* ('father of the family') (Fitzmyer 1985: 1300–1368). Arthur Just (1993: 241) notes that this passage narrates the first act of breaking bread after the Last Supper and thus fulfils Jesus' command to perform the ceremony in remembrance of him. But it likewise recalls Jesus' entire ministry of table fellowship. Nolland (1993b: 1205–1206) finds the primary motif as entertaining angels unawares

---

[32] Nolland (1993b: 1205) also cites Judges 19:9.

[33] Fitzmyer helpfully nuances this view by recognizing that at the level of the historical Jesus such an allusion may not be present, while still affirming that by the stage of Lukan redaction it is surely intended. Yet even this last claim seems to outstrip what the evidence can actually demonstrate.

(as in Genesis 18) and thus uncovers no allusion to the Eucharist at all.

Whatever the precise kind of meal, this is the occasion in which the disciples' 'eyes were opened' (v. 31), probably a divine passive implying that God was the one who granted them the spiritual insight into their mysterious companion's identity. This is the only instance of this expression in the New Testament (Bock 1996: 1920). The disciples recognized Jesus, but he immediately disappeared from their midst. Apparently his purposes for this resurrection appearance have been accomplished in giving the two their extensive 'Old Testament survey' lecture.

This is not a passage depicting Jesus' table fellowship with sinners as such, nor even with milder outcasts, yet Cleopas and his companion, who had followed Jesus at some level, at best are confused and at worst have given up on him. They may well also feel that *they* are now threatened, or at least marginalized, in their own society. Just (1993: 138) goes even further, believing that while the disciples are not full-fledged apostates, they have lost all hope and left the large overall group of Jesus' followers. Nevertheless, Jesus stoops to eat with them.

The brief recognition scene (v. 31) leads the two to ask themselves after Jesus has disappeared again, 'Were not our hearts burning within us while he talked with us on the road and opened the Scriptures to us' (v. 32)? 'Luke sought to convey to Theophilus and his readers that as certainty came to the disciples in the sharing of Scripture and the "breaking of bread", so too could they experience this certainty as they heard the Scriptures in the context of the church's breaking of bread (cf. Acts 2:42–47)' (R. Stein 1992: 613). This observation likewise makes it less probable that Luke intends to allude to the Eucharist, for then one would expect different references (e.g., to the words of institution about the bread and the wine) and more of a focus on the meal itself. Instead, one thinks again of the coming eschatological banquet. As Andy Johnson (2002: 137) explains, if Jesus' table fellowship prior to the resurrection foreshadowed the Messianic banquet, and if his resurrection implies that the Messianic age has begun, then 'This scene is a foretaste or anticipation of the messianic banquet with Jesus as host.'

The passage concludes with the two disciples returning to Jerusalem, reporting their encounter, and learning how Jesus has appeared to Simon Peter as well (v. 34). The two narrate what happened to them (v. 35), and before they finish Jesus interrupts them with another appearance (v. 36). This verse forms a transition to the penultimate passage of the Gospel (vv. 37–49), which moves beyond our topic, except that Jesus eats a piece of broiled fish (vv. 42–43) to demonstrate the genuineness and physicality of his resurrection.

What then are we to make of our narrative and the meal which forms the setting for Christ's climactic revelation in Luke? The details suggest that his hosts knew he was someone special, thus allowing him to take over the lead role in the conversation and in the distribution of the food. But only when he drops his mask, as it were, do they realize his full identity, and the telltale sign that should have disclosed him to them was his Scriptural exposition, not the dinner itself. Bock (1996: 1919) opines: 'This meal is not a reenactment of the Lord's Supper since there is no wine and nothing is said over the elements ... Neither is this the messianic banquet, though it may anticipate this decisive banquet meal that takes place in the eschaton after the gathering of all the saints. The meal simply pictures Jesus as raised and present with his disciples in fellowship.' But to the extent that his fellowship meals often foreshadowed the end-times feast, perhaps this anticipation plays a larger role here than Bock acknowledges.

The generally restrained nature of the narrative, however, particularly surrounding the meal, and the ambiguity created by Jesus' immediate disappearance after the disciples recognized him, all support authenticity. A purely legendary story would disclose Christ far more clearly and fill in the obvious gaps Luke has left in his narrative (as in fact the apocryphal Gospel accounts regularly do). The verb for eating 'at the table' in verse 30 comes from *kataklinō*. Other than that single word and the presence of a meal, nothing here suggests a symposium. Indeed, all the significant dialogue comes before the meal, on the road to the village, rather than during it (cf. Just 1993: 220). Conversely, Jesus' disappearance interrupts the meal almost before it is under way. But, together, Jesus' teaching and his fellowship meal form the climax of Luke's Gospel, with Jesus now manifest as both the suffering and the risen Christ prophesied in the Hebrew Scriptures (Just 1993: 242).

Summary and conclusion

Even adding the texts Luke takes over from one of his sources to his distinctive material, it would be difficult to argue that Jesus' table fellowship with sinners formed the central theme in his Gospel (see the 'Introduction' to this chapter). Nevertheless, it clearly plays a prominent role in his narrative. Indeed, a wide array of people dine with Jesus, all of whom had problems of various kinds, but not necessarily those conventionally associated then or now with sinful lifestyles. In 7:36–50 a woman who probably, though not demonstrably, was a prostitute fits the classic conception of a 'sinner'. In 10:38–42 Jesus merely lodges at the home of two sisters, but potentially scandalizes the male disciples by allowing Mary to sit at his feet on equal terms with them. In 11:37–54 the sinners turn out to be the Pharisees and scribes, despite the fact that they would have considered themselves among the most upright in the land. The same is true of 14:1–24, in which the 'great reversal' theme central to Luke dominates. Whether at the literal feast described in this chapter or in the parables with banquet imagery that Jesus narrates on this occasion, those with social status are humbled, while the poor and outcasts are exalted. The chapter on lostness (15:1–32) reverts to the complaint that Jesus associates with tax collectors and 'sinners' as the Pharisees and scribes defined them. Luke 19:1–10 illustrates that propensity with a classic example of the chief toll collector, Zacchaeus. A large chunk of chapter 24, finally, involves Jesus' appearance to two of the larger group of his disciples beyond the Twelve, who may themselves have been feeling marginalized.

The kinds of table fellowship involved in each of these passages likewise varies greatly. There are banquets thrown by Pharisees in chapters 7, 11, and 14, in which, to one degree or another, Jesus plays the part of a 'rude' guest, challenging the behaviours and attitudes of his hosts and the other invitees. This one kind of meal *does* reflect a unique feature of Luke's Gospel, but the only time clear elements of a symposium emerge, Jesus tries to turn it into an anti-symposium (14:1–24)! Chapter 15:2 generalizes about Jesus' intimacy at table with the notoriously wicked, which 7:36–50 and 19:1–10 illustrate with the specific examples of the unnamed prostitute and the tax collector Zacchaeus. In the latter text, however, a meal is merely presupposed, not explicitly narrated. The same is true with the accounts of Jesus with Mary and Martha (10:38–42) and with Cleopas and his anonymous companion in Emmaus. In the latter instance, the meal begins, but as soon as the two travellers recognize Jesus he disappears from them (24:30–31).

The similarities with the passages from the other strata of the Gospel tradition make it difficult to argue that Luke's redactional emphasis in any way plays fast and loose with the history he inherited. If the anonymous woman in Luke 7:36–50 truly is a prostitute, then this account illustrates what Matthew 21:31–32 describes as a general trend: the tax collectors and prostitutes coming into the kingdom of God ahead of the Jewish leaders. The parallelism of imagery with the anointing of Jesus by Mary of Bethany during the last week of Jesus' life (John 12:1–8 pars.) creates further multiple attestation of other imagery in the story. While Mary and Martha figure elsewhere in the Gospels only in John 11, the Synoptics likewise depict unusually positive interactions between Jesus and women. In Mark alone, one thinks of Jairus' daughter, the woman with the haemorrhage, the widow and her mite, and the women who go to the empty tomb (cf. further Kinukawa 1994). The invective unleashed at scribes and Pharisees in Luke 11 closely matches the contents of Matthew 23, even if there Jesus does not utter his tirade at mealtime. The very banquet parable of Luke 14:15–24 finds a close parallel in the account of the wedding feast in Matthew 22:1–10. Luke 15:1–2 generalizes about incidents like the call of Levi attested in the triple tradition. The conversion of Zacchaeus affords one further example of Jesus' shocking intimacy at table with 'tax collectors and sinners', the refrain found in both Matthew's and Luke's accounts of the children in the marketplace, not just in Luke 15:1–2. Finally, the recognition of Jesus in the breaking of the bread in Luke 24 echoes themes of Jesus feeding the five thousand and the four thousand in Matthew and Mark. Luke obviously has an interest in narrating more of these accounts than either Matthew or Mark does, but they hardly differ in theme or import.

While it is not impossible that one or more of these meals adopted aspects of the Greco-Roman symposium, no actual evidence for that claim has emerged. Most Pharisees were not Hellenized, yet few other Jews would have amassed the wealth to throw such a banquet. Zacchaeus probably could have done so, but Luke does not even mention his dining in the account of his conversion. Jesus' meals with Mary and Martha or with the unnamed disciples in Emmaus seem unrelated to the symposium form, and the truly distinctive elements of dialogue, entertainment, games with wine, the amenities of a 'social club', and the like are missing altogether. If we are to look for parallels to other banquets, we would do far better to see anticipations of the eschatological and Messianic banquet for which so many Jews longed. Here even outcasts, even the wicked will be present, but only if they have repented and followed Christ. The parable of the great banquet indicates this discipleship by the depiction of those who respond positively to the rich man's invitation. The accounts of the meals with the prostitute and Zacchaeus include their explicit changes in belief or behaviour along with their gratitude. But many who think they will participate in the great end-times celebration of God's people will find themselves excluded, as in the confrontations between Jesus and his Pharisaic hosts in chapters 7, 11, and 14. And this is precisely what Christ emphasized already in the 'Q' passage of the healing of the centurion's servant. While possible echoes of the eschatological feast are not heard as frequently in the uniquely Lukan texts,[34] they remain present. Again, no *significant* difference emerges in comparing the uniquely Lukan material with passages from other Gospel strata. All the themes that we saw in the latter are reinforced and promoted in the former. What McMahan (1987: 1) concludes about Luke fairly summarizes what we have seen throughout the Gospels:

Of all the means by which Jesus could have chosen to be remembered, he chose to be remembered by a meal. What he considered memorable and characteristic of his ministry was his table-fellowship. The meal, one of humankind's most basic and common practices, was transformed by Jesus into an occasion of divine encounter. It was in the sharing of food and drink that he invited his companions to share in the grace of God. The quintessence of Jesus' redemptive mission was revealed in his eating with sinners, repentant and unrepentant alike.

---

[34] Not surprisingly, given that Luke's more Hellenistic audience would not be as familiar with the Jewish tradition of a Messianic banquet.

Chapter Six

The potential of
contemporary Christian meals
Conclusions and applications

Summary

Until recently, Jesus' table fellowship with sinners was widely agreed
to form a central part of the fundamental core of authentic historical
Jesus material derivable from the Synoptic Gospels. Several recent
challenges make this conclusion somewhat less secure today. The
most significant of these is the claim that the meals in which Jesus
participates regularly take the form of Greco-Roman symposia,
which probably did not permeate Israel to the extent required for all
the Gospel meal-narratives to be authentic. Even if they had proved
this pervasive, was Jesus likely to have participated in them to the
extent he is portrayed as doing? Given that Luke contains more than
twice as many references to Jesus' feasting than any other Gospel or
Gospel stratum, and given that Luke is by far the most Hellenistic of
the Synoptics, it is easy to conclude that his meal-narratives represent
at least a redactional emphasis, if not an entire creation of the third
evangelist, which does not reflect the true, more limited extent of
Jesus' involvement in such celebrations.

A second debate involves the 'sinners' with whom Jesus joins in
fellowship. Since the ground-breaking work of E. P. Sanders, it has
become increasingly common to argue that these were the most
notoriously wicked of Israel's society, not merely the ritually impure
or those who did not satisfy the ultra-strict Pharisaic standards for
holiness. Also, thanks to Sanders, doubt has been cast on whether
Jesus truly called such people to repentance or, if he did, how
centrally he featured such preaching in his mission.

In both debates, valid criteria of authenticity must be established in
order to make progress toward a resolution, but then one must also
assess the meaning and significance of Jesus' behaviour. The double

similarity and dissimilarity criterion holds out the greatest promise for making progress on the first front, while the Jewish hope of an eschatological banquet becomes suggestive on the second.

The two prongs of the double similarity and dissimilarity criterion involving early Christianity prove the easiest to assess. The fledgling Jesus movement continued the practice of celebrating special meals, demonstrating continuity with the Jesus tradition, but very quickly narrowed their practice almost exclusively to the celebration of the Eucharist or Lord's Supper. Were our purpose to analyse the authenticity and meaning of the Last Supper, our task would become far more complex. But, given the paucity of other forms of table fellowship in Acts through Revelation, and in early Christianity beyond the first century, it appears relatively straightforward to argue that Jesus' table fellowship with sinners remained quite distinctive.

Comparing Jesus' practice with Jewish backgrounds requires far more detailed analysis. Meals appear in many contexts for many different reasons throughout the Old Testament. They may reflect the typical intimacy of a family, often including neighbours and friends, in a world in which the evening meals were often prolonged, drawn-out affairs, not least because there was little else to do after a strenuous working day in a world without electricity. In other cases, meals ratify covenants; celebrate military victories; accompany the anointing of kings and the establishment of their reigns; celebrate special family occasions, such as birth, marriage and death; and accompany prescribed festivals that memorialize key events in the salvation history of God's people.

Even more specialized meals accompanied animal sacrifices for the forgiveness of sins, while the unique combination of Jewish dietary laws distinguish Israel from its neighbours. The promised land of Canaan was set aside for this uniquely chosen people as 'a land flowing with milk and honey', an expression that emphasized the prosperity and abundance with which God wanted to bless Israel. Eating with the wrong people, or not eating with the right people, could at times prove disastrous, while the decadence of lavish banquets, both inside and outside Israel, remained a regular temptation for leading Israelites into sin. Food itself remains an inherently good gift from God, but, as with all such gifts, people can easily abuse it.

Isaiah 25:6–8 introduces a theme that recurs in later prophecy and takes on greater significance in the centuries after the completion of the Hebrew Scriptures. An eschatological banquet, sometimes explicitly portrayed as including a Messiah, envisions a future day when God's material blessings are so plentiful that none of his people lack any good thing. All may rejoice together in unending camaraderie, as the evil and suffering of previous eras is finally obliterated.

While meals and other forms of hospitality should be extended to the resident aliens sojourning in the land, and can be offered to total strangers in ways that create new friendships and loyalties, the Old Testament contains comparatively few references to meals as building bridges between those previously estranged. Even less often do we find the command to love one's enemies or the illustration of warring parties eating together. The numerous ways in which Israel was to remain distinct from the Gentiles around her naturally led to the use of food to draw boundaries far more often than to break them down.

The intertestamental literature pursues most of the themes of the Hebrew Scriptures with respect to food and meals. If anything, their role as boundary markers increases, as hostility between Jews and Gentiles is often magnified. Preoccupation with ritual purity, represented in meals by keeping a kosher table, also increases. Some of the most poignant accounts of Jewish martyrdom involve the faithful who refuse to compromise and disobey the dietary laws. Once again, references to feeding the needy or showing hospitality to strangers do appear, but much more rarely than in the Old Testament.

The concept of an eschatological banquet continues to develop, and it is given particular prominence in the hopes of Qumran for a day in the near future in which the Messiah or Messiahs will eat together with a completely purified and holy people. Daily meals among the Dead Sea sectarians, like those Philo describes among the Therapeutae, form important precursors to feasting in the eschaton.

During the centuries leading up to the time of Christ, a quite different tradition was evolving in the Greco-Roman world. The symposium involved a two-part banquet that began with an elaborate meal, which was then followed by a 'drinking party' with forms of entertainment that could range from a drunken orgy to a refined philosophical discourse. The latter, however, seems to have occurred far more rarely than the former. While Hellenistic customs had significantly intruded into Israel in the centuries of Greek hegemony, it is unclear how widespread the practice of symposia actually became, particularly among Jewish leaders like the Pharisees, concerned to separate themselves from Hellenism. Tellingly, one of the most common ways of describing Jewish meals, from a simple daily lunch to an elaborate, festive banquet, was as 'the breaking of bread', the one element which did not feature prominently in Greco-Roman symposia. This suggests that the meals in the two cultures remained more distinct than those scholars acknowledge who want to interpret the Gospel banquets as symposia. The frequent appeal to 'reclining' as the telltale sign of a symposium reads far more into that single word than it can bear. It is likewise improbable that the format of the symposium had substantially influenced the developing concept of the eschatological banquet. The practice of reclining on couches for banquets had indeed permeated Judaism, but it had done so to such an extent that it was adopted in other formal meals besides symposia. 'Reclining' even became a metaphor for eating meals in certain contexts in which the literal posture was not adopted at all.

When we turn to the Synoptic Gospels, we discover Jesus challenging the purity laws of his day, or at least the way in which they are applied to exclude various categories of Israelites. Scandalously, he associates with the notoriously wicked, but he is willing to feast with the scrupulous religious leaders as well. Jesus' table fellowship with sinners reflects his willingness to associate with them at an intimate level, but not merely for the sake of defying convention or enjoying a party. In each case various textual clues, if not explicit statements, demonstrate that Christ is indeed calling them to repentance and summoning them to become his followers. At the same time, he is ready to accept them at the slightest sign of a positive response and does not follow the Essene pattern of requiring a lengthy period of probation for them to prove themselves. In various ways, Jesus' meals, and especially his wilderness feedings, evoke the theme of the Messianic banquet but again suggest a far more inclusive guest list than most Jews anticipated. Little wonder that when his behaviour is caricatured he is described as 'a glutton and a drunkard'.

While all of Jesus' practices find points of continuity with antecedent Judaism, their cumulative effect is rather to distance him from his tradition than to reinforce it. Thus the two prongs of the double similarity and dissimilarity criterion are satisfied with respect to Jewish backgrounds just as the two prongs with respect to subsequent Christianity had been. As to the meaning of Jesus' behaviour, the unifying theme that emerges is one that may be called 'contagious holiness'. Jesus discloses not one instance of fearing contamination, whether moral or ritual, by associating with the wicked or impure. Rather, he believes that his purity can rub off on them, and he hopes that his magnanimity toward them will lead them to heed his calls to discipleship.

167

A survey of the peculiarly Lukan texts turns out not to demonstrate any substantially different emphases from those already unearthed in other layers of the Synoptic tradition. It is true that Luke stresses repentance a little more, but this theme has been regularly implicit, and occasionally explicit, throughout the passages previously surveyed. Luke likewise paints a more variegated picture of the Pharisees and thus includes several examples of them inviting Jesus to meals, to which invitations he at first responds favourably. But in every instance these episodes eventually find him criticizing his hosts' behaviour, showing that it is the religious elite, rather than the outcasts of society, who have most seriously misunderstood God's will. Finally, Luke highlights Jesus' concern for the outcast more than any other Gospel or Gospel source, but in so doing only builds on motifs already present in those earlier documents and traditions.

Applications

Obviously meals do not mean the same thing in every contemporary culture that they did in the biblical cultures and the societies that surrounded them. In our hectic Western lifestyle, we are used to fast food on the run, bag lunches for work or school, and family members eating at home at whatever times suit them best, whether or not the entire family can sit down together.[1] Even when we go out to nice restaurants, time is often at a premium, and we scarcely anticipate spending three or four hours over a meal. Of course there are exceptions, and adjacent to the Mediterranean, even in the developed world, formal dinners can indeed occupy numerous courses over several hours.

In more traditional societies and in subcultures that preserve older customs within our modern world, meals can still reflect times of special intimacy. Families may expect to eat together; close friends or relatives may be invited, especially for the evening meal; and leisurely conversation, perhaps with after-dinner games around the table, still forms an important recurring ritual. Even while eating at a fast-food restaurant, most of us are not likely to join just anyone at table, although some Europeans still preserve the custom of feeding total strangers at the same table in a restaurant when there are vacant

---

[1] 'A recent survey, taken in a school for upper-middle-class American children, surfaced a startling statistic. When asked how many times *per month* each child sat down to an evening meal with the family, the average answer was *once*' (Nangle 1996: 49).

chairs available but not entirely vacant tables. Even then, however, the unwritten custom is that people will take this opportunity to get to know one another a little. Similarly, guests at a traditional bed and breakfast will often eat together in the mornings and start to become acquainted. In other words, while table fellowship by no means consistently reflects the degree of intimacy it usually represented during Old or New Testament times, we can relate to their customs to some degree, because we have experienced at least partial analogies in our cultures (cf. further Douglas 1975).

Even closer parallels emerge during the celebration of special events: wedding receptions, funeral wakes, parties for rites of passage (though they may well be secular as well as religious: for example, graduation from a school rather than a confirmation or bar mitzvah), the inauguration of a head of state, or the announcement of a company merger. While specifics change from one time and place to another, the felt need to honour special occasions with elaborate meals in the company of particularly close friends remains relatively constant across the cultures (Wilkins and Harvey 1996; Juengst 1992). More mundanely, church potlucks prove perennially popular, usually more for the fellowship than for the food. Those congregations, though few and far between, that have instituted Sunday or mid-week meals as a regular feature of church life consistently testify to the added meaningfulness the dining creates. For many, it is the closest thing to true Christian *koinōnia* they will ever experience (Sack 1999). With a little planning and creativity, a fellowship meal can produce even deeper community.[2]

Christians, particularly in Western cultures, have a difficult time appreciating the pervasive influence of ancient Israel's dietary laws, though believers who represent minority communities in primarily orthodox Jewish towns or neighbourhoods understand better, as do those who live in predominantly Muslim or Hindu societies. Our easy access to an abundance of food and drink in the West makes it likewise difficult to appreciate the spectacular promise to Israel that it could inhabit 'a land flowing with milk and honey'. Some of us, quite frankly, eat a greater quantity and better quality of food on a regular basis than all but the very richest people did in the biblical cultures, even at their special feasts.

A theme that did not fall within our purview in surveying the biblical material is nevertheless amply represented in the Scriptures:

---

[2] Again, see the suggestions in Nangle 1996.

the need for God's people to share from their surplus, especially of foodstuffs, with the poor and needy at home and abroad. In a world of almost record disparities between haves and have-nots and more than one billion of starving, sick or malnourished individuals, the contemporary task takes on an unprecedented urgency (see esp. Sider 1997). Perhaps it is not too much of a stretch to suggest that, when Jesus asked his disciples to 'duplicate' his miracle of feeding the multitudes, he envisioned a later day when they would do so by non-miraculous means (cf. esp. Campbell 2003). The majority of our world's inhabitants have no difficulty looking forward to the prospects of a future age when material as well as spiritual sustenance will know no bounds. Even we who remain satiated most of the time can usually reflect on special meals that whetted our appetites for the biblical vision of an eschatological banquet in which all God's people will enjoy one another and all of God's good material provisions for ever, with none of the selfishness, injustice, or alienation that so often mar even the best of our celebrations in this age. Meanwhile,

> Jesus' promiscuous table-fellowship should commit us to a world where all human beings regardless of race, gender, economic status, class, sexual orientation, or religious belief have access to the goods of the earth bestowed on us by our Creator God. There is no avoiding the economic and political implications of genuine table-fellowship.
>
> (Joncas 2000: 363–364)

Archie Smith (1998: 140), a psychology and counselling professor at the Graduate Theological Union in Berkeley, tells the story of his wife and him giving a party in their home for colleagues from each of their respective workplaces. The gathering was apparently large enough that not everyone had a chance to meet everyone else. One appropriately dressed, friendly man circulated comfortably, eating and drinking copiously, and thanked his hosts graciously when he left. Later that evening, Smith asked his wife who the man was, only to discover that she did not know either. He then reflected: 'the stranger was generously received, fed, and treated the same as everyone. When leaving, he said he had a great time. But would he have been so well received had we known that he was uninvited – a party crasher?' A. Smith (1998: 150) concludes that to this day he does not know who the uninvited man was. 'Nothing is certain about his emotional, social, spiritual states, or his situation before God. But these things need not be perceived in order to extend hospitality. Maybe he was hungry and we fed him; maybe he was thirsty and we provided something for him to drink; maybe he was lonely and found a way to stem the tide of loneliness by circulating among a hospitable crowd.' If any of these possibilities proved true, 'then he found a hospitable spirit. God's healing Spirit can move among us in ways of which we are unaware.'

More challenging is how to implement Jesus' comparatively unique vision in extending the intimacy of table fellowship not merely to the stranger, but also to the outcast and even the enemy. A number of years ago, when my wife and I were living in England, we decided to celebrate an American Thanksgiving by inviting a pair of other American couples we knew to join us, but we also extended the invitation to nearby international residents of very different ages along with a few British acquaintances, including two older men from our church who struggled with mental illness and frequently had to be hospitalized. My wife's Mormon niece, who was visiting us, also participated. Conversations proved noticeably awkward that day. The clash in the customs of the various cultures became nowhere more evident than in the length of time various people chose to stay. Our final guests (a Norwegian pastor and his wife) did not leave until after 11pm, even though our meal had begun in the middle of the afternoon, and then only when they saw our niece emerge from her bedroom in more casual clothes than she had been wearing. We wondered if they mistook them for pyjamas! But as we looked back on that day, we had the sense that perhaps we had captured something more of the spirit of the holiday and – more significantly – of biblical meals than in most of our comfortable, homogeneously grouped gatherings.

On another occasion, when we were living in Scotland, we went out of our way to befriend an Iraqi couple and have them to dinner. The husband was a Shia Muslim. Those were the days of the American hostage crisis in Iran and of the United States' support for Saddam Hussein's regime in Iraq, but our Iraqi friend minced no words about his approval of the revolutionary takeover by the Ayatollah Khomeini in his neighbouring country. That may be the closest we have ever come to dining with an enemy! But most of the time we do not even do a good job of heeding Jesus' injunction to focus on inviting those too poor to be able to pay us back (unless I count all the students we have over). Indeed, recovering hospitality as a Christian tradition more generally is widely needed in our fast-paced, self-centred lifestyles (Pohl 1999: iii).

Perhaps a more challenging example of such a recovery is inviting a non-Christian to live with a Christian family, both to provide for his or her needs for 'room and board', but also in the hopes that the person might find Christ.[3] We have welcomed younger adults into our home on three occasions for two-year stretches at a time, including a divorced woman and our first-ever Russian student at Denver Seminary, but all three of our guests were Christians. But good friends of ours did bring a troubled young adult into their home for several years and see him turn his life over to Jesus.

Of course, there are other ways to be involved with the needy. We support (and Denver houses) a large number of Christian organizations which reach out to the marginalized and dispossessed in a whole host of arenas. Our own church has a thriving 'home and health ministry', complete with food bank, which helps a surprisingly large and ever-growing number of suburban poor. Our seminary's food closet does the same, especially for international students. These various ministries regularly solicit not merely donations but Christian people willing to take turns in preparing food, hosting meals, coming to organizational outlets where the poor are fed, and delivering food in person to people's homes, all to give us opportunity for actual personal interaction and meal-sharing with those we are helping. Most of us would do well to be more extensively involved with such ministries. If all we ever do is overeat and overdrink with our own kind, our dining will, ironically, resemble more closely the Old Testament *marzēaḥ* and the Greco-Roman symposium than the meals that God's people in both testaments were commanded to celebrate. At the same time, Christine Pohl (1999: 160) observes that 'churches have generally done better with offering food programs and providing clothing closets than with welcoming into worship people significantly different from their congregations. Because we are unaware of the significance of our friendship and fellowship, our best resources often remain inaccessible to strangers.'

At the same time, if we emulate Jesus, we will move as freely among the 'up and out' as among the 'down and out'. We will not hesitate to eat with non-Christian friends in their homes, in restaurants and pubs, or in other places of meaningful festivity. Michael Prior's diagnosis from two decades ago (1985: 83, 162) remains as accurate today as then. There is a 'desperate need for Christians to excise innumerable church meetings, in order to free their diaries for

---

[3] On which, see esp. Rupprecht 1983.

proper meeting with unbelievers'. Again, Jesus' model of ministering to people of all backgrounds 'challenges us to cross the culture-gap between the Christian sub-culture of cozy meetings and holy talk and the pagan culture of our local community. The task of identification with and incarnation into our contemporary paganism, of all kinds, is one of the biggest tasks confronting the church.'

If Jesus was right, and the prevailing view in ancient Judaism wrong, so that holiness can be more contagious than impurity, then we need not fear such activity. The sad examples of Christians being corrupted and adopting the sinful practices of their non-Christian acquaintances with whom they associate is a testimony to their unwillingness to rely on the Spirit's power and not a disproof of the viability of Jesus' model. I still recall vividly the college friend who finally let down her guard and allowed the gospel to lead her to Christ after she saw a group of us Christians willing to drink wine in moderation with her friends and her. She had never seen that among born-again believers before and thought that Christianity required teetotalling. Each year I meet seminarians who have come to the Lord because Christians reached out to them in unorthodox places, despite their sinful lifestyles, and each year we send out various interns and graduates to minister in similar fashion.

One entire church in downtown Denver, which voluntarily chose for itself the name 'Scum of the Earth' (from 1 Cor. 4:13), has been particularly successful in recent years in reaching young street and city people, as well as countercultural teens and twenty-somethings from the suburbs. Worship styles, messages, and discipleship and outreach ministries are all geared for this target population, which forms a sizeable majority of the congregation. Not surprisingly, they serve a full dinner in conjunction with their weekly Sunday evening services. Of course, as in Jesus' ministry, the point of all such outreach efforts is not merely to provide food for the hungry, break down cultural barriers, or develop friendships with those with whom one might not naturally associate. However contextualized it is, the offer of salvation must still be our culminating objective, or our activity may have no eternal significance. So, too, the religious insider who does nothing but object to and stand in the way of such creative outreach must be rebuked in no uncertain terms, just as Jesus regularly did (see further Blomberg 2002).

God has uniquely blessed 'Scum', as it is abbreviated, enabling the church to reach people no one else seems to be able to. On a 'story night' one summer evening in 2004, in lieu of a message, four individuals shared their testimonies. One involved 'a man who grew up in the church but was raped by a pastor as a child, and so walked away from all things Christian (except to try to tear Christians down)', until he discovered Scum. The second, a twenty-seven-year-old man, 'grew up in a dysfunctional family, ran away when he was 15 and joined a gang, was imprisoned by 17 for attempted murder', and was now finally putting his life back in God's hands at the Denver Rescue Mission. A third was a young woman, a recent college graduate 'who grew up in a good home, but got into cutting herself, sleeping around and partying, and walked away from Christianity till she met a group of "credible" Christians at her college to help her turn her life around'. The final speaker 'commented that when he is asked for directions anywhere in Denver, he'll give the person directions to Scum first and then will tell them how to get where they're trying to go' (Kamell 2004).

A second urban Denver congregation, reflecting a broader spectrum of ages of attenders, still finds twenty- and thirty-somethings predominating, but more among the professional ranks. One distinctive of this congregation is its openness to gay and lesbian seekers. Unlike many of the mainline Protestant churches, it does not condone this lifestyle. But neither does it exaggerate the evil of this sin as if it were the worst one imaginable; the church stresses that all believers struggle throughout their lives with certain temptations. Through public teaching and private friendships, it has created a climate in which one American subculture that almost without exception perceives hostility from the evangelical church has recognized a genuine welcome. People come to Christ but are still not required to change instantly. Rather they are encouraged to become part of specialized Christian ministries that help homosexuals set personalized, realistic goals for themselves on what often remains a long path to full wholeness. And all newcomers are encouraged to get involved in a small-group ministry, for growth toward or in Christian discipleship, which frequently incorporates meals into its fellowship.

Additional contemporary applications are limited only by our lack of creativity, even in our fast-paced Western world. A ministry in Colorado a few years back attempted to reduce some of the polarization in a city that housed a number of high-profile conservative Christian organizations but also a fair number of ideologically liberal and secular groups and individuals, by organizing supper clubs which brought representatives of both communities together with a prescribed series of discussion questions in hopes that each side could understand the other somewhat better. Obviously the Christians who participated had the opportunity to foster relationships that could extend beyond the period covered by the formal programme and hopefully lead to later opportunities for more explicit outreach.

Some writers even speak explicitly of 'hospitality evangelism', which regularly involves Christians inviting unbelievers to share meals with them (Noll and Price 1999). More than twenty years ago, Mortimer Arias (1982) wrote of the need to practice 'centripetal' as well as 'centrifugal' mission: that is, 'evangelization by hospitality'. The evangelical church, comparatively speaking, has done better in taking a holistic gospel abroad to diverse cultures than in reaching members of those cultures when they move to our countries, cities and neighbourhoods. We also somehow avoid prejudice more when we go to 'their turf' than when they come to ours. A surprising amount of that prejudice has to do with what foods we are willing to eat in which locales!

As I write these words in September 2004, America continues to occupy Iraq, despite the formal transition of power to an indigenous government. Violence and murder still occur daily. Individual Christian civilians and representatives of Christian relief and out-reach organizations are risking their lives not only to provide humanitarian aid for the 'enemy' but also to distance themselves in the perception of the Iraqi people from our government, to encourage local believers, and to plant seeds among unbelievers that may later ripen into Christian commitments. All kinds of ministry efforts throughout the Middle East (and among Middle Eastern refugees elsewhere, particularly in Europe) are labouring to demonstrate true Christian love and to refute the notion that the average American television-show export depicts what true Christianity involves when it portrays American wealth, consumption and sexual promiscuity! Even our multinational military coalition, despite the appalling scandals and abuse perpetrated by a small minority of American soldiers, includes numerous unsung heroes, many of them Christians, who are working hard to rebuild the country, befriend the people, model peacemaking and reconciliation, and share the gospel in culturally sensitive ways when appropriate occasions arise. The brother of a close friend of mine, a mid-level officer in the American army and a strong believer, this summer described to me some of the incredible work his troops performed in a city of over 100,000 people to help restore its infrastructure. Numerous friendships developed between coalition forces and the local Iraqis, and not a single person has died there as a casualty of the war. Not surprisingly, when he told me the name of the city I had never heard of it, and he assured me that no attention has ever been paid to it by the media! Once again, in almost all these contexts, eating together with people of other cultures forms an integral part of establishing goodwill and building trust. At a personal level, it also smooths the way for believing individuals to share their faith more explicitly.

The Christian futurologist Tom Sine (1999: 191–240) charts some of the most imaginative efforts around the English-speaking world in what he calls 'reinventing Christian life and community' and 'reinventing Christian mission' for this new millennium. Not surprisingly, a large number of these ventures place shared meals in the centre of their activity. A congregation in east London prepared a lavish feast in a festively decorated hall with a huge fruit and vegetable display, offering residents in its richly multicultural neighbourhood a dinner for only one pound sterling per person. As far as they know, this was the first time anyone has brought together the entire community. Participants were amazed and hoped that the experience could be repeated, even while being introduced to the church and its convictions. Parallels with the eschatological banquet come immediately to mind.

Another example from London involves 'twenty-somethings' reaching out to Caribbean young people in a neighbourhood pub. They created a reggae band to lead worship and invited the community to join them. People did not even realize, at first, that they were in a 'church' and, as a result, some are coming to Christ. In Auckland, New Zealand, two Christian men willing to break the mould rented a nightclub, set up what they called 'Parallel Universe', and produced multi-screen, multi-media presentations with a thoughtfully contextualized gospel message while patrons ate, drank and socialized.

Even more radically, small groups of Christians in various countries have created intentional communities in which groups of families and individuals live in proximity to one another, or even more communally. Sharing dinner regularly is often the most central way they keep in touch with one another for fellowship and common service, though the actual amount of shared activity and ministry can vary widely. Cooperative gardening for food may form an important portion of that additional activity. Practitioners have also recognized a link between shared meals and working for social justice. The co-founders of the Open Door Community in Atlanta, a residential Christian home for about thirty men and women who minister to prisoners and the homeless, comment: 'justice is important, but supper is essential.' After all, 'without supper, without love, without table companionship, justice can become [simply] a program that we *do* to other people' (cited in Pohl 1999: 74).

A DVD recording of a unique dialogue between evangelical pastor and founder of the Standing Together parachurch ministry in Utah Greg Johnson and Robert Millet, the Richard L. Evans Professor of Religious Understanding at Latter-day Saint-operated Brigham Young University, explains on its case, 'truth matters, people matter, relationships matter, lunch matters' (Johnson and Millet 2004), for exactly the same reason. The friendship between these two men began over lunch, and their ongoing conversations are nurtured over lunch as, among other things, they are forced to acknowledge their shared humanity despite their religious differences. They have also discovered far more points of common ground than they ever expected to find.

In the Majority World, such ventures move beyond creating optional new lifestyles and greater openness among individuals, at times making the difference between life and death for some people. A decade and a half ago I had the privilege of visiting and spending considerable time in various neighbourhoods in the slums of Lima, Peru, in which Christian clergy had helped to organize cooperative soup kitchens. The poor residents pooled their financial resources so that they could buy foodstuffs in bulk at considerably cheaper prices than they would have had to pay otherwise. The women set up a rota for helping to prepare a decent-sized, nourishing meal every day at midday for all in the community who needed it. Each participant paid a small amount for his or her lunch, but the sum was more meagre than what individuals would have had to pay to feed themselves or their families on their own. In the high Andes mountains outside Cuzco, also in Peru, we saw a similar rural enterprise, adjacent to the local church, involving the shared cultivation of fields for edible vegetables.

In other parts of the world, 'a growing number of bootstrap agricultural programs are being started to enable the poor to become more self-reliant in providing their supply of nutritious food. Vegetable gardens are being planted in vacant lots, rooftop tomato patches, and backyard beehives. Some 750 cities have community gardening programs' (Sine 1999: 230). Even in our developed countries the poor often need similar help. The Evangelical Lutheran Church in America established food banks for Chicago's urban poor that included various vegetables grown in wading pools on top of a parking garage near that city's largest airport. And in both developed and developing countries, the International Heifer Project enables families to raise small live-stock in order to become more self-supporting (Sine 1999: 230–231). While there are plenty of once-Christian organizations that have deteriorated into mere social-action agencies, those mentioned here, along with many others, continue to include a vibrant Christian witness in keeping with Jesus' own practice.[4]

I have assiduously avoided turning this study into yet one more work on the Last Supper and/or Lord's Supper. Yet perhaps a few brief remarks on this topic at the end of this volume may be permitted. The intention of Jesus and of first-generation Christians was not, in my opinion, to take all aspects of ritual ceremony out of religious life. It is true that the ethical teaching of the New Testament regularly applies terminology of Old Testament ritual metaphorically to moral arenas, but that does not mean that it jettisons all elements of symbolic routine. Anthropologists of religion have highlighted the ubiquity of such 'ritual' throughout the history of the world, whether or not it is always recognized or acknowledged as such, along with the positive, stabilizing role it plays in the lives or individuals and societies (see classically Eliade 1965). Of course, ritual can always deteriorate into mindless behaviour or be thought to convey the blessing of God or the gods automatically, at which point it is better labelled in *Religionsgeschichtliche* terminology as magic.

But with respect to the meals of the New Testament, instead of using the insights of this study to de-sacramentalize or play down the

---

[4] Of course, food need not form a part of every of outreach effort! If the point of Jesus' practice was to demonstrate surprising intimacy through table fellowship with people with whom his culture expected him not to associate, then faithful contextual-ization of his model today should consider other opportunities to do things together with people our societies deem outcasts or enemies. It is increasingly common in the United States for twenty-year-olds to bridge traditional ethnic barriers as they form study groups in universities, business partnerships in the workplace, and civic clubs for recreation and service. By their own admission, ageism remains a far greater problem than racism or ethnocentricity (Ballard 2004). The older university student who has already raised a family may find it as hard to fit in as the person of the wrong 'race' did a generation ago. Intentional Christian student ministry could target this kind of population as an unexpected example of the marginalized. The physically challenged, the hospitalized, and the elderly (and others) in need of assisted-care living are forgotten, ignored or stigmatized by people in almost every age group, particularly by virtue of the fact that they are hidden away. Yet individuals in these unhealthy circumstances often prove remarkably open to the gospel, even after years of hardened cynicism, especially when the messengers are first of all caring for their physical needs. Are we taking advantage of all the opportunities to minister in these arenas that we could?

role and significance of the Last Supper or Lord's Supper, it seems to me that the right application is to elevate the significance and 'sacramentalize' the role of other fellowship meals, *when Christians celebrate them intentionally for the sake of creating greater intimacy with fellow human beings or reconciling them to each other and to God.* In similar vein, the upshot of our research does not support the replacement of the Lord's Supper (as is the case in a tiny minority of Protestant churches) with church meals in which no bread and wine are ever consumed in conscious remembrance of the death of Jesus, in honour of the spiritual presence of the Risen Christ with his people as host at a table, and in anticipation of his return and re-enactment of his Last Supper at the eschatological banquet (or the wedding feast of the Lamb: Rev. 19:9).[5] Nor, as is more common in Protestant and especially evangelical circles, is the point to celebrate the Eucharist infrequently and as more of an afterthought to worship than a central part of it. Rather, churches should creatively consider ways in which the *agapē* meal or love-feast might be restored: an entire sacral meal culminating in the Lord's Supper.

One of the most personally moving examples of this that I have experienced took place years ago, when our Evangelical Free church in Deerfield, Illinois, arranged our fellowship hall to seat everyone who came to an evening service so that we would be divided into tables of about eight persons, each with a designated leader. After a simple meal, worship and a message, each table leader led in a brief reflection on the Lord's Supper. The people at each table then passed the elements to one another, pronouncing a blessing on each person in turn. A second example occurred just this summer in our Baptist church in the suburban Denver area. At an elders' meeting, in which several members whose terms had expired were rotating off while new members were rotating on, we shared a meal, discussed our business, and then gave the elements of Communion, one person at a time, to the person next to us. As we proceeded around the circle, each elder prayed out loud for the one sitting to his left to whom he had given the bread and wine, while also laying hands on him.

Of course, such creative celebrations require participants to recognize that no biblical text anywhere even remotely hints at limiting the administration or distribution of the elements to any category of

---

[5] For this tripartite understanding of the theology of the Last Supper and Lord's Supper, see esp. Marshall (1980), whose work on the topic has scarcely been improved on in the quarter century since its publication.

Christian: not to the ordained clergy; not to any particular office-holder; not even to one gender. 'Low church' Baptists, who have otherwise rejected the post-biblical superstructures erected to prevent the laity from performing numerous ecclesiastical tasks, somehow seem to have as much difficulty coming to grips with this last vestige of Roman Catholic canon law intruding into Protestantism as do 'high church' Anglicans. And so do all kinds of Christians in between.

On the other hand, to the extent that an *agapē* meal, complete with Lord's Supper, is celebrated in a context in which non-Christians (or Christians unwilling to share with the poor and needy in their midst) are present, those who do administer the table will need to exercise the identical precautions as at a more traditional Eucharist. The explicit and implicit warnings of 1 Cor. 11:17–34 and Jude 12 will have to be presented, so that people do not participate in the partaking of the bread and wine who should be refraining. There may be contexts in which this is a little more awkward than in a service involving only Communion, but to the extent that the sharing of the elements occurs at a discrete moment during the larger meal, the safeguards should not be insurmountable. And the Christian fellowship extended during the rest of the meal to those who refrain from the bread and wine may actually compensate for that exclusion, more than in a traditional worship service, where frequently little or no intimate interpersonal fellowship occurs. This may precisely have been the dynamic in Old Testament times, when the Passover meal was extended to certain 'outsiders' while at the same time preserving various boundaries (recall above, pp. 36–37, 47).

More than I expected when I first undertook the research for this project, as I repeatedly described to friends that I was investigating 'Jesus, Sinners and Table Fellowship' I would receive blank stares. 'So just what would that involve?' became a frequent rejoinder. As I would then explain several of the exegetical issues that this volume has explored, the lights would come on and interest would awaken. Almost always the next comment involved some contemporary application along the lines of one of the suggestions we have presented in this chapter. The relevance of the issue was suddenly recognized. If these final reflections on the possibilities for current Christian meals form the shortest and least systematic part of this study, then let readers 'take up the ball and run with it'. Our desperately lost and hurting world demands no less!

Bibliography

Abrahams, I. (1967), *Studies in Pharisaism and the Gospels*, New York: KTAV, repr. of 1924 ed.

Ackerman, S. (1989), 'A Marzeah in Ezekiel 8:7–13?' *HTR* 82: 267–281.

Aitken, K. T. (1986), *Proverbs*, Edinburgh: Saint Andrews; Philadelphia: Westminster.

Allen, L. C. (1976), *The Books of Joel, Obadiah, Jonah and Micah*, Grand Rapids: Eerdmans.

—— (1983), *Psalms 101 – 150*, Waco: Word.

—— (1990), *Ezekiel 20 – 48*, Dallas: Word.

Andersen, F. I. (1976), *Job*, Leicester and Downers Grove: IVP.

—— (1983), '2 (Slavonic Apocalypse of) Enoch', in J. H. Charlesworth (ed.), *Old Testament Pseudepigrapha*, vol. 1, 91–213, Garden City: Doubleday.

Anderson, A. A. (1972), *The Book of Psalms*, 2 vols, London: Marshall, Morgan & Scott, 1972; Grand Rapids: Eerdmans, 1981.

—— (1989), *2 Samuel*, Dallas: Word.

Appler, D. A. (1999), 'From Queen to Cuisine: Food Imagery in the Jezebel Narrative', *Semeia* 86: 55–71.

Arias, M. (1982), 'Centripetal Mission or Evangelization by Hospitality', *Missiology* 10: 69–81.

Asen, B. A. (1996), 'The Garlands of Ephraim: Isaiah 28:1–6 and the Marzeah', *JSOT* 71: 73–87.

Ashby, G. (1998), *Go Out and Meet God: A Commentary on the Book of Exodus*, Edinburgh: Handsel; Grand Rapids: Eerdmans.

Ashley, T. R. (1993), *The Book of Numbers*, Grand Rapids: Eerdmans.

Aus, R. (1988), *Water into Wine and the Beheading of John the Baptist*, Atlanta: Scholars.

Averbeck, R. E. (2003), 'Sacrifices and Offerings', in T. D. Alexander and D. W. Baker (eds.), *Dictionary of the Old Testament: Pentateuch*, 706–733, Leicester and Downers Grove: IVP.

Baarda, T. (1985), 'The Sentences of the Syriac Menander', in J. H. Charlesworth (ed.), *Old Testament Pseudepigrapha*, vol. 2, 583–606, Garden City: Doubleday.

Badian, E. (1972), *Publicans and Sinners: Private Enterprise in the Service of the Roman Republic*, Oxford: Blackwell; Ithaca: Cornell.

Bailey, K. E. (1976), *Poet and Peasant: A Literary-Cultural Approach to the Parables of Luke*, Grand Rapids: Eerdmans.

——— (1980), *Through Peasant Eyes: More Lucan Parables*, Grand Rapids: Eerdmans.

——— (1992), *Finding the Lost: Cultural Keys to Luke 15*, St. Louis: Concordia.

——— (2003), *Jacob and the Prodigal: How Jesus Retold Israel's Story*, Downers Grove: IVP.

Baldwin, J. G. (1978), *Daniel*, Leicester and Downers Grove: IVP.

——— (1984), *Esther*, Leicester and Downers Grove: IVP.

Ballard, R. (April 2004), 'Biblical Teaching on the Generations', Mission Hills Church, Greenwood Village, CO: Bridges Adult Sunday School Class.

Balsdon, J. P. V. D. (1979), *Romans and Aliens*, London: Duckworth; Chapel Hill, University of North Carolina Press.

Balz, H. and G. Schneider (eds.) (1990, 1991, 1993), *Exegetical Dictionary of the New Testament*, 3 vols, Grand Rapids and Cambridge: Eerdmans.

Bartchy, S. S. (2002), 'The Historical Jesus and Honor Reversal at the Table', in W. Stegemann, B. J. Malina and G. Theissen (eds.), *The Social Setting of Jesus and the Gospels*, 175–185, Minneapolis: Fortress.

Bauer, W. (ed.) (2000), *A Greek-English Lexicon of the New Testament and Other Early Christian Literature*, rev. and ed. F. W. Danker, W. F. Arndt and F. W. Gingrich, Chicago: University of Chicago Press.

Bechtel, L. M. (1999), 'Boundary Issues in Genesis 19.1–38', in H. C. Washington, S. L. Graham, and P. L. Thimmes (eds.), *Escaping Eden: New Feminist Perspectives on the Bible*, 22–40, Sheffield: SAP.

Bergant, D. (1994), 'An Anthropological Approach to Biblical Interpretation: The Passover Supper in Exodus 12:1–20 as a Case Study', *Semeia* 67: 43–62.

Bergen, R. D. (1996), *1, 2 Samuel*, Nashville: Broadman & Holman.

Berger, K. (1993), *Manna, Mehl und Sauerteig*, Stuttgart: Quell.

Bilde, P. (1998), 'The Common Meal in the Qumran-Essene Communities', in I. Nielsen and H. S. Nielsen (eds.), *Meals in a Social Context: Aspects of the Communal Meal in the Hellenistic and Roman World*, 145–166, Aarhus: Aarhus University Press.

Black, M. (1985), *The Book of Enoch, or, 1 Enoch*, Leiden: Brill.

Block, D. I. (1997, 1998), *The Book of Ezekiel*, 2 vols, Grand Rapids and Cambridge: Eerdmans.

——— (1999), *Judges, Ruth*, Nashville: Broadman & Holman.

Blomberg, C. L. (1986), 'The Miracles as Parables', in D. Wenham and C. Blomberg (eds.), *Gospel Perspectives*, vol. 6, 327–359, Sheffield: JSOT.

——— (1987), *The Historical Reliability of the Gospels*, Leicester and Downers Grove: IVP.

——— (1990), *Interpreting the Parables*, Downers Grove: InterVarsity Press; Leicester: Apollos.

——— (1992), *Matthew*, Nashville: Broadman.

——— (1994a), *1 Corinthians*, Grand Rapids: Zondervan.

——— (1994b), ' "Your Faith Has Made You Whole": The Evangelical Liberation Theology of Jesus', in J. B. Green and M. Turner (eds.), *Jesus of Nazareth: Lord and Christ*, 75–93, Carlisle: Paternoster; Grand Rapids: Eerdmans.

——— (1997), *Jesus and the Gospels: An Introduction and Survey*, Nashville: Broadman & Holman; Leicester: Apollos.

——— (1999), *Neither Poverty Nor Riches: A Biblical Theology of Possessions*, Leicester: Apollos; Downers Grove: InterVarsity Press.

——— (2001), *The Historical Reliability of John's Gospel: Issues and Commentary*, Leicester: Apollos; Downers Grove: InterVarsity Press.

——— (2002), 'The New Testament Definition of Heresy (or When Do Jesus and the Apostles Really Get Mad?)', *JETS* 45: 59–72.

——— (2005 forthcoming), 'Women in Ministry: A Complementarian Perspective', in J. R. Beck (ed.), *Two Views on Women in Ministry*, Grand Rapids: Zondervan, rev.

Blümner, H. (1966), *The Home Life of the Ancient Greeks*, New York: Cooper Square Publishers, rev.

Bock, D. L. (1994, 1996), *Luke*, 2 vols, Grand Rapids: Baker.

Bohnen, J. (2000), ' "Watch How You're Eating": Judas and Jesus and Table Manners: An Intertextual Reading of John 13:26, Matthew 26:23 and Sirach 31:12 – 32:13', *Scriptura* 74: 259–283.

Bolyki, J. (1998), *Jesu Tischgemeinschaften*, Tübingen: Mohr.

Booth, R. P. (1986), *Jesus and the Laws of Purity*, Sheffield: JSOT.

Borg, M. J. (1984), *Conflict, Holiness, and Politics in the Teaching of Jesus*, New York and Toronto: Mellen.

Bovon, F. (2002), *Luke 1*, Minneapolis: Fortress.

Braun, W. (1992), 'Symposium or Anti-Symposium? Reflections on Luke 14:1–24', *TJT* 8: 70–84.

——— (1995), *Feasting and Social Rhetoric in Luke 14*, Cambridge: Cambridge University Press.

Brawley, R. L. (1995), 'Table Fellowship: Bane and Blessing for the Historical Jesus', *PRS* 22: 13–31.

Breneman, M. (1993), *Ezra, Nehemiah, Esther*, Nashville: Broadman & Holman.

Brenner, A. (1999), 'The Food of Love: Gendered Food and Food Imagery in the Song of Songs', *Semeia* 86: 101–112.

Brownlee, W. H. (1986), *Ezekiel 1 – 19*, Waco: Word.

Brueggemann, W. (1968), 'Isaiah 55 and Deuteronomic Theology', *ZAW* 80: 191–203.

——— (1998), *Isaiah 1 – 39*, Louisville: WJKP.

——— (2000), *1 and 2 Kings*, Macon: Smyth & Helwys.

Budd, P. J. (1996), *Leviticus*, London: Marshall Pickering; Grand Rapids: Eerdmans.

Bultmann, R. (1971), *The Gospel of John*, Oxford: Blackwell; Philadelphia: Westminster.

Burchard, C. (1987), 'The Importance of Joseph and Aseneth for the Study of the New Testament: A General Survey and a Fresh Look at the Lord's Supper', *NTS* 33: 102–134.

Burkert, W. (1991), 'Oriental Symposia: Contrasts and Parallels', in W. J. Slater (ed.), *Dining in a Classical Context*, 7–24, Ann Arbor: University of Michigan Press.

Bush, F. (1996), *Ruth, Esther*, Dallas: Word.

Byrne, B. (2000), *The Hospitality of God: A Reading of Luke's Gospel*, Collegeville: Liturgical.

Campbell, C. C. (2003), *Stations of the Banquet: Faith Foundations for Food Justice*, Collegeville: Liturgical.

Carroll, M. P. (1985), 'One More Time: Leviticus Revisited', in B. Lang (ed.), *Anthropological Approaches to the Old Testament*, 117–126, Philadelphia: Fortress.

Carroll, R. P. (1999), 'YHWH's Sour Grapes: Images of Food and Drink in the Prophetic Discourses of the Hebrew Bible', *Semeia* 86: 113–131.

Carroll R., M. D. (1992), *Contexts for Amos: Prophetic Poetics in Latin American Perspective*, Sheffield: JSOT.

——— (2002), *Amos – The Prophet and His Oracles*, Louisville and London: WJKP.

Carter, W. (1996), 'Getting Martha Out of the Kitchen: Luke 10:38–42 Again', *CBQ* 58: 264–280.

Cassuto, U. (1967), *A Commentary on the Book of Exodus*, Jerusalem: Magnes.

Charlesworth, J. H. (ed.) (1983, 1985), *The Old Testament Pseudepigrapha*, 2 vols, Garden City: Doubleday.

Charlesworth, J. H. and J. A. Sanders (1985), 'More Psalms of David', in J. H. Charlesworth (ed.), *Old Testament Pseudepigrapha*, vol. 2, 609–624, Garden City: Doubleday.

Chesnutt, R. D. (1989), 'Bread of Life in Joseph and Aseneth and in John 6', in J. E. Priest (ed.), *Johannine Studies*, 1–16, Malibu: Pepperdine University Press.

Childs, B. S. (2001), *Isaiah*, Louisville: WJKP.

Chilton, B. (1988), 'Jesus and the Repentance of E. P. Sanders', *TynB* 39: 1–18.

——— (1992), 'The Purity of the Kingdom as Conveyed in Jesus' Meals', *SBL Seminar Papers* 31: 473–488.

——— (2000), *Rabbi Jesus: An Intimate Biography*, New York and London: Doubleday.

Christiansen, E. J. (1998), 'The Consciousness of Belonging to God's Covenant and What It Entails according to the Damascus Document and the Community Rule', in F. H. Cryer and T. L. Thompson (eds.), *Qumran Between the Old and New Testaments*, 69–97, Sheffield: SAP.

Clifford, R. J. (1999), *Proverbs: A Commentary*, Louisville and London: WJKP.

Clines, D. J. A. (1984), *Ezra, Nehemiah, Esther*, London: Marshall, Morgan & Scott; Grand Rapids: Eerdmans.

Collins, J. J. (2000), 'Enoch, Books of', in C. A. Evans and S. E. Porter (eds.), *Dictionary of New Testament Background*, 313–318, Downers Grove and Leicester: IVP.

Cooper, F. and S. Morris (1990), 'Dining in Round Buildings', in O. Murray (ed.), *Sympotica: A Symposium on the* Symposion, 66–85, Oxford: Clarendon.

Cooper, L. E. Sr (1994), *Ezekiel*, Nashville: Broadman & Holman.

Corley, K. E. (1993a), 'Jesus' Table Practice: Dining with "Tax

Collectors and Sinners", Including Women', *SBL Seminar Papers* 32: 444–459.

———(1993b), *Private Women, Public Meals: Social Conflict and Women in the Synoptic Tradition*, Peabody: Hendrickson.

———(2002), *Women and the Historical Jesus: Feminist Myths of Christian Origins*, Santa Rosa: Polebridge.

Crawford, S. W. (2000), *The Temple Scroll and Related Texts*, Sheffield: SAP.

Crenshaw, J. L. (1987), *Ecclesiastes: A Commentary*, Philadelphia: Westminster.

Crossan, J. D. (1991), *The Historical Jesus: The Life of a Mediterranean Jewish Peasant*, San Francisco: HarperSanFrancisco.

———(1994), *Jesus: A Revolutionary Biography*, San Francisco: HarperSanFrancisco.

Dahood, M. (1965), *Psalms I: 1 – 50*, Garden City: Doubleday.

Danby, H. (ed.) (1933), *The Mishnah*, London: Oxford University Press.

Davidson, R. (1998), *The Vitality of Worship: A Commentary on the Book of Psalms*, Edinburgh: Handsel; Grand Rapids: Eerdmans.

Davies, P. R. (1999), 'Food, Drink and Sects: The Question of Ingestion in the Qumran Texts', *Semeia* 86: 151–163.

Davies, W. D. and D. C. Allison Jr (1988, 1991, 1997), *A Critical and Exegetical Commentary on the Gospel according to St Matthew*, 3 vols, Edinburgh: T. & T. Clark.

Davis, E. C. (1967), 'The Significance of the Shared Meal in Luke-Acts', PhD dissertation, Southern Baptist Theological Seminary, Louisville.

Decker, R. J. (2001), *Temporal Deixis of the Greek Verb in the Gospel of Mark with Reference to Verbal Aspect*, New York: Peter Lang.

Deines, R. (2001), 'The Pharisees Between "Judaisms" and "Common Judaism"', in D. A. Carson, P. T. O'Brien, and M. A. Seifrid (eds.), *Justification and Variegated Nomism*, vol. 1, 443–504, Tübingen: Mohr; Grand Rapids: Baker.

De Meeus, X. (1961), 'Composition de Lc., xiv, et genre symposiaque', *ETL* 37: 847–870.

Denaux, A. (1999), 'The Theme of Divine Visits and Human (In)hospitality in Luke-Acts: Its Old Testament and Graeco-Roman Antecedents', in J. Verhuyden (ed.), *The Unity of Luke-Acts*, 255–279, Leuven: LUP and Peeters.

Derrett, J. D. M. (1970), *Law in the New Testament*, London: Darton, Longman & Todd.

DeVries, S. J. (1997), 'Festival Ideology in Chronicles', in H. T. C. Sun and K. L. Eads (eds.), *Problems in Biblical Theology*, 104–124, Grand Rapids: Eerdmans.

Donahue, J. R. (1971), 'Tax Collectors and Sinners: An Attempt at Identification', *CBQ* 33: 39–61.

Douglas, M. (1966), *Purity and Danger: An Analysis of the Concepts of Pollution and Taboo*, New York: Praeger.

———(1975), *Implicit Meanings: Essays in Anthropology*, London: Routledge and Kegan Paul.

Duguid, I. M. (1999), *Ezekiel*, Grand Rapids: Zondervan.

Duke, R. K. (1980), 'Toward an Understanding of Hospitality in the Old Testament', MCS thesis, Regent College, Vancouver.

Dunn, J. D. G. (1990), 'Pharisees, Sinners, and Jesus', in *Jesus, Paul and the Law: Studies in Mark and Galatians*, 61–88, London: SPCK; Louisville: WJKP.

———(1992), 'Jesus, Table-Fellowship, and Qumran', in J. H. Charlesworth (ed.), *Jesus and the Dead Sea Scrolls*, 254–272, New York and London: Doubleday.

———(2003), *Jesus Remembered*, Grand Rapids and Cambridge: Eerdmans.

Dupont, F. (1999), 'De l'ous à la comme: La *cena* romaine', in J.-L. Slandrin and J. Cobbi (eds.), *Tables d'hier, tables d'ailleurs: Histoire et ethnologie du repas*, 59–85, Paris: Odile Jacob.

Durham, J. I. (1987), *Exodus*, Waco: Word.

Eaton, M. A. (1983), *Ecclesiastes*, Leicester and Downers Grove: IVP.

Edwards, J. R. (2002), *The Gospel according to Mark*, Grand Rapids: Eerdmans; Leicester: Inter-Varsity Press.

Eisenman, R. H. and M. Wise (1992), *The Dead Sea Scrolls Uncovered*, Shaftesbury, Dorset; Rockport, MA: Element.

Elgvin, T. (2000), 'Wisdom and Apocalypticism in the Early Second Century BCE – The Evidence of 4QInstruction', in L. H. Schiffman, E. Tov, and J. C. Vanderkam (eds.), *The Dead Sea Scrolls, Fifty Years after their Discovery*, 226–247, Jerusalem: Israel Exploration Society.

Eliade, M. (1965), *Rites and Symbols of Initiation*, New York: Harper & Row, rev.

Elliott, J. H. (1991), 'Household and Meals vs. Temple Purity Replication Patterns in Luke-Acts', *BTB* 21: 102–108.

Enns, P. (2000), *Exodus*, Grand Rapids: Zondervan.

Eshel, H. and E. Eshel (2000), '4Q448, Psalm 154 (Syriac), Sirach 48:20, and 4QpIsa^a', *JBL* 119: 645–659.

Esler, P. F. (1987), *Community and Gospel in Luke-Acts*, Cambridge: Cambridge University Press.

Evans, C. A. and P. W. Flint (eds.) (1997), *Eschatology, Messianism, and the Dead Sea Scrolls*, Grand Rapids and Cambridge: Eerdmans.

Evans, C. F. (1990), *Saint Luke*, London: SCM; Philadelphia: Trinity.

Evans, M. J. (2000), *1 and 2 Samuel*, Peabody: Hendrickson; Carlisle: Paternoster.

Farmer, W. R. (1978), 'Who Are the "Tax Collectors and Sinners"' in the Synoptic Tradition?' in D. Y. Hadidian (ed.), *From Faith to Faith*, 167–174, Pittsburgh: Pickwick.

Feeley-Harnik, G. (1981), *The Lord's Table: Eucharist and Passover in Early Christianity*, Philadelphia: University of Pennsylvania Press.

Fensham, F. C. (1982), *The Books of Ezra and Nehemiah*, Grand Rapids: Eerdmans.

Fiedler, P. (1976), *Jesus und die Sünder*, Frankfurt and Bern: Lang.

Finley, T. J. (1990), *Joel, Amos, Obadiah*, Chicago: Moody.

Firmage, E. (1990), 'The Biblical Dietary Laws and the Concept of Holiness', in J. A. Emerton (ed.), *Studies in the Pentateuch*, 177–208, Leiden: Brill.

Fisher, N. R. E. (1988a), 'Greek Associations, Symposia, and Clubs', in M. R. Grant and M. R. Kitzinger (eds.), *Civilization of the Ancient Mediterranean: Greece and Rome*, vol. 2, 1167–1197, New York: Charles Scribner's Sons.

——— (1988b), 'Roman Associations, Dinner Parties and Clubs', in M. R. Grant and M. R. Kitzinger (eds.), *Civilization of the Ancient Mediterranean: Greece and Rome*, vol. 2, 1199–1225, New York: Charles Scribner's Sons.

Fitzmyer, J. A. (1981, 1985), *The Gospel according to Luke*, 2 vols, Garden City: Doubleday.

Fleishman, J. (1998), 'An Echo of Optimism in Ezra 6:19–22', *HUCA* 69: 15–29.

Flusser, D. (1988), *Judaism and the Origins of Christianity*, Jerusalem: Magnes.

Ford, J. M. (1984), *My Enemy is My Guest: Jesus and Violence in Luke*, Maryknoll: Orbis.

France, R. T. (1985), *The Gospel according to Matthew*, Leicester: Inter-Varsity Press; Grand Rapids: Eerdmans.

——— (2002), *The Gospel of Mark*, Carlisle: Paternoster; Grand Rapids: Eerdmans.

Franzmann, M. (1992), 'Of Food, Bodies, and the Boundless Reign of God in the Synoptic Gospels', *Pacifica* 5: 17–31.

Fretheim, T. E. (1999), *First and Second Kings*, Louisville and London: WJKP.

Freyne, S. (2000), *Galilee and Gospel: Collected Essays*, Tübingen: Mohr; Leiden: Brill, 2002.

Fyall, R. S. (2002), *Now My Eyes Have Seen You: Images of Creation and Evil in the Book of Job*, Downers Grove and Leicester: IVP.

García Martínez, F. and E. J. C. Tigchelaar (eds.) (1997, 1998), *The Dead Sea Scrolls: Study Edition*, 2 vols, Leiden: Brill; Grand Rapids and Cambridge: Eerdmans.

Garland, D. E. (1993), *Reading Matthew*, New York: Crossroad.

Garnsey, P. (1999), *Food and Society in Classical Antiquity*, Cambridge: Cambridge University Press.

Garrett, D. A. (1993), *Proverbs, Ecclesiastes, Song of Songs*, Nashville: Broadman & Holman.

——— (1997), *Hosea, Joel*, Nashville: Broadman & Holman.

Gibson, J. (1981), '*Hoi telōnai kai hai pornai*', *JTS* 32: 429–433.

Gnilka, J. (1997), *Jesus of Nazareth: Message and History*, Peabody: Hendrickson.

Goldingay, J. E. (1989), *Daniel*, Dallas: Word.

——— (2001), *Isaiah*, Peabody: Hendrickson; Carlisle: Paternoster.

Goldstein, J. A. (1976), *1 Maccabees*, Garden City: Doubleday.

Gordon, R. P. (1986), *I and II Samuel*, Grand Rapids: Zondervan; Exeter: Paternoster.

Graham, M. P. (1999), 'Setting the Heart to Seek God: Worship in 2 Chronicles 30:1 – 31:7', in M. P. Graham, R. R. Marrs, and S. L. McKenzie (eds.), *Worship and the Hebrew Bible*, 124–141, Sheffield: SAP.

Green, J. B. (1997), *The Gospel of Luke*, Grand Rapids and Cambridge: Eerdmans.

——— (2003), 'Which Conversation Shall We Have? History, Historicism and Historical Narrative in Theological Interpretation: A Response to Peter van Inwagen', in C. Bartholomew, C. S. Evans, M. Healy and M. Rae (eds.), *'Behind' the Text: History and Biblical Interpretation*, 141–150, Carlisle: Paternoster; Grand Rapids: Zondervan.

Grimm, V. (1996), *From Feasting to Fasting, The Evolution of a Sin: Attitudes to Food in Late Antiquity*, London and New York: Routledge.

Guelich, R. A. (1989), *Mark 1 – 8:26*, Dallas: Word.

Gundry, R. H. (1982), *Matthew: A Commentary on His Literary and Theological Art*, Grand Rapids: Eerdmans.

—— (1993), *Mark: A Commentary on His Apology for the Cross*, Grand Rapids: Eerdmans.

Hadas, M. (1953), *The Third and Fourth Books of Maccabees*, New York: Harper and Brothers.

Hagner, D. A. (1993, 1995), *Matthew*, 2 vols, Dallas: Word.

Hamilton, V. P. (1990, 1995), *The Book of Genesis*, 2 vols, Grand Rapids: Eerdmans.

Hamm, D. (1991), 'Zacchaeus Revisited Once More: A Story of Vindication or Conversion?' *Bib* 72: 249–252.

Harrelson, W. (1994), 'Isaiah 35 in Recent Research and Translation', in S. E. Ballantine and J. Barton (eds.), *Language, Theology, and the Bible*, 247–260, Oxford: Clarendon.

Harrington, H. K. (1997), 'Holiness in the Laws of 4QMMT', in M. Bernstein, F. García Martínez, and J. Kampen (eds.), *Legal Texts and Legal Issues: Proceedings of the Second Meeting of the International Organization for Qumran Studies*, 109–128, Leiden: Brill.

Hartley, J. E. (1988), *The Book of Job*, Grand Rapids: Eerdmans.

—— (1992), *Leviticus*, Dallas: Word.

Hempel, C. (1997), 'Qumran Communities: Beyond the Fringes of Second Temple Society', in S. E. Porter and C. A. Evans (eds.), *The Scrolls and the Scriptures: Qumran Fifty Years After*, 43–53, Sheffield: SAP.

Hengel, M. and R. Deines (1995), 'E. P. Sanders' "Common Judaism", Jesus, and the Pharisees', *JTS* 46: 1–70.

Herrenbrück, F. (1981), 'Wer waren die Zöllner?' *ZNW* 72: 178–194.

—— (1987), 'Zum Vorwurf der Kollaboration des Zöllners mit Rom', *ZNW* 78: 186–199.

—— (1990), *Jesus und die Zöllner: Historische und neutestamentlich-exegetische Untersuchungen*, Tübingen: Mohr.

Hertzberg, H. W. (1964), *I and II Samuel*, London: SCM; Philadelphia: Westminster.

Hobbs, T. R. (1985), *2 Kings*, Waco: Word.

—— (1993), 'Man, Woman, and Hospitality – 2 Kings 4:8–36', *BTB* 23: 91–100.

—— (2001), 'Hospitality in the First Testament and the "Teleological Fallacy"', *JSOT* 95: 3–30.

Hofius, O. (1967), *Jesu Tischgemeinschaft mit den Sündern*, Stuttgart: Calwer.

Holgate, D. A. (1999), *Prodigality, Liberality and Meanness: The Prodigal Son in Greco-Roman Perspective*, Sheffield: SAP.

Holm-Nielsen, S. (1960), *Hodayot: Psalms from Qumran*, Aarhus: Universitetsforlaget.

Hooker, M. D. (1991), *The Gospel according to St. Mark*, London: Black; Peabody: Hendrickson.

Horsley, R. A. (1987), *Jesus and the Spiral of Violence*, San Francisco: Harper and Row.

House, P. R. (1995), *1, 2 Kings*, Nashville: Broadman & Holman.

Houston, W. (1993), *Purity and Monotheism: Clean and Unclean Animals in Biblical Law*, Sheffield: JSOT.

Hubbard, D. A. (1989), *Joel and Amos*, Leicester and Downers Grove: IVP.

Hubbard, R. L. Jr (1988), *The Book of Ruth*, Grand Rapids: Eerdmans.

——— (1991), *First and Second Kings*, Chicago: Moody.

Hultgren, A. J. (1979), *Jesus and His Adversaries: The Form and Function of the Conflict Stories in the Synoptic Tradition*, Minneapolis: Augsburg.

Ishida, T. (1987), 'Adonijah, The Son of Haggith and His Supporters: An Inquiry into Problems about History and Historiography', in R. E. Friedman and H. G. M. Williamson (eds.), *The Future of Biblical Studies: The Hebrew Scriptures*, 165–187, Atlanta: Scholars.

Jenks, A. W. (1993), 'Eating and Drinking in the Old Testament', in D. N. Freedman (ed.), *Anchor Bible Dictionary*, vol. 2, 250–254, New York and London: Doubleday.

Jeremias, J. (1931), 'Zöllner und Sünder', *ZNW* 30: 293–300.

——— (1969), *Jerusalem in the Time of Jesus*, London: SCM; Philadelphia: Fortress.

Jobes, K. H. (1999), *Esther*, Grand Rapids: Zondervan.

Johnson, A. (2002), 'Our God Reigns: The Body of the Risen Lord in Luke 24', *WW* 22: 133–143.

Johnson, G. and R. Millet (2004), 'A Mormon and an Evangelical in Conversation', Provo: CD-ROM.

Joncas, J. M. (2000), 'Tasting the Kingdom of God: The Meal Ministry of Jesus and Its Implications for Contemporary Worship', *Worship* 74: 329–365.

Jones, I. (2003), *The Apocrypha*, Werrington, Peterborough: Epworth.

Juengst, S. C. (1992), *Breaking Bread: The Spiritual Significance of Food*, Louisville and London: WJKP.

Just, A. A. Jr (1993), *The Ongoing Feast: Table Fellowship and Eschatology at Emmaus*, Collegeville: Liturgical.

Kaiser, W. C. Jr (1979), *Ecclesiastes: Total Life*, Chicago: Moody.

Kamell, M. (June 2004), 'Scum of the Earth Newsletter', Denver: privately circulated.

Karris, R. J. (1985), *Luke: Artist and Theologian*, New York: Paulist.

Kayama, H. (1997), 'Christianity as Table Fellowship', in D. J. Adams (ed.), *From East to West*, 51–62, Lanham: UPA.

Kee, H. C. (1996), 'Jesus: A Glutton and a Drunkard', *NTS* 42: 374–393.

Keener, C. S. (1999), *A Commentary on the Gospel of Matthew*, Grand Rapids and Cambridge: Eerdmans.

——— (2003), *The Gospel of John*, 2 vols, Peabody: Hendrickson.

Kelley, R. L. (1995), 'Meals with Jesus in Luke's Gospel', *HBT* 17: 123–131.

Kidner, D. (1964), *Proverbs*, Leicester and Downers Grove: IVP.

——— (1973, 1975), *Psalms*, 2 vols, Leicester and Downers Grove: IVP.

——— (1976), *The Message of Ecclesiastes: A Time to Mourn and a Time to Dance*, Leicester and Downers Grove: IVP.

Kieweler, H. V. (1998), 'Benehmen bei Tisch', in R. Egger-Wenzel and I. Krammer (eds.), *Der Einzelne und seine Gemeinschaft bei Ben Sira*, 191–215, Berlin: de Gruyter.

Kilgallen, J. J. (1985), 'John the Baptist, the Sinful Woman, and the Pharisee', *JBL* 104: 675–679.

——— (1992), 'A Suggestion Regarding *gar* in Luke 10:42', *Bib* 73: 255–258.

——— (1998), 'Forgiveness of Sins (Luke 7:36–50)', *NovT* 40: 105–116.

——— (1999), 'Luke 7:41–42 and Forgiveness of Sins', *ET* 111: 46–47.

——— (2001), 'Faith and Forgiveness: Luke 7:36–50', *RB* 108: 214–227.

King, P. J. (1988), 'Using Archaeology to Interpret a Biblical Text: The Marzeah Amos Denounces', *BAR* 14.4: 34–44.

——— (1998), 'Commensality in the Biblical World', in J. Magness and S. Gitin (eds.), *Hesed Ve-Emet*, 53–62, Atlanta: Scholars.

King, P. J. and L. E. Stager (2001), *Life in Biblical Israel*, Louisville and London: WJKP.

Kinukawa, H. (1994), *Women and Jesus in Mark*, Maryknoll: Orbis.

Klein, R. W. (1983), *1 Samuel*, Waco: Word.

Klinghardt, M. (1996), *Gemeinschaftsmahl und Mahlgemeinschaft: Soziologie und Liturgie frühchristlicher Mahlfeiern*, Tübingen: Francke.

Klosinski, L. E. (1998), 'The Meals in Mark', PhD dissertation, Claremont Graduate School, Claremont, CA.

Knibb, M. A. (1987), *The Qumran Community*, Cambridge: Cambridge University Press.

Knoppers, G. N. (1995), 'Aaron's Calf and Jeroboam's Calves', in A. B. Beck (ed.), *Fortunate the Eyes That See*, Grand Rapids: Eerdmans.

Koenig, J. (1985), *New Testament Hospitality: Partnership with Strangers as Promise and Mission*, Philadelphia: Fortress.

Kollmann, B. (1990), *Ursprung und Gestalt in der frühchristlichen Mahlfeier*, Göttingen: Vandenhoeck und Ruprecht.

Koptak, P. E. (2003), *Proverbs*, Grand Rapids: Zondervan.

Kruse, C. (2003), *The Gospel according to John*, Leicester: Inter-Varsity Press, 2003; Grand Rapids: Eerdmans, 2004.

Kügler, J. (1998), 'Der König als Brotspender', *ZNW* 89: 118–124.

Kuhn, K. G. (1957), 'The Lord's Supper and the Communal Meal at Qumran', in K. Stendahl (ed.), *The Scrolls and the New Testament*, 65–93, London: SCM; New York: Harper and Brothers.

Lamb, W. R. M., intro. and trans. (1975), *Plato*, vol. 3, London: Heinemann; Cambridge: Harvard University Press.

Lane, W. L. (1974), *The Gospel according to Mark*, Grand Rapids: Eerdmans.

Langley, W. E. (1996), 'The Parable of the Two Sons (Matthew 21:28–32) against Its Semitic and Rabbinic Backdrop', *CBQ* 58: 228–243.

Lee, D. (1996), 'Women as "Sinners" ', *ABR* 44: 1–15.

Levenson, J. D. (1997), *Esther: A Commentary*, Louisville: WJKP.

Levine, B. (2000), 'The Land of Milk and Honey', *JSOT* 87: 43–57.

Lindars, B. (1972), *The Gospel of John*, London: Marshall, Morgan & Scott, 1972; Grand Rapids: Eerdmans, 1981.

Lissarrague, F. (1990), *The Aesthetics of the Greek Banquet: Images of Wine and Ritual*, Princeton: Princeton University Press.

Lohfink, N. (1990), 'Qoheleth 5:17–19 – Revelation by Joy', *CBQ* 52: 625–635.

Long, J. C. Jr (2002), *1 and 2 Kings*, Joplin: College Press.

Longman, T. III (1998), *The Book of Ecclesiastes*, Grand Rapids and Cambridge: Eerdmans.

——— (1999), *Daniel*, Grand Rapids: Zondervan.

Louw, J. P. and Nida, E. A. (1988), *A Greek-English Lexicon of the New Testament Based on Semantic Domains*, 2 vols, New York: UBS.

Love, S. L. (1995), 'Women and Men at Hellenistic Symposia Meals in Luke', in P. F. Esler (ed.), *Modeling Early Christianity*, 198–210, London and New York: Routledge.

Marcus, J. (2000), *Mark 1 – 8*, New York and London: Doubleday.

Marshall, I. H. (1978), *The Gospel of Luke*, Exeter: Paternoster; Grand Rapids: Eerdmans.

——— (1980), *Last Supper and Lord's Supper*, Exeter: Paternoster; Grand Rapids: Eerdmans.

——— (1988), *Luke: Historian and Theologian*, Exeter: Paternoster; Grand Rapids: Zondervan, rev.

Mathews, K. A. (1996), *Genesis 1 – 11:26*, Nashville: Broadman & Holman.

Matthews, V. H. (1991), 'Hospitality and Hostility in Judges 4', *BTB* 21: 13–21.

——— (1992), 'Hospitality and Hostility in Genesis 19 and Judges 19', *BTB* 22: 3–11.

May, D. M. (1993), 'Mark 2:15: The Home of Jesus or Levi?', *NTS* 39: 147–149.

McGowan, A. (1997), 'Naming the Feast: The *Agapē* and the Diversity of Early Christian Meals', in E. A. Livingstone (ed.), *Studia Patristica XXX*, 314–318, Leuven: LUP and Peeters.

McKinlay, J. E. (1999), 'To Eat or Not to Eat: Where Is Wisdom in This Choice?', *Semeia* 86: 73–84.

McMahan, C. T. (1987), 'Meals as Type-Scenes in the Gospel of Luke', PhD dissertation, Southern Baptist Theological Seminary, Louisville.

Mendels, D. (1979), 'Hellenistic Utopia and the Essenes', *HTR* 72: 207–222.

Metzger, B. M. (ed.) (1977), *The Apocrypha of the Old Testament (RSV)*, Oxford and New York: Oxford University Press.

Miller, G. T. (1995), 'Isaiah 25:6–9', *Int* 49: 175–178.

Miller, M. (1991), 'Foreigners at the Greek Symposium?' in W. J. Slater (ed.), *Dining in a Classical Context*, 59–81, Ann Arbor: University of Michigan Press.

Miller, S. R. (1994), *Daniel*, Nashville: Broadman & Holman.

Mitchell, A. C. (1991), 'The Use of *sykophantein* in Luke 19:8: Further Evidence for Zacchaeus's Defense', *Bib* 72: 546–547.

Montague, G. T. (1989), *Companion God: A Cross-Cultural Comment-ary on the Gospel of Matthew*, New York: Paulist.

Moore, C. A. (1977), *Daniel, Esther, and Jeremiah: The Additions*, Garden City: Doubleday.

—— (1985), *Judith*, Garden City: Doubleday.

—— (1996), *Tobit*, New York and London: Doubleday.

Moritz, T. (1996), 'Dinner Talk and Ideology in Luke: The Role of the Sinners', *EJT* 5: 47–69.

Morris, L. (1992), *The Gospel according to Matthew*, Grand Rapids: Eerdmans; Leicester: Inter-Varsity Press.

Mosca, F. (1985), 'Meals in the Gospels and Their Old Testament and Jewish Antecedents', MTh thesis, Andrews University, Berrien Springs, MI.

Moshala, J. (2001), 'Categorization and Evaluation of Different Kinds of Interpretation of the Laws of Clean and Unclean Animals in Leviticus 11', *BR* 46: 5–41.

Motyer, J. A. (1993), *The Prophecy of Isaiah: An Introduction and Commentary*, Leicester and Downers Grove: IVP.

—— (1999), *Isaiah*, Leicester and Downers Grove: IVP.

Moxnes, H. (1986), 'Meals and the New Community in Luke', *SEÅ* 51: 158–167.

Murphy, R. (1992), *Ecclesiastes*, Dallas: Word.

—— (1998), *Proverbs*, Nashville: Nelson.

Myers, J. M. (1974), *I and II Esdras*, Garden City: Doubleday.

Nangle, J. (1996), 'The Breaking of Bread (Luke 24)', *Sojourners* 25 (November–December): 49.

Nave, G. D. (2002), *The Role and Function of Repentance in Luke-Acts*, Atlanta: SBL; Leiden: Brill.

Neale, D. A. (1991), *None But the Sinners: Religious Categories in the Gospel of Luke*, Sheffield: JSOT.

Neufeld, D. (2000), 'Jesus' Eating Transgressions and Social Impro-priety in the Gospel of Mark: A Social Scientific Approach', *BTB* 30: 15–26.

Neusner, J. (1982), 'Two Pictures of the Pharisees: Philosophical Circle or Eating Club', *ATR* 64: 525–538.

—— (1991), 'Mr. Sanders' Pharisees and Mine', *SJT* 44: 73–95.

Newton, M. (1985), *The Concept of Purity at Qumran and the Letters of Paul*, Cambridge: Cambridge University Press.

Neyrey, J. H. (1991), 'Ceremonies in Luke-Acts: The Case of Meals and Table-Fellowship', in J. H. Neyrey (ed.), *The Social World of Luke-Acts: Models for Interpretation*, 361–387, Peabody: Hendrickson.

———(1996), 'Meals, Food, and Table Fellowship', in R. Rohrbaugh (ed.), *The Social Sciences and New Testament Interpretation*, 159–182, Peabody: Hendrickson.

Nicol, G. G. (1996), 'The Narrative Structure and Interpretation of Genesis xxvi 1–33', *VT* 46: 339–360.

Nitzan, B. (2000), 'The Idea of Holiness in Qumran Poetry and Liturgy', in D. K. Falk, F. García Martínez, and E. M. Schuller (eds.), *Sapiential, Liturgical and Poetical Texts from Qumran*, Leiden: Brill.

Noll, P. and M. Price (1999), *Hospitality Evangelism: Sharing the Bread of Life*, Atlanta: CBF.

Nolland, J. (1989, 1993a, 1993b), *Luke*, 3 vols, Dallas: Word.

North, J. L. (1997), '*oligōn de estin chreia ē henos* (Luke 10:42): Text, Subtext and Context', *JSNT* 66: 3–13.

Noy, D. (1998), 'The Sixth Hour is the Mealtime for Scholars: Jewish Meals in the Roman World', in I. Nielsen and H. S. Nielsen (eds.), *Meals in a Social Context*, 134–144, Aarhus: Aarhus University Press.

Odeberg, H. (1973), *3 Enoch or the Hebrew Book of Enoch*, New York: KTAV.

Oden, A. G. (ed.) (2001), *And You Welcomed Me: A Sourcebook on Hospitality in Early Christianity*, Nashville: Abingdon.

Ogden, G. S. (1979), 'Qoheleth's Use of the "Nothing is Better"-Form', *JBL* 98: 339–350.

Oswalt, J. N. (1986, 1998), *The Book of Isaiah*, 2 vols, Grand Rapids and Cambridge: Eerdmans.

O'Toole, R. F. (1991), 'The Literary Form of Luke 19:1–10', *JBL* 110: 107–116.

Overman, J. A. (1996), *Church and Community in Crisis: The Gospel according to Matthew*, Valley Forge: Trinity.

Pantel, P. S. (1999), 'Manger entre citoyens: Les repas dans les cités grecques antiques', in J.-L. Slandrin and J. Cobbi (eds.), *Tables d'hier, tables d'ailleurs: histoire et ethnologie du repas*, 39–57, Paris: Odile Jacob.

Parsons, M. C. (2001), ' "Short in Stature": Luke's Physical Description of Zacchaeus', *NTS* 47: 50–57.

Paul, G. (1991), 'Symposia and *Deipna* in Plutarch's *Lives* and in Other Historical Writings', in W. J. Slater (ed.), *Dining in a Classical Context*, 157–169, Ann Arbor: University of Michigan Press.

Perrin, N. (1967), *Rediscovering the Teaching of Jesus*, New York: Harper & Row; London: SCM.

Pervo, R. I. (1985), 'Wisdom and Power: Petronius' *Satyricon* and the Social World of Early Christianity', *ATR* 67: 307–325.

——— (1994), '*Panta Koina*: The Feeding Stories in the Light of Economic Data and Social Practice', in L. Bormann, K. del Tredici, and A. Standhartinger (eds.), *Religious Propaganda and Missionary Competition in the New Testament World*, 163–194, Leiden: Brill.

Pilgrim, W. E. (1981), *Good News to the Poor*, Minneapolis: Augsburg.

Pohl, C. D. (1999), *Making Room: Recovering Hospitality as a Christian Tradition*, Grand Rapids and Cambridge: Eerdmans.

Polaski, S. H. (1999), 'Identifying the Unnamed Disciple: An Exercise in Reader-Response Criticism', *PRS* 26: 193–202.

Poon, W. C. K. (2003), 'Superabundant Table Fellowship in the Kingdom: The Feeding of the Five Thousand and the Meal Motif in Luke', *ET* 114: 224–230.

Pope, M. H. (1972), 'A Divine Banquet at Ugarit', in J. Efird (ed.), *The Use of the Old Testament in the New*, 170–203, Durham: Duke.

Porter, S. E. (1992), *Idioms of the Greek New Testament*, Sheffield: JSOT.

Priest, J. F. (1963), 'The Messiah and the Meal in IQSa', *JBL* 82: 95–100.

——— (1992), 'A Note on the Messianic Banquet', in J. H. Charlesworth (ed.), *The Messiah: Developments in Earliest Judaism and Christianity*, 222–238, Minneapolis: Fortress.

Prior, M. (1985), *The Message of 1 Corinthians: Life in the Local Church*, Leicester and Downers Grove: IVP.

Pryke, E. J. (1966), 'The Sacraments of Holy Baptism and Holy Communion in the Light of the Ritual Washings and Sacred Meals at Qumran', *RQ* 5: 543–552.

Raney, W. H. (1930), 'Who Were the Sinners?', *JR* 10: 578–591.

Rau, E. (1998), 'Jesu Auseinandersetzung mit Pharisäern über seine Zuwendung zu Sünderinnen und Sündern: Lk 15:11–32 und Lk 18:10–14a als Worte des historischen Jesus', *ZNW* 89: 5–29.

Ravens, D. A. S. (1991), 'Zacchaeus: The Final Part of a Lucan Triptych?', *JSNT* 41: 19–32.

Reed, Stephen A. (1987), 'Food in the Psalms', PhD dissertation, Claremont Graduate School, Claremont, CA.

Reich, R. (1995), '6 Stone Water Jars', *Jerusalem Perspective* 48: 30–33.

Reid, B. E. (1995), ' "Do You See This Woman?" Luke 7:36–50 as a Paradigm for Feminist Hermeneutics', *BR* 40: 37–49.

Rice, G. (1980), 'Dining with Deutero-Isaiah', *JRT* 37: 23–30.

Richardson, P. (2002), 'What Has Cana to Do With Capernaum?' *NTS* 48: 314–331.

Ringgren, H. (1993), *The Faith of Qumran: Theology of the Dead Sea Scrolls*, New York: Crossroad, rev.

Rupprecht, D. and R. Rupprecht (1983), *Radical Hospitality*, Phillipsburg, NJ: Presbyterian and Reformed.

Sack, D. (1999), 'Every Meal Has A Meaning', *Christian Ministry*, 30 (May–June): 14–17.

Safrai, S. (1976), 'Home and Family', in S. Safrai and M. Stern (eds.), *The Jewish People in the First Century*, vol. 2, 728–792, Assen: Van Gorcum.

Sanders, E. P. (1983), 'Jesus and the Sinners', *JSNT* 19: 5–36.

——— (1985), *Jesus and Judaism*, London: SCM; Philadelphia: Fortress.

——— (1993), *The Historical Figure of Jesus*, London: Penguin.

——— (2000), 'The Dead Sea Sect and Other Jews: Commonalities, Overlaps and Differences', in T. H. Lim, (ed.), *The Dead Sea Scrolls in their Historical Context*, 7–43, Edinburgh: T. & T. Clark.

Sarna, N. (1989), *Genesis*, Philadelphia: Jewish Publication Society.

——— (1991), *Exodus*, Philadelphia: Jewish Publication Society.

Sasson, J. M. (1979), *Ruth*, Baltimore: Johns Hopkins.

Satterthwaite, P. E. (1993), ' "No King in Israel": Narrative Criticism and Judges 17 – 21', *TynB* 44: 75–88.

Schiffman, L. H. (1979), 'Communal Meals at Qumran', *RQ* 10: 45–56.

——— (1983), *Sectarian Law in the Dead Sea Scrolls: Courts, Testimony and the Penal Code*, Chico: Scholars.

——— (1989), *The Eschatological Community of the Dead Sea Scrolls*, Atlanta: Scholars.

Schiffman, L. H. and J. C. VanderKam (eds.) (2000), *Encyclopedia of the Dead Sea Scrolls*, 2 vols, Oxford: Oxford University Press.

Schnackenburg, R. (2002), *The Gospel of Matthew*, Grand Rapids and Cambridge: Eerdmans.

Schnider, F. (1977), *Die verlorenen Söhne*, Göttingen: Vandenhoeck und Ruprecht.

Schramm, G. (1993), 'Meal Customs (Jewish)', in D. N. Freedman (ed.), *Anchor Bible Dictionary*, vol. 4, 648–650, New York and London: Doubleday.

Schultz, U. (ed.) (1993), *Speisen, Schlemmen, Fasten: Eine Kultur-geschichte des Essens*, Frankfurt am Main: Insel.

Seccombe, D. (2002), *The King of God's Kingdom: A Solution to the Puzzle of Jesus*, Carlisle and Waynesboro: Paternoster.

Seland, T. (1996), 'Philo and the Clubs and Associations of Alexandria', in J. S. Kloppenborg and S. G. Wilson (eds.), *Voluntary Associations in the Graeco-Roman World*, 110–127, London and New York: Routledge.

Selman, M. J. (1994), *1 Chronicles*, Leicester and Downers Grove: IVP.

Shantz, C. (2001), 'Wisdom is as Wisdom Does: The Use of Folk Proverbs in Q 7:31–35', *TJT* 17: 249–262.

Sharon, D. M. (1999), 'When Fathers Refuse to Eat: The Trope of Rejecting Food and Drink in Biblical Narrative', *Semeia* 86: 135–148.

——— (2002), *Patterns of Destiny: Narrative Structures of Foundation and Doom in the Hebrew Bible*, Winona Lake: Eisenbrauns.

Sharp, D. B. (1980), 'In Defense of Rebecca', *BTB* 10: 164–168.

Shimoff, S. R. (1996), 'Banquets: The Limits of Hellenization', *JSJ* 27: 440–452.

Shirock, R. J. (1993), 'The Growth of the Kingdom in Light of Israel's Rejection of Jesus: Structure and Theology in Luke 13:1–35', *NovT* 35: 15–29.

Sider, R. J. (1997), *Rich Christians in an Age of Hunger*, 3rd ed., Dallas and London: Word.

Sine, T. (1999), *Mustard Seed Vs. McWorld*, Grand Rapids: Baker.

Skehan, P. W. (1987), *The Wisdom of ben Sira*, New York: Doubleday.

Smend, R. (1977), 'Essen und Trinken – ein Stück Weltlichkeit des Alten Testaments', in H. Donner, R. Hanhart and R. Smend (eds.), *Beiträge zur Alttestamentlichen Theologie*, 446–459, Göttingen: Vandenhoeck und Ruprecht.

Smith, A. Jr (1998), 'Hospitality: A Spiritual Resource for Building Community', *JITC* 25: 139–151.

Smith, B. K. (1995), 'Amos, Obadiah', in B. K. Smith and F. S. Page, *Amos, Obadiah, Jonah*, 22–201, Nashville: Broadman & Holman.

Smith, D. E. (1980), 'Social Obligation in the Context of Communal Meals: A Study of the Christian Meal in 1 Corinthians in Comparison with Graeco-Roman Communal Meals', ThD dissertation, Harvard Divinity School, Cambridge, MA.

—— (1987), 'Table Fellowship as a Literary Motif in the Gospel of Luke', *JBL* 106: 613–638.

—— (1989), 'The Historical Jesus at Table', *SBL Seminar Papers*, 28: 466–486.

—— (1991), 'The Messianic Banquet Reconsidered', in B. A. Pearson (ed.), *The Future of Early Christianity*, 64–73, Minneapolis: Fortress.

—— (2003), *From Symposium to Eucharist: The Banquet in the Early Christian World*, Minneapolis: Fortress.

Speiser, E. A. (1964), *Genesis*, Garden City: Doubleday.

Spencer, A. B. (1985), *Beyond the Curse: Women Called to Ministry*, Nashville: Nelson.

Stallman, R. C. (2000), 'Divine Hospitality and Wisdom's Banquet in Proverbs 9:1–6', in J. I. Packer and S. K. Soderlund (eds.), *The Way of Wisdom*, 117–133, Grand Rapids: Zondervan.

Steele, E. S. (1984), 'Luke 11:37–54 – A Modified Hellenistic Symposium?' *JBL* 103: 379–394.

Stegemann, H. (1998), *The Library of Qumran: On the Essenes, Qumran, John the Baptist and Jesus*, Leiden: Brill; Grand Rapids: Eerdmans.

Stein, R. H. (1992), *Luke*, Nashville: Broadman.

Stein, S. (1957), 'The Influence of Symposia Literature on the Literary Form of the Pesah Haggadah', *JJS* 8: 13–44.

Stinson, M. A. (2000), 'Dining in the Kingdom: Jesus and Table Fellowship in the Gospel of Luke', MA thesis, Denver Seminary, Denver, CO.

Sutcliffe, E. F. (1960), 'Sacred Meals at Qumran?', *HeyJ* 1: 48–65.

Taussig, H. (1991), 'The Sexual Politics of Luke's Mary and Martha Account: An Evaluation of the Historicity of Luke 10:38–42', *Forum* 7: 317–319.

Taylor, J. B. (1969), *Ezekiel*, London: Tyndale; Downers Grove: IVP.

Terrien, S. L. (2003), *The Psalms: Strophic Structure and Theological Commentary*, Grand Rapids and Cambridge: Eerdmans.

Theissen, G. and A. Merz (1997), *The Historical Jesus: A Comprehensive Guide*, London: SCM; Minneapolis: Fortress, 1998.

Theissen, G. and D. Winter (2002), *The Quest for the Plausible Jesus*, Louisville and London: WJKP.

Thompson, J. A. (1994), *1, 2 Chronicles*, Nashville: Broadman & Holman.

Todd, O. J., intro. and trans. (1979), *Xenophon*, vol. 4, London: Heinemann and Cambridge, MA: Harvard University Press.

Tonson, P. (2001), 'Mercy Without Covenant: A Literary Analysis of Genesis 19', *JSOT* 95: 95–116.

Tyson, J. B. (ed.) (1988), *Luke-Acts and the Jewish People: Eight Critical Perspectives*, Minneapolis: Augsburg.

VanderKam, J. and P. Flint (2002), *The Meaning of the Dead Sea Scrolls*, San Francisco: Harper.

Van der Ploeg, J. P. M. (1957), 'The Meals of the Essenes', *JSS* 2: 163–175.

VanGemeren, W. (1991), 'Psalms', in F. E. Gaebelein (ed.), *Expositor's Bible Commentary*, vol. 5, 1–880, Grand Rapids: Zondervan.

Van Ruiten, J. T. A. G. M. (1992), 'The Intertextual Relationship Between Isa 11:6–9 and Isa 65:25', in F. García Martínez, A. Hilhorst and C. J. Labuschagne (eds.), *Scriptures and the Scrolls*, 31–42, Leiden: Brill.

Via, E. J. (1985), 'Women, the Discipleship of Service, and the Early Christian Ritual Meal in the Gospel of Luke', *SLJT* 29: 37–60.

Vledder, E.-J. (1997), *Conflict in the Miracle Stories: A Socio-Exegetical Study of Matthew 8 and 9*, Sheffield: SAP.

Völkel, M. (1978), ' "Freund der Zöllner und Sünder" ', *ZNW* 69: 1–10.

Vrudny, K. (1999), 'Medieval Fascination with the Queen of Heaven: Esther as the Queen of Heaven and Host of the Messianic Banquet', *ARTS* 11.2: 36–43.

Walker, W. O. (1978), 'Jesus and the Tax Collectors', *JBL* 97: 221–238.

Wall, R. W. (1989), 'Martha and Mary (Luke 10.38–42) in the Context of a Christian Deuteronomy', *JSNT* 35: 19–35.

Waltke, B. K. with C. J. Fredricks (2001), *Genesis*, Grand Rapids: Zondervan.

Watts, J. D. W. (1985–87), *Isaiah*, Waco: Word.

Weinfeld, M. (1986), *The Organizational Pattern and the Penal Code of the Qumran Sect*, Fribourg: Editions Universitaires; Göttingen: Vandenhoeck und Ruprecht.

Wendland, E. R. (1997), ' "Blessed is the Man Who Will Eat at the Feast in the Kingdom of God" (Luke 14:15)', *Neot* 31: 159–194.

Wenham, G. (1987, 1994), *Genesis*, 2 vols, Waco and Dallas: Word.

Westerholm, S. (1978), *Jesus and Scribal Authority*, Lund: Gleerup.

White, L. M. (1988), 'Regulating Fellowship in the Communal Meal: Early Jewish and Christian Evidence', in I. Nielsen and H. S. Nielsen (eds.), *Meals in a Social Context: Aspects of the Communal Meal in the Hellenistic and Roman World*, 177–205, Aarhus: Aarhus University Press.

Whybray, R. N. (1989), *Ecclesiastes*, London: Marshall, Morgan & Scott; Grand Rapids: Eerdmans.

——— (1994), *Proverbs*, London: Marshall Pickering; Grand Rapids: Eerdmans.

Widyapranawa, S. H. (1990), *The Lord Is Savior: Faith in National Crisis – A Commentary on the Book of Isaiah 1 – 39*, Edinburgh: Handsel; Grand Rapids: Eerdmans.

Wilkins, J. and F. D. Harvey (1996), *Food in Antiquity*, Exeter: University of Exeter Press.

Wilkins, M. (2001), 'Women in the Teaching and Example of Jesus', in R. L. Saucy and J. K. Tenelshof (eds.), *Women and Men in Ministry: A Complementary Perspective*, 91–112, Chicago: Moody.

Wilson, G. H. (2002), *Psalms*, vol. 1, Grand Rapids: Zondervan.

Winter, B. (2003), *Roman Wives, Roman Widows: The Appearance of New Women and the Pauline Communities*, Grand Rapids and Cambridge: Eerdmans.

Wintermute, O. S. (1985), 'Jubilees', in J. H. Charlesworth (ed.), *The Old Testament Pseudepigrapha*, vol. 2, 35–142, Garden City: Doubleday.

Wiseman, D. J. (1993), *1 and 2 Kings*, Leicester and Downers Grove: IVP.

Witherington, B. III (2001), *The Gospel of Mark: A Socio-Rhetorical Commentary*, Grand Rapids and Cambridge: Eerdmans.

Wright, C. J. H. (1996), *Deuteronomy*, Peabody: Hendrickson; Carlisle: Paternoster.

Wright, N. T. (1996), *Jesus and the Victory of God*, London: SPCK; Minneapolis: Fortress.

Young, B. H. (1998), *The Parables: Jewish Tradition and Christian Interpretation*, Peabody: Hendrickson.

Young, N. H. (1985), ' "Jesus and the Sinners": Some Queries', *JSNT* 24: 73–75.

Young, R. A. (1994), *Intermediate New Testament Greek: A Linguistic and Exegetical Approach*, Nashville: Broadman & Holman.

Younger, K. L. Jr (2002), *Judges and Ruth*, Grand Rapids: Zondervan.

Youtie, H. C. (1937), 'Publicans and Sinners', *ZPE* 1: 1–20.

Zeitlin, S. (1954), *The Second Book of Maccabees*, New York: Harper and Brothers.

Ziesler, J. A. (1979), 'Luke and the Pharisees', *NTS* 25: 146–157.

Index of modern authors

Index of Scripture references

1:11–53 44
2:7 44
4:22–28 44
4:25 44
8 44
8:62–66 44
13 45
17:1–6 45
17:7–24 45
17 – 19 45
18:19 45
19:6–8 46

2 Kings
4:1–7 46
4:18–37 46
4:38–41 46
4:42–44 46, 105,
  106
5:1–27 46
6:18–20 47
6:22–23 46, 63
23:21 47
23:21–23 47
25:27–30 44

2 Chronicles
30:15–23 47
30:25 47
35:1–19 47

Ezra
6:19–22 47

Nehemiah
5:15–18 47

Esther
1:5–12 48
2:18 48
8:17 48
9:18–22 48

Job
1:4 49
1:5 49

31:17–18 49
42:10–17 49

Psalms
22:26–29 49–50
23 50
23:5 50
23:6 50
36:8–9 50
36:12 50
41:9 51
78:15–31 51
78:18–30 106
81:17 106
99:4 51
104:10–30 51
105:40 106
107:3 112, 114
111:5 51
128:2–3 51
141:4 51
145:16 51
146:7 51

Proverbs
3:9–10 52
9 52
9:2 52
9:3 52
9:4 52
9:11 52
9:14–16 52
9:18 52
14:20 67
15:17 52
16:7 36
17:1 52
21:20 52
22:9 52
23:1–3 52
23:6–8 52
23:20–21 119
24:11 53
24:12 53
24:13 52
24:17 53

24:18 53
24:29 53
25:16 52
25:21–22 53, 64
25:27 52
27:7 52
31:10–31 52

Ecclesiastes
2:24–26 53–54
3:9–22 54
3:12–15 54
3:13 54, 55
4:2 55
5:18 54
5:18–20 54
6:7–8 54
6:9 54–55
8:14 55
8:15 55
9:7 55
9:9 55
9:16 67

Isaiah
2:2–3 114
2:2–4 50, 58
5:11–12 56
5:22–23 57
11:1–5 58
11:6–9 58
11:7 58, 60
22:13 57
25:6 113, 116,
  148
25:6–8 114, 165
25:6–9 50, 58–59,
  101, 104
25:8 59
25:10–12 59
26 – 27 59
28:1–6 57
34:6–7 61
35:6–7 59
43:5–6 114
45:23–24 50

Index of ancient sources